D1230345

317-1
7

TWICE A MINORITY

Mexican American women

TWICE A MINORITY

Mexican American women

Edited by

MARGARITA B. MELVILLE, Ph.D.

Department of Anthropology,
University of Houston, Houston, Texas

With 29 illustrations

The C. V. Mosby Company

ST. LOUIS · TORONTO · LONDON   1980

Copyright © 1980 by The C. V. Mosby Company

All rights reserved. No part of this book may be reproduced
in any manner without written permission of the publisher.

Printed in the United States of America

The C. V. Mosby Company
11830 Westline Industrial Drive, St. Louis, Missouri 63141

Library of Congress Cataloging in Publication Data

Main entry under title:

Twice a minority.

   Includes bibliographical references and index.
   1. Mexican American women—Addresses, essays, lectures. I. Melville, Margarita B., 1929-
E184.M5T84   305.4'8'0973   80-11177
ISBN 0-8016-3386-9

AC/CB/CB 9 8 7 6 5 4 3 2 1   01/D/059

811649   LIBRARY
ALMA COLLEGE
ALMA, MICHIGAN

Contributors

ANITA L. ALVARADO, R.N., Ph.D.

Associate Professor, Department of Anthropology,
University of New Mexico, Albuquerque, New Mexico

SALLY J. ANDRADE, Ph.D.

National Science Foundation Postdoctoral Fellow,
Institute of Human Development and Family Studies,
The University of Texas at Austin, Austin, Texas

ZENA SMITH BLAU, Ph.D.

Sociology Department,
University of Houston, Houston, Texas

MARTA COTERA, M.Ed.

Information Systems, Austin, Texas

CARMEN ACOSTA JOHNSON, Ph.D.

Assistant Professor of Pediatrics,
Baylor College of Medicine, Houston, Texas

MARGARITA A. KAY, R.N., Ph.D.

University of Arizona, College of Nursing,
Tucson, Arizona

JOSÉ E. LIMÓN, Ph.D.

Department of Anthropology,
The University of Texas at Austin, Austin, Texas

JOHN M. LONG, M.A.

University of California at Los Angeles and
East Los Angeles College, Los Angeles, California

KATE R. LORIG, R.N., M.P.H.

School of Medicine, Stanford University,
Stanford, California

JUNE MACKLIN, Ph.D.

Professor and Chairman, Department of Anthropology,
Connecticut College, New London, Connecticut

HECTOR GARCIA MANZANEDO, Dr. P.H.

Professor, School of Social Work,
San Jose State University, San Jose, California

TERRY MASON, M.A.

Department of Anthropology,
The University of Texas at Austin, Austin, Texas

MARGARITA B. MELVILLE, Ph.D.

Department of Anthropology,
University of Houston, Houston, Texas

GEORGE T. OSER, Ph.D.

Sociology Department,
University of Houston, Houston, Texas

DIANE M. SCHAFFER, Ph.D.

Assistant Professor, School of Social Work,
San Jose State University, San Jose, California

RICHARD C. STEPHENS, Ph.D.

Sociology Department,
University of Houston, Houston, Texas

MARIA LUISA URDANETA, R.N., Ph.D.

College of Humanities and Social Science,
Division of Social Science,
University of Texas at San Antonio,
San Antonio, Texas

LIBRARY
ALMA COLLEGE
ALMA, MICHIGAN

CARLOS G. VELEZ-I., Ph.D.

Assistant Professor of Anthropology,
Department of Anthropology,
University of California, Los Angeles, California

DIEGO VIGIL, Ph.D.

Social Science Department, Chaffey College,
Rancho Cucamonga, California;
The Chicano Pinto Research Project,
East Los Angeles, California

ESPERANZA GARCIA WALTERS, R.N., M.P.H.

Santa Clara County Health Systems Agency,
San Jose, California

ROLAND M. WAGNER, Ph.D.

Assistant Professor, School of Social Work,
San Jose State University, San Jose, California

LINDA WHITEFORD, Ph.D.

Department of Anthropology,
Southern Methodist University, Dallas, Texas

Preface

Although the literature on the study of women has increased in recent years, a dearth of firsthand materials dealing with minority females in the United States remains. This fact brought a group of us together to present a symposium focusing on Mexican American women at the American Anthropological Association Meetings in Houston, Texas in 1977. We found that we had much high-quality information based on empirical research to share and decided that the quality and diversity of the materials warranted an attempt to publish them. The idea was supported enthusiastically by other researchers who became contributors to this book. We were able to gather enough material to present a well-rounded profile of the Mexican American female.

Unfortunately, in the area of labor participation we were able to locate only research in progress and were therefore unable to include it here. This is probably the most neglected and misunderstood aspect of all women's lives. This vacuum is even more significant when we consider that about 41% of adult Mexican American females are wage earners and the vast majority of Mexican American women, except perhaps for the incapacitated, are engaged in productive but unrecognized labor in their homes and communities. We hope that the results of firsthand research in this field will soon be made public.

This book presents a range of perspectives, including those of both female and male researchers as well as Anglos and Mexican Americans. We thus present outsider and insider perceptions or, as some anthropologists would say, the "etic" and "emic" perspectives.

The authors of Chapter 17 would like to thank Suzanne Underwood and Cathy Williams for typing assistance. I wish to thank Hilda Castillo Phariss of the Mexican American Studies Program at the University of Houston who helped me coordinate the difficult task of maintaining active contact with sixteen widely located contributors. I am especially grateful to Thomas R. Melville, my husband and in-house editor and consultant, who supported and applauded this effort from its inception.

Margarita B. Melville

Contents

TABLES

Chapter 1

Introduction

Margarita B. Melville

Mexican Americans have been called the silent minority. Mexican American women could in addition be called invisible. Until now they have never been featured in empirical social science literature. This information we have on Mexican American women comes mostly from the sections on family life in those monographs dealing with the Mexican American population.

The vast majority of such monographs dealt only with rural communities. There have been some few exceptions, such as Baca's work (1975) that speculates about the participation of Mexican American women in the Chicano political movement, Apodaca's treatise (1977), and the work of Sanchez and Cruz (1977) regarding the present status of Mexican American women as it has evolved from Aztec tradition and the Spanish conquest.

This volume is a first attempt, to my knowledge, to gather in one text a variety of empirical data on Mexican American women collected by both Mexican American and Anglo American social scientists. Its purpose is to modify the stereotypes of Mexican American women found in much of the social science literature, which often views females as passive sufferers. For example, Madsen says: "Where he [the Latin male] is strong, she [the Latin woman] is weak. Where he is aggressive, she is submissive. While he is condescending toward her, she is respectful toward him" (1973:22).

The picture that emerges from our research is that of a population of women who attempt, with varying degrees of success, to fit into the mainstream of American life without losing their identity as Mexicans or their love of many aspects of Mexican culture. Most of the authors have purposefully investigated the life-styles of urban Mexican American women, avoiding the rural stereotype, although Whiteford's insightful work does keep us in touch with the rural setting.

This book concerns a representative cross section of American women who are 14 years old and over. They comprise only 2½ percent of the adult women in the United States, but their relative numbers are increasing because of their younger median age (20.8 years in 1977) as compared to that of the overall population (29.2 years in 1977) according to the United States Bureau of the Census (1978).

Because Mexican American women have been neglected in social science literature, this book is designed as an important step in making Mexican American women visible and vocal. It is undoubtedly a work of political and social advocacy. It is intended to reach Mexican American women so that they might come to know themselves—to be fully aware of their status and its causes, to be familiar with their strengths and weaknesses—in order that they might be able to increase and improve their efforts to alter their social situation. Understanding by Anglo society and by Mexican American men can also contribute to change and improvement, and it is the authors' collective hope that members of both these populations will also read the present volume and gain insight.

Advocative social science is a stumbling block for those who still hold to pristine notions of value-free science. One would think such naivete disappeared in the period of soul-searching that accompanied the academic upheavals of the late 1960s and early 1970s (Berreman 1968; Melville and Melville 1978). But such is not the case. To those who would deny advocacy a legitimate role in social science, I might point out that this volume intends to be responsive to the needs and values of the population that was studied and not merely to elicit a new theoretical perspective.

MINORITY STATUS

Minority status has come to mean a dependency status that makes no necessary reference to the numerical size of the population. It means that the members of such a population face inferior treatment and opportunities. Such a situation is due to the lack of social power of the population in that its members do not possess an equitable share of political and economic resources. Mexican American women, as Mexican Americans, are a minority population in this sense in their relationship to Anglo American society, as all the government statistics on employment, income, education, health, life expectancy, and so on reveal. This situation is, in part, the legacy of the colonial-like relationship that the United States has maintained over the centuries with Mexico, as well as the result of Anglo American's chauvinistic ethnic conception of the "white man's burden," which has never allowed Anglos to see Mexicans as all that "white." Furthermore, Mexican American women possess a minority status in relation to their own brothers and husbands, as do so many of their gender counterparts around the globe. They are "twice a minority." The reasons for their inferior social status based on their sexual identity are too complex to go into here. However, in her chapter, Cotera faces this issue straightforwardly. It is appropriate to recall, however, that Azteco-Mexican culture in general is essentially that which has developed over the centuries in conjunction with, or as a result of, an agriculturally based economy. Martin and Voorhies (1975), among others, have shown that women's status has consistently deteriorated in the transition from foraging and horticultural economies to an agricultural economy, as males appropriate the females' roles as primary producers.

This does not mean that there are no women of Mexican heritage who have passed the education barrier, have egalitarian marriage relationships, and have achieved positions of power. These do exist, but they are so few and exceptional that they are not representative. Even when there are capable, qualified Mexican American women who could assume positions of responsibility, they are often overlooked, even more than their male counterparts.

Mexican American women are generally identified by the population at large through one or more very visible characteristics. It might be their physical appearance, especially if it reflects Indian or mestizo features. It might be their Spanish surname. It might be a Spanish accent in their speech. Whatever it is, discrimination is the result. As a young woman with strong Indian features remarked to me, ''When I ask about a position over the telephone and indicate my qualifications, my inquiry is received with enthusiasm. Then when I present myself for an interview, I am told that the position has been filled.'' Job discrimination, however, is not the only source of economic minority status.

It is difficult to break out of the vicious circle of powerlessness created by the interdependency between education and employment. Poor educational opportunities lead to poor paying employment. Poorly educated, impoverished parents lack the resources to stimulate educational development in their children. As has been so often noted, it is unlikely that the children of the poor will become high achievers, motivated to pursue the few educational opportunities open to them. And it is education, of which occupation and income are often functions, that determines social class and the degree of power to which an individual will have access.

Power is another topic too broad to handle in the present context. Yet, the lack of it is the essence of the problems discussed throughout this volume. Power is generally defined to be the ability to control the behaviors of others (Adams 1975). Many theorists attempt to classify power according to the resources used to influence the behavior of others (cf. Schermerhorn 1963). Melville (1976) discusses four of these as the most basic: physical force, knowledge, material wealth, and ideological control. The latter two are effectively dependent on physical force. Only knowledge is relatively independent of physical control, but the sources of knowledge are not. Where education is systematized, especially in an extradomestic context, it is easy for the powers-that-be to control the dissemination of knowledge, albeit by budgetary and legislative means. In this sense, it is interesting to note that Mexican American women, according to the United States Bureau of the Census (1978), are the most poorly educated population in the nation. The median years of school completed by all women 25 years of age and older was 12.3 years in 1977. Mexican women of the same age had completed 8.8 years, and Mexican men had completed 9.3 years. This is the lowest educational level of any Hispanic group in the United States, and it is also lower than that of blacks (U.S. Bureau of the Census 1978). It is appropriate to point out that educational opportunities have improved in recent years and that the population 24 years old and younger will undoubtedly have a better educational level. Bilingual education, where it is being adequately implemented, is a major breakthrough increasing educational opportunities for Mexican Americans.

Poor education affects employment. This is evident in the dismal picture of Mexican American women's economic situation. The labor force participation for all women in 1975 was 46 percent. Mexican American women had a participation of 42 percent. The unemployment rate was 9.5 percent for all women but 11.9 percent for Mexican Americans (MALDEF Newsletter 1979). In 1976, the median annual income for Mexican American women was $2,925, roughly three fourths of the median income for all women. One out of three Mexican origin women had an income under $2,000; Puerto Ricans ranked next with one out of five women earning less than $2,000. Mexican men, 14 years old and over, were in a considerably better position with a median income of $7,050, a figure lower than the $9,580 for men not of Spanish origin. About 21 percent of all employed women in the United States work in the higher paying professional, technical, and managerial positions where they earn median salaries over $7,000 annually. Only 7 percent of Mexican American women hold these types of jobs. At the other end of the scale, 28 percent of employed Mexican American women are operatives where they earn an average of only $3,200 per year (MALDEF Newsletter 1979).

As has been noted, social power depends not only on the control of physical force, knowledge, and material resources but on the control of ideology. If Mexican Americans in general, and Mexican American women in particular, are to be denied an equitable share of political and economic resources, this condition must be ideologically justified. Justification of inferior status is generally attributed to biological capabilities. Owing to the state of the art in understanding and explaining human behavioral patterns, such justifications can appropriately and quite simply be called prejudice. If prejudice were merely the ideological ingredient of the inequities of power institutions in a given society, we might drop the subject here. However, prejudice and the discrimination that is its behavioral expression have a far more insidious effect than the justification of an inequitable social system. Such social rejection is turned in on oneself, and individuals and groups become convinced that derogatory statements and treatment are based on objective, usually biological, reality. Prejudice, as Allport (1954) demonstrated years ago, distorts experience as well as perception. Victims are often socialized so that they come to believe the distortion about their group. It is simply a case of psychological and social adaptation. Prejudice thus leads to lowered self-esteem, to a lack of incentive for self-improvement, and to pejorative attitudes toward one's own group. As O'Leary points out (1977:99), if a woman feels she has little personal control because of sexism or racism, her tendency will be to blame herself rather than the social system. She will then have diminished her striving for achievement.

WHAT IS IN A NAME?

There are three principal labels that are used either by Mexican women to identify themselves or are ascribed to them by others. These are "Mexican American," "Chicana," and "Mexicana." The names "Hispanic," "Latin American," and "Latino" are not culturally specific; they encompass a much larger population that includes people of Puerto Rican, Cuban, Spanish, Central and South American, as well as Mexican descent. The term "Mexican American" has the longest history and is probably the most generally accepted term today. It originated in the 1940s as one of the terms for "hyphenated" Americans. Before that time, people of Mexican descent were generally concerned with being recognized as legitimately and fully "American" as any other immigrant population. For example, when it was founded in 1929, the League of United Latin American Citizens (LULAC), which is one of the largest and strongest Mexican American organizations today, avoided the name Mexican because of its negative connotations. The members wanted to emphasize their citizenship status and their loyalty to the United States.

The name Chicano or Chicana was self-appropriated by political activists during the 1960s as a conscious identification with laborers and farm workers who, within the Mexican American population, were called Chicanos in a derogatory sense. It also avoids the hyphen and is a catchy, short name, a nickname. It has become more widely acceptable as the Mexican American population becomes more politically active. It has been picked up by the media and by government agencies and is at present being used more widely by Anglo Americans than by Mexican Americans. Many Mexican Americans reject its use because of its identification with political radicals or a despised social status.

Mexicana (pronounced in Spanish as Mejicana) is an in-house self-identification that is being used more frequently even when identifying oneself to outsiders (Limón 1979). The growth of ethnic pride is eliminating the inhibitions against such self-identification. In fact, it is encouraged. The hyphen is rejected by those persons who consider it demeaning to have to remind Anglo Americans that Mexican Americans are equal citizens with equal rights.

HETEROGENEITY OF MEXICAN AMERICANS

These labels just discussed attest in part to the heterogeneity of the Mexican population in the United States. It is difficult to generalize and attribute common characteristics to all persons of Mexican heritage. In fact, the only uncontestable characteristic that people of Mexican heritage in the United States have in common is that somewhere in their genealogies there was an ancestor who came from Mexico.

Speaking Spanish is not a general characteristic although ''Spanish-speaking'' is a frequently used label. There are many Mexican American people who do not speak Spanish fluently. For some, this resulted from parents who spoke only English to their children in order to protect them from the discrimination that comes with poor language ability or accented speech. For others it was the schools that eradicated their native language in their effort to assure fluent English speakers and, until very recently, often punished children for speaking Spanish, even on the playground. What was a functional educational technique in the North and East for European immigrants was quite dysfunctional, particularly in the West and Southwest, for Mexicanos. The proximity of Mexico and a tradition of strong family networks that extended across an invisible border mandated that Mexicanos maintain a Spanish-language capability. To do so limited their fluency in English to a degree not experienced by other Americans. To go along with Anglo American society and struggle to develop English as their first and only language necessitated the sacrifice of relationships and values that their culture cherished with a passion. The latter alternative was embraced by many generations of Mexicanos whose descendants today bemoan such a choice.

Another frequently used label is the Spanish surname. Even this is not always accurate. Culture can be inherited from both the father and the mother. In fact, it is inherited in greater degree from the mother because it is she who nurtures and contributes most to the enculturation process. In New Mexico, especially, there have been many Anglo husband–Mexican wife marriages (Gonzalez 1967:165-172) from which Anglo-surnamed children, who are either Mexican culturally or at least biculturally, have resulted.

The heterogeneity of the Mexican American population is marked by regional, generational, and class differences. The chapters in this book feature women who live in Texas, California, New Mexico, Arizona, and Indiana. Some are members of the working class and others are middle class and upward bound. Some are first generation, while others can trace roots that go back more than 300 years to ancestors who occupied these lands long before there ever was a United States of America. It is not accurate to generalize for all Mexican American women those characteristics discovered in one region, or for one generation, or for one class. Further study and corroboration are necessary.

Regional differences

There are regional differences among people who settled in Texas or California, Colorado or Michigan, New Mexico or Illinois. These differences are not only due to the ecological adaptation to each geographical region but to the kinds of relationships and attitudes that prevail between Mexicans and Anglos that mandated a certain type of social adaptation. The war fought in Texas in the 1840s generated a bitterness that developed into a long-lasting discriminatory attitude prevalent there that is not present, for example, in Michigan. New Mexico was settled in the 1600s when the territory of Mexico was still a Spanish colony and when ethnicity differentiated between Spaniards, Indians, and mestizos. This created a tradition of pride and self-identity such that when the Anglo settlers moved in a mix was produced that is very distinct from that which exists in California for example.

The rural-urban contrast is another type of regional difference that inhibits generalization. Out of a total of 1,455,000 Mexican families in the United States in 1977, 1,157,000 families lived in cities and only 298,000 families lived in nonmetropolitan areas (U.S. Bureau of the Census 1978). Yet, until recently, most of the research on Mexican Americans has been done among rural dwellers (Kluckhohn and Strodtbeck 1961; Madsen 1973; Rubel 1966; Saunders 1949), with a resulting bias in social science thinking and literature.

Generational differences

Differences can be dramatic between a person who can trace her ancestors as having lived in what is now United States territory since the 1600s and another who remembers coming to the United States as a child with her parents. Some people of Mexican heritage can trace their ancestors to the early colonists who settled some of the oldest cities in the United States: Santa Fe in 1618, San Antonio in 1718, and San Francisco in 1776. A large number of people can trace their settlement in the United States to the 1910 to 1918 period when many families had to leave revolution-torn Mexico for the land to the north, where World War I opened up many jobs. Mexican men were welcomed to farming, railroading, and industry to replace United States men fighting on the European front. Still other families can trace their history as coming and going between these two neighboring countries. Some people who were born in the United States were deported to Mexico in 1930s and then returned in the 1940s or 1950s. Still others who were deported in the 1950s have seen their United States–born children return home in the last two decades. The ebb and flow of population between these two countries have left many with uncles and aunts and cousins on both sides of the border and reinforce the need to maintain a Spanish linguistic capability. The number of generations of residence in the United States contributes to the heterogeneity. It also contributes to strained relations between those who are longtime residents and who feel they are making their way through the mire of discrimination and those newcomers who still reflect the walk and talk of a Mexican peasant but can take advantage of gains made by those who preceded them. The latter remind both the Anglo American and the Mexican American about origins and stereotypes.

Class status

Class status is still another dimension that contributes to differences and is probably the most difficult to assess. As has already been noted, the type of job that sustains a family is not the only component of class. Educational level and class aspirations also contribute to a person's class attitudes and behavior. There is no doubt that family income will influence the behavior, values, and choices made by individuals. One cannot ignore class differences when attempting to describe and define Mexican women in the United States. Most of the chapters in this book deal with lower-class persons. They are the most numerous. Some, however, do examine the women who at least aspire to middle-class status.

• • •

This book is divided into three parts. The first deals with several aspects of the staus of womanhood, which among Mexican Americans is considered a near-essential component of femaleness, an ideological reflection of the extradomestic powerlessness of the Mexican American female. When a young couple is childless, an older woman may be heard to remark: "That marriage is not confirmed, it won't be sealed until there are children."

The second part explores gender roles and the changes that seem to be occurring in their conceptualization. These chapters also demonstrate the dynamic push-pull between tradition and modernity, between the ideals of a culture that is still basically in an agricultural economy and/or that has adapted to industrialization. The result is not Angloization but a contemporary edition of Mexican American ethnicity.

The final chapters are the most numerous. It is a difficult task to explain cross-cultural dynamics. They deal with cultural conflict. This does not imply that contact and conflict between two cultures are not evident in the chapters of the first two parts. They most certainly are. In this last section, however, the investigators focus on the dialectic and dilemmas of Mexican American–Anglo American relations.

I would venture three conclusions. One is that the empirical facts herein recorded give evidence that income and the relations with the majority society are more clearly the determinants of people's options than are tradition or ethnicity per se. It is likely that research based on hypotheses that focus on correlations between religion, belief systems, traditional roles, values, and other similar themes, which are not founded on economic considerations or minority status, will yield incomplete or even false information.

Secondly, the process of acculturation, conceived as the adoption of the cultural traits of a dominant group by the members of a dependent population, when prolonged and in close proximity does not appear to be experienced by Mexican American women. Selective acculturation does. But this does not have a melting pot effect. It stimulates a constant redefinition of ethnic identity.

Finally, the moral strength of Mexican American women lies in their self-identification as members of the Family of la Raza. Within that Family, they believe they have a uniquely female role to fill. It is the role of the mother who nurtures and sustains her children, a role of power based on love. It is only when she sacrifices this perspective and accepts the male definition of power as based primarily on domination, or the Anglo definition of power as based on control of economic resources, that she sacrifices her own self-respect and becomes truly twice a minority. It is for Mexican American women to show Mexican American men and Anglo American society that female power can never mean the rejection of motherhood and the capacity to nurture but rather is its fulfillment in all aspects of social life.

REFERENCES

Adams, Richard N.
1975 Energy and Structure: A Theory of Social Power. Austin, Texas: University of Texas Press.

Allport, Gordon W.
1954 The Nature of Prejudice. Cambridge, Massachusetts: Addison-Wesley Publishing Co., Inc.

Apodaca, Maria Linda
1977 "The Chicana women: a historical materialist perspective." Latin American Perspectives. Winter and Spring.

Baca, Maxine Zinn
1975 "Political familism: toward sex role equality in Chicano families." Aztlan, VI(1):13-26.

Berreman, Gerald D.
1968 "Is anthropology alive? Social responsibility in social anthropology." Current Anthropology 9:391-396.

Gonzalez, Nancie L.
1967 The Spanish-Americans of New Mexico: Heritage of Pride. Albuquerque: University of New Mexico Press.

Kluckhohn, Florence and Fred Strodtbeck
1961 Variations in Value Orientations. Evanston, Illinois: Row, Peterson & Co.

Limón, Jose E.
1979 "The folk performance of Chicano and the cultural limits of political ideology." Unpublished paper.

Madsen, William
1973 Mexican Americans of South Texas, ed. 2. New York: Holt, Rinehart & Winston.

MALDEF (Mexican American Legal Defense and Educational Fund) Newsletter
1979 "Chicana rights: a major MALDEF issue." Comadre III:30-35.

Martin, M. Kay and Barbara Voorhies
1975 Female of the Species. New York: Columbia University Press.

Melville, Margarita and Thomas R. Melville
1978 "Anthropologists and political action." In D. Shimkin and S. Stax (eds.), Anthropology for the Future. Urbana, Illinois: Department of Anthropology, University of Illinois.

Melville, Thomas R.
   1976 "The nature of Mapuche social power." Unpublished doctoral dissertation. Washington, D.C.: The American University, Anthropology Department.

O'Leary, Virginia E.
   1977 Understanding Women. Belmont, California: Wadsworth Publishing Co.

Rubel, Arthur J.
   1966 Across the Tracks: Mexican Americans in a Texas City. Austin, Texas: Hogg Foundation.

Sanchez, Rosaura and Rosa M. Cruz
   1977 Essays on la Mujer. Los Angeles: UCLA Chicano Studies.

Saunders, Lyle
   1949 The Spanish-speaking Population of Texas. Inter-American Education, Occasional Papers, No. 5. Austin, Texas: University of Texas Press.

Schermerhorn, R. A.
   1963 El Poder y la sociedad. Buenos Aires: Paidos.

U.S. Bureau of the Census
   1978 "Current population reports: persons of Spanish origin in the United States, March 1977." Series P-20, No. 329.

Part I

MATRESCENCE

Motherhood, in Mexican culture, is considered to be the fulfillment of womanhood. To be a mother is to be respected in a way that is unequaled by that accorded to any other role, male or female. It is a respect founded on love and admiration that gives to a mother a degree of domestic power that is seldom fully recognized by outside observers. Merely to mention the words "tu madre" in an antagonistic manner is the gravest insult one Mexican can extend to another. It is no mere happenstance that the Virgin of Guadalupe is Mexico's national patroness and that she has been extended the title of General of the Mexican Army.

Power based on love is intransitive; that is, it extends only to those who love and not to those who love them in turn. Therefore, it cannot by systematized, much like the power of charisma that Weber expounded, and is distinct from economic and political power. Economic power is transitive, giving one power over one's employees and over their employees as well, if they have any. Political power functions in the same way. But the power of Mexican motherhood extends only to those she loves, that is, to her children. Thus, although Mexican mothers are universally held in very high esteem, it is not a source of extradomestic power.

Mexican American culture reflects this same value regarding the role of motherhood, but it has been tempered by contact with and adaptation to Anglo American culture and its emphasis on economic productivity fostered by industrialism. Mexican American women are expected to be mothers, first and foremost, but they are also expected to be economically active outside the domestic sphere wherever possible, contributing to the well-being of their families and their communities.

Part I of this volume deals with some aspects of Mexican American motherhood. Becoming a mother is a biological event and, as often happens when a biological event signals an important social change, the event is shrouded in ritual so that it becomes a veritable rite of passage. When a Mexican American woman becomes a mother for the first time, she is expected to initiate a whole series of new relationships and to effect entirely new behavior patterns befitting a mother. Andrade shows that the high birthrate of Mexican Americans has eluded satisfactory explanation. Recent studies of family planning reveal that consistent and effective birth control among Mexican American women is

11

not primarily affected by ethnic-specific ideological or cultural factors. Rather, services are frequently inaccessible—whether it be for economic reasons or caused by the attitudes and behavior of service personnel, who are most often members of the majority culture. Stereotyping or generalizing the behavior of Mexican American women in this regard becomes a self-fulfilling prophecy and is particularly damaging if one wants to provide necessary services or even to predict accurately the fertility trends within this population.

The restricted use of abortion services by Mexican American women after these were legalized led to speculation about whether traditional cultural patterns and Roman Catholicism were the impediments to the use of this method of fertility regulation. Urdaneta discovered instead that economics and bureaucracy were the hindrances. Medically indigent Mexican Americans have few options for services available to terminate

pregnancies. Yet, their attitudes favoring abortion and their expressed needs make it evident that such services are desired and urgently needed.

Childbirth beliefs and practices of Mexican American women can be correlated with how many generations a woman is removed from Mexico. Kay found that Mexican American women are returning to their grandmothers' custom of giving birth at home, with selectivity as to the precise practices they want to adopt. However, new migrants from Mexico still opt for hospital births when they can afford them because of the specific obstetrical care they believe they will obtain there. Kay records that the support of female relatives is especially important and functional during the childbirth period for Mexican

American women. In fact, the adoption of home birth by Mexican Americans seems to have as an important motivation the return to the family of the functions that have gradually been relegated to scientific medical personnel but were never adequately provided because of a lack of appreciation for the psychological, cultural, and social correlates of biological health.

Johnson shows that the practice of breast-feeding babies correlates with social class, with the middle class being the least likely to opt for breast-feeding. In her research, she

found that Mexican women see migration to the United States as their only opportunity to improve their living conditions. After migration, 60 percent of the sample being investigated chose not to breast-feed. This is considerably higher than the normal practice in Mexico for women of similar background. Two variables seem to contribute to their decision. The decrease in the intensity and extensiveness of the social support network women experienced after migration seems to be an important factor influencing women to choose commercial milks for their babies over their own. But even more importantly, the advice they received in hospitals and clinics inhibits the practice of breast-feeding. It is evident that nutritional education regarding the importance of breast-feeding is seriously lacking and vitally necessary for the survival and health of Mexican American children.

REFERENCE

Raphael, Dana
    1975 "Matrescence, becoming a mother, a 'new/old'
          rite de passage." In Dana Raphael (ed.), Being
          Female. Reproduction, Power and Change. The
          Hague: Mouton.

Chapter 2

Family planning practices of Mexican Americans[1]

Sally J. Andrade

A 1974 survey of Hispanic women suggested that the median age of Mexican-origin women was 19.7 years, with almost 42 percent being under the age of 16 (U.S. Bureau of the Census 1975). Analyses of census data on children ever born to women aged 35 to 44 indicate that in 1969 Mexican-origin women tended to have about 47 percent more children than all other women (Bradshaw and Bean 1972). These and other tabulations led the authors to suggest that it was possible that the Mexican-origin population would double itself in a generation or less. In another article comparing differential fertility rates among Mexican Americans and Anglo Americans, the same authors concluded that it is not clear whether the high fertility of Mexican Americans is due to economic factors or to a unique cultural orientation of that group (Bradshaw and Bean 1973).

Population research in Third World countries has often tried to explain the high fertility rates of those societies by concluding that their "traditional" values support large-sized families. This is contrasted to the two-child norm that is assumed to be more typical of nations with "modern" values in the West. A similar process has occurred in the United States in reaction to analyses of census data over the last 25 years that documents the unusually high fertility rates of Mexican Americans.

While several possible explanations might be offered to account for this finding, the one that is common in much social science literature is that of cultural differences. Mexican American values are assumed to differ from those of Anglos and blacks with regard to their perception of large families.

The two concepts that are often emphasized are "familism" (the Mexican American woman is described as defining herself almost exclusively in a maternal role) and "machismo" (the Mexican American man's self-esteem is conceptualized as being determined by how many children he procreates). Support for this explanation is sometimes given in the form of data showing that Mexican American women do not participate in the labor force to the extent of Anglo and black women.

Many of the studies from which the preceding interpretation has emerged were done in primarily rural settings, and almost all of them investigated lower-class samples. Results of current research indicate that socioeconomic status is usually confounded in any such cultural explanation of fertility behavior. In the past, farm-working families may have viewed large numbers of children as economic assets. Over 81 percent of the Mexican American population in 1978, however, is urban (U.S. Bureau of the Census 1978). Mexican Americans in the Southwest have the lowest educational level of any other ethnic group (U.S. Commission on Civil Rights 1971). Furthermore, most Mexican American women (more than 72 percent) do not complete high school (U.S. Bureau of the Census 1975). Thus, it is possible that monolingual Spanish-speaking Mexican Americans and those from impoverished families may have difficulties utilizing contraception effectively because of their limited education or their lack of sophistication about the health care delivery system.

There continues to be a general shortage of accurate, comprehensive national and regional demographic data and, until recently, of nonethnocentric social science investigations sensitive to the hetereogeneity of Mexican Americans. This chapter will attempt to highlight some of the problems of doing bicultural research on contraceptives and fertility, the relevant information currently available about Mexican Americans, and major research areas that need to be initiated.

PSYCHOLOGICAL STUDIES OF POPULATION ISSUES

Population psychology provides a pertinent example of the difficulties faced by the social sciences in studying Mexican Americans and family planning issues.

Only since the 1960s have a noticeable number of psychologists begun to take a serious interest in population issues and research (Pohlman 1969). The formation of a Task Force on Psychology, Family Planning and Population Policy by the American Psychological Association in 1969 was testimony to the influence of the few (APA Task Force 1972). With the establishment of a Division of Population Psychology within the APA in 1973, a commitment by some psychologists to the scientific study of population phenomena was officially recognized and legitimized.

Nevertheless, the conclusion of an exhaustive collection of scholarly reviews in 1973 asserts that a tremendous amount and variety of psychological research on population issues are yet to be undertaken (Fawcett 1973). Almost every author complains about the limited number of investigations and especially the lack of systematic, controlled research. While numerous studies have been completed, there remain large theoretical gaps and very serious methodological difficulties. Since the volume is a basic reference for the field of population studies, the lack of citations to Mexican Americans or Chicanos is noteworthy. Only one unpublished study, a survey of black and Chicano college students, is mentioned in the 500+ page book.

Theoretical issues in population psychology generally revolve around two basic areas. One is the urgent need for a motivational theory of childbearing. As several authors emphasize (Bardwick 1973; Russo and Brackbill 1973), psychologists do not have a well-founded explanation for sexual roles, motivation for parenthood or the value of children, the psychology of women, changes in life-style and psychological state that occur with increased number of children, the rationale for assumption or discontinuation of contraceptive use, and so forth—all of which are fundamentally important to any theory of fertility behavior.

The second major area of concern to psychology is the well-known gap between attitudes and behaviors. This discrepancy is particularly evident in research on birth control. People all over the world are described as increasingly favorable toward fertility regulation when interviewed in a variety of survey research methods, yet measures of their individual verbal commitment to family planning (for example, their desired number of children) and especially of their subsequent behavior indicates that the socially desirable norm of a two-child family is far from being accepted. This is as true of the United States as it is of international samples (Blake 1974).

Although there has been considerable cross-cultural, international work on fertility and family planning, very little systematic research on Mexican Americans has been undertaken. Given the criticisms of ethnocentrism that have been leveled against the discipline of psychology by Chicano researchers (Casas and Keefe 1978; Padilla 1976), this fact is not surprising. Yet there are several interesting investigations available, a number of which are doctoral dissertations and some studies from other disciplines, that have been overlooked by psychologists. This research offers provocative data and speculations about family planning practices of Mexican Americans. These studies have not made it into the mainstream of social science, however. For example, a recent summary on adolescent sexuality closes the chapter on contraceptive use with the following statement:

> No mention has been made in this chapter of the contraceptive behaviors of such minority ethnic groups as American Indians or Spanish-speaking Americans because no research is available on these groups (Chilman 1978:180).

The publication of the present work will hopefully suffice to refute such a declaration.

MEXICAN AMERICAN CULTURE AND FAMILY SIZE

In some respects, one expects to find a lack of information about the attitudes and behaviors of Mexican Americans in the United States regarding fertility. As noted, the field of population psychology is an emerging one, and there is a lack of empirical studies on fertility as a general topic in the other disciplines. In addition, Mexican Americans have only recently become the topic of national social policy and of intensive social science research projects. Yet in light of the high fertility patterns historically characterizing the Mexican American population of the Southwest for more than a century (Bradshaw and Bean 1972), one is puzzled, nevertheless, that so little is known about the dynamics behind this sociocultural phenomenon.

Analysis of the census data over the last 25 years allows one to conclude that Mexican American fertility rates are unusually high (Bradshaw and Bean 1972, 1973). According to the 1960 census (the first year that data were systematically collected on this group), Spanish-surnamed women in the southwestern states tended to be about 41 percent more fertile than Anglos, the former averaging a 4.8 family size in contrast to the 3.4 of the latter (Grebler, Moore, and Guzmán 1970). The 1970 census reported that although the average number of children ever born had declined significantly, at least for women under 30, the fertility of Spanish-surnamed women in the Southwest remained almost 40% higher than that of Anglos in the region (Bradshaw and Bean 1972).

There are major problems involved in basing one's analysis of Mexican Americans on census data, for example, the problem of actually defining the group (Hernández, Estrada, and Alvírez 1972), of estimating conceptions vs. children ever born, and the serious difficulty of the methodological problems that result in undercounting that particular ethnic group (U.S. Commission on Civil Rights 1974). In spite of these limitations, such descriptive analyses underline a demographic variable that has been of considerable interest to sociologists, public health officials, educators, politicians, and demographers in recent decades.

At least three possible explanations or interpretations have traditionally been offered in social science literature to account for the higher fertility of Mexican Americans. The first focuses on religion, the second on socioeconomic class, and the third on culture.

With reference to religion as an explanation, the question is whether Mexican Americans, who as a group overwhelmingly self-identify as Catholic (Moore 1970), support the national pattern of Catholics being less supportive of contraceptives and more positive about larger families. A recent sociological study by Alvírez (1973) suggests that the Catholic Church's official position against the use of "artificial" means of contraception does not affect the increase nor the nonuse of the more effective means of contraception (for example, the pill) by Mexican American women. The generally weak association between religion and fertility that he found in his analysis of data from the Austin Family Survey was explained as the result of the culturally unique Catholicism practiced by Mexican Americans.

Alvírez's findings, which might be questioned because of his generally middle-class sample in a university town with a low percentage of Mexican Americans, have been supported by the findings of Urdaneta (1977) with indigent family planning clinic clients in the same university community as Alvírez, by a random survey of lower-income Mexican American women in Tucson (O'Grady 1973), by ethnographic work in a Mexican American community in South Texas (Hotvedt 1976), and by a survey of low-income Mexican and Mexican American couples at a community mental health center in Detroit (Esparza 1977). Some Mexican American couples practice birth control, with varying degrees of effectiveness, and some do not; but religion does not appear to be a major factor in their decision-making process.

A second explanation has emphasized the generally low socioeconomic status of Mexican Americans, explaining that their low income and lack of education make fertility control difficult for them. Several authors have pointed out that this is an incomplete interpretation in terms of the actual way that income relates to fertility (Bean 1973) and that Mexican American families are consistently larger than those of blacks, although the latter share similar economic deprivation (Uhlenberg 1972).

In a reanalysis of 1970 census data utilizing more precise definitions of ethnic/minority membership, Roberts and Lee (1974) concluded that the distinctive fertility patterns of Spanish-surnamed women in the five southwestern states persist even after controlling for socioeconomic status. None of the socioeconomic indicators used, including education of women, however, was a good predictor of current fertility for younger women, regardless of ethnicity.

The third and predominant interpretation in the literature focuses on a cultural explanation to account for high Mexican American fertility; that is, Mexican American values are assumed to be significantly different from those of Anglos and blacks in terms of the way large numbers of children are perceived. This explanation emphasizes the social pressure of "familism," suggesting that Mexican American women especially value the maternal role and a high number of children, preferring not to work outside the home for that reason. For example, Johnson (1970), with an analysis of census data, concludes that the most important predictor of the fertility of Mexican American women is whether or not they work and that the low percentage of Spanish-surnamed women in the labor force is due to their traditional style of family life.

In contrast, Cooney (1975) suggests that when one controls for socioeconomic factors, the most important predictors for Mexican American and black women in terms of participation in the labor force is their level of education (in contrast to Anglos, for whom it is a factor of the presence of preschool children at home and their husbands' income). She also found that two groups of Mexican American wives now have a higher rate of labor force participation than comparable Anglo groups—those with a college education and those with preschool children.

An alternative cultural theme has been developed by some social scientists in their study of Mexican American health care practices. Drawing heavily on a theory of acculturation/assimilation, these primarily Anglo writers have tended to portray the Mexican American family as deficient and sometimes even pathological, the male dominated by *machismo* and the woman by a masochistic submissive role, with the children suffering the consequences. The conclusion emerges that the father and mother produce large families in order to meet their cultural norms and ego needs, resulting in an endless struggle with the economic repercussions of such personality dynamics. Several examples of earlier research that present variations of these parental roles include Clark (1959), Madsen (1961, 1964), Rubel (1966), and Kiev (1968).

Alvírez and Bean (1976) utilize a very different perspective in their description of the Mexican American family as an illustration of the importance of analyzing ethnic factors in order to understand family life-styles. They discuss at length three major characteristics often emphasized in most social science literature as typical of the Mexican American family—familism, male dominance, and the subordination of younger persons to older persons. They also present demographic data from the census surveys emphasizing the higher fertility characteristic of Mexican American women as well as the disadvantaged socioeconomic position of that population in general.

The thesis of the Alvírez and Bean article is that Mexican American families (like all families throughout history) are changing in adaptation to new situations and new opportunities. There is considerable diversity among Mexican American families partially caused by the differing impacts of Indian, Spanish, and Mexican influences in the different regions of the Southwest and partially to the diverse social and economic histories of those areas. The authors point out that one of the great problems of social science research has been its tendency to "base descriptions of Mexican American family patterns on observations made only upon poor families of predominantly Mexican background" and thereby ignore cultural factors that better characterize other segments of the population. The result has been one generally of perpetuating ethnic stereotypes in the styles of Madsen (1964) or Rubel (1966).

Alvírez and Bean suggest that there is another serious problem in a too narrowly anthropological approach to Mexican American family life:

> . . . the interpretation of Mexican American family life in terms of monolithic stereotypes implicitly assigns too great a role to the influence of cultural factors in shaping the family patterns of Mexican Americans. It invites the idea that certain patterns are derivatives of beliefs and values passed from generation to generation rather than functional adaptations to a difficult environment (Alvírez and Bean 1976:33).

Thus, the reader must cultivate a questioning attitude concerning the cultural "traditionalism" so regularly ascribed to Mexican American families as he or she begins to examine issues of family planning in this group. One must be sensitive to the disproportionate poverty and racial/linguistic discrimination experienced by Mexican Americans as factors influencing their perception and use of the health care delivery system.

MEXICAN AMERICAN FERTILITY REGULATION PATTERNS

Social science research on the Mexican American family and population issues is characterized by the cultural interpretation described in the preceding. For example, the massive U.C.L.A. study (Grebler, Moore, and Guzmán 1970) challenged whether the cultural ideal of the traditional family (that is, in which the male makes all important decisions unilaterally, while the submissive wife unquestioningly carries out his will) has ever been the behavioral norm among Mexican Americans. Yet the authors suggest that the issue of family size and attitudes toward birth control are intimately associated with *machismo* and norms about the role of women. They note a brief pilot study in a small California community in 1976, reporting that it was the "traditionalistic lower-class Mexican American" husbands more often than their wives who objected to the use of contraceptives.

From the surveys that their research teams did, the U.C.L.A. authors report further a generally high verbal acceptance of birth control by Mexican Americans (64 percent in Los Angeles and 50 percent in San Antonio, in contrast to a comparable national sample of 62 percent at that time). Low-income respondents were much less positive about birth control, as were older individuals. A majority of all subjects agreed that "the most important thing" that a married woman could do was to have children. But there was a notable age differential of about 20 percent between people under 30 (73.5 percent agreement) in contrast to those over 50 (93.5 percent). Placing the family role "in perspective'' with regard to achievement, Grebler, Moore, and Guzmán emphasize the concept of ''cultural lag'' and the influence of social class to supplement findings regarding the traditional Mexican American family's way of life.

Bradshaw and Bean (1972), in their discussion of Mexican American fertility for the U.S. Commission on Population Growth, conclude that the ''cultural context of childbearing'' is the most significant explanation for the group's high fertility. They reached this conclusion after examining and rejecting several other possible explanations for the higher Mexican American birth rate (including earlier age of marriage, prevalence and stability of marriage, spacing of children). Utilizing data from the Mexican American husbands and wives who participated in the Austin Family Survey, Bradshaw and Bean report the couples' desires for numerous children that are ''evidently supported by and are congruent with a generalized high valuation of large families'' (1972:160). They note that, with a more inclusive sample, greater variation should emerge and that the cultural context of fertility for Mexican Americans may vary with differing ethnic compositions of neighborhoods.

Bradshaw and Bean also remark on the lack of information about contraceptive use among Mexican Americans. They present findings from the Austin investigation regarding the apparently ineffective use and nonuse of contraceptives, even though the cumulative contraceptive experience of the respondents was fairly extensive.

The authors also discuss individual variation in fertility and suggest that:

> . . . the values of Mexican-American women who have relatively small families are likely to differ somewhat from the general cultural values, though not to such an extent that such women consistently prefer small families. Rather, their values are sufficiently different that women cannot unequivocally endorse the valuation of large families (Bradshaw and Bean 1972:160).

The expected finding obtained that the higher the social status of the families (as indicated by the husband's and wife's education), the smaller the family size tended to be. The interesting aspect of this result was that the wife's education apparently exerted the stronger influence, partially caused by the fact that better educated wives married later.

Uhlenberg (1973) utilized 1970 census data to point out that it is the poorly educated segment of Mexican Americans that is responsible for the group's exceptionally high fertility:

> The fact that a very small percent of all Mexican Americans have completed four years of high school means that the low fertility of the better educated has little influence upon the minority's overall rate (Uhlenberg 1973:35).

Because of the lack of data regarding Mexican American desired family size, he concludes that it is impossible to determine how much of their high fertility is due to lack of access to contraceptives and how much to their desire for large families.

Kay (1972) did an ethnographic study of low-income Mexican American women in Tucson, Arizona, focusing on their beliefs about health and illness. In the chapter, ''Childbearing and Health,'' she discusses fertility regulation, noting traditional means of spacing children by prolonging lactation and practicing withdrawal.

Kay dismisses *machismo* as an explanation for the high fertility of Mexican American women. Instead, she emphasizes the women's lack of knowledge about reproduction and sex, which leads to a modesty that hinders their interaction with the medical system.

In a later paper, Kay (1974) provides the results of an apparent follow-up survey of Mexican American informants in Tucson about their fertility regulation. She reports positive support for the concept of family planning, although the subjects' knowledge was not always accurate. The pill was the favorite method of contraception; the average number of children was three. Kay concludes that the typically stereotyped sex roles often used to describe Mexican Americans were not supported by her interview data; for example, many men spoke of equality within marriage, and more than half believed that spouses should share the responsibilities of family planning.

Bradshaw and Bean (1973), in their short summary on the trends in Mexican American fertility from 1950 to 1970, point out that both Mexican Americans and Anglos in the Southwest followed similar patterns during that 20-year period. That is, their average fertility increased from 1950 to 1960 and decreased from 1960 to 1970. The fertility differential between the two populations, however, remains about the same. The authors note that the continued high fertility of Mexican Americans has apparently been less influenced by socioeconomic conditions than that of other groups. Their summary raises the question that continues to challenge social science researchers—is the high birthrate of Mexican Americans the result of:

—discrimination (which may have impeded the flow of economic benefits to Mexican Americans during periods of economic prosperity) or [of]
—cultural orientations in the population supportive of having large families. . . . (Bradshaw and Bean 1973:696).

DISSERTATIONS ON MEXICAN AMERICAN CONTRACEPTIVE USE (1974 to 1979)

In recent years, several interesting doctoral dissertations have focused on various aspects of contraceptive use among Mexican Americans. Coming from different disciplines in the social sciences, their findings bring into question many of the traditional stereotypes about Mexican American women and contraceptives.

Nies (1974) developed a multiple regression equation to predict contraceptive use or nonuse among low-income Mexican American women. The 262 subjects were interviewed immediately after giving birth at the county hospital in San Antonio, Texas. They were contacted 2 months following delivery regarding their use of either birth control pills or an IUD. He found that the wife's perception of her husband's feelings proved to be the strongest single predictor of subsequent contraceptive practices.

Nies also utilized a dichotomized version of the Personal Values Abstract (Gough 1973) and found that the more modern woman, as identified by this instrument, tended to adopt contraceptive measures more frequently. The other psychological variables that he investigated (impulsiveness, social warmth, social abrasiveness, ego organization, introversion/extroversion, neurotic anxiety, individualism, social attractiveness, attitudes toward fate and efficacy, and intelligence), however, did not correlate with birth planning behavior. This proved to be a major disappointment for the author, in light of the time and effort expended on measuring those variables.

Nies concluded, nevertheless, that one of the "most surprising and important findings" of his study was the high percentage of women who were entering into family planning programs. He found that almost 80 percent of his cross-validation sample could be classified as successful users of contraception.

Urdaneta (1977) did an intensive participant/observer study of a low-income family planning clinic in a city in Texas, interviewing 125 Mexican American female clients. She found that 96 percent of her respondents had used some type of contraception at one period or another—but sporadically and haphazardly. She concludes that their generally high fertility rate was not due to ideological or cultural components of their value systems nor to their disinterest. Rather their fecundity was due to more empirically grounded sociocultural and poverty variables that vitiate "correct" use of birth control measures. Specifically, Urdaneta zeroes in on variables within the health care delivery system (for example, access, in the sense of awareness, knowledge, transportation and finances, as well as the cultural and linguistic acceptability of service providers' methods) as the explanation for whatever lack of motivation for reproduction control may have existed on the part of the Mexican American women in the neighborhood. It is the disjuncture of the Anglo, English-speaking, middle-class health care delivery system in terms of implementation as it intersects with the Mexican American system of utilization that causes the problem—not the microsystem of the Mexican American population and their beliefs.

Naranjo (1976) examined attitudes of 117 college undergraduates, including 28 Mexican American females, with respect to alternatives in genetic counseling therapy. During the course of her investigation, she discovered highly significant sex by ethnic interactions on a number of issues related to family planning. Mexican American females were frequently the most positive advocates of birth control measures in the described cases of genetic risk (for example, in the absence of pregnancy, approval of sterilization advice), and both Mexican American and Anglo females were quite close in their approval of therapeutic abortion, with or without positive diagnosis of an affected fetus. On this latter issue, Anglo males were more negative than Mexican American males, while both male groups diverged significantly from the more accepting position of the two female groups. It thus appeared that, counter to what might be expected from the familism literature:

> . . . in general, the Mexican American female desired the most effective means of contraception in family planning complicated by the increased risk of genetic disease (Naranjo 1976:83).

Hotvedt (1976) did an ethnographic study in a South Texas Mexican American community, focusing on the motivational factors influencing women in their decision to utilize or reject contraceptives. Her anthropological project utilized participant observation, an open-ended interview schedule, and questionnaires administered to elementary school, high school, and adult samples.

She concludes that there was a large degree of intracommunity acceptance of utilization of contraceptives by married couples. She identified, however, three fairly distinct groups of users or potential users:

1. Lower socioeconomic status women who used contraceptives only after several children were born and who appeared to be interested in birth control for primarily economic reasons
2. Middle-class women who began to use contraceptives immediately on marrying or after the birth of one child and who expressed concerns about the quality of family life and about career advancement
3. Adolescents who were faced with conflicting sexual mores and increased possibilities for premarital intercourse in a community that was generally opposed to the premarital use of contraceptives

Hotvedt suggests that the acceptance of birth control by married adults is not a measure of assimilation to Anglo culture but rather a cultural adaptation that is consistent with norms in Mexican American culture. The one major area of possible conflict lay with the potential needs and problems of adolescents regarding pregnancy or abortion, but adults expressed very little reservation about family planning per se.

Chavira (1978) did an exploratory study of the family organizational factors among impoverished Mexican Americans in San Antonio, which he postulated would affect their contraceptive use and health behavior. He emphasized the difference between ineffective users and nonusers and the point that lower-class couples' inability to regulate their fertility may be simply one additional indicator of their difficulties in solving many other problems as well.

The results of interviews with the 51 couples, all of whom were practicing some form of contraception at the time (although not necessarily effectively), permitted a dichotomization into a group with a strong family organization and another with a weak family organization (based on the degree of compatibility, cooperative decision making, husband's history of employment, husband's willingness to assist with household chores, and emotional and economic support from the extended kin network).

Contrary to Chavira's expectations, there was no relationship between the index of family organization strength as broadly construed and contraceptive effectiveness or with desirable health behavior. He concludes that our incomplete understanding of the multidimensional nature of family organization strength, contraceptive effectiveness, and good health practices limits our ability to understand the family dynamics underlying fertility behavior.

For example, one of the surprising findings was that the "objective" economic circumstances of a family apparently do not directly influence their contraceptive use or health behavior. The "subjective" dimension (that is, compatibility, decision making, and kinfolks' emotional support), however, appears to allow the family to deal with its internal affairs effectively in spite of economic hardships and to practice effective birth control and desirable health care.

Esparza (1977) investigated motivational factors related to fertility behavior among

120 low-income couples in Detroit, Michigan, with 30 couples from each of the following groups: Mexican Catholics (MCs), Mexican American Catholics (MACs), Anglo Catholics (ACs), and Anglo Protestants (APs). The questionnaire and interview process generated data on the value of children, the costs and barriers to fertility, and family planning methods and decision-making processes regarding contraceptive use. Utilizing the Hoffman and Hoffman (1973) model of values, Esparza reported that the four groups ordered their responses under five major categories:

1. Primary group ties—The MCs were the strongest advocates of the value that children are the essence of family life, whereas the MACs differed by stressing the value of communication between parents and children. Anglo couples focused more on the children's benefiting the marital relationship itself.
2. Stimulation—Both Latino groups emphasized that the joys of children were to be found within the context of family life, and they differed from the Anglo groups in their perception that younger children provided them with more happiness than did older children.
3. Expansion of self—MC fathers were the most adamant about the importance of having male children to carry on the family name, while MAC women emphasized this aspect the least. Most APs, ACs and MACs (in contrast to the MCs) indicated a tolerance for those parents who chose not to have children.
4. Adult status—The majority of all the women appeared to doubt their adequacy as mothers, as did the majority of MAC and AC men in terms of their parental roles. However, APs and MACs appeared to feel more in control of their destiny than did MCs. Both AP and MC women complained that their husbands were not sufficiently involved in child-rearing.
5. Economic utility—MACs and APs cited economic reasons the most frequently as the major disadvantage of having children. Contrary to some findings, however, Esparza's study found a sizable group of parents who denied any major disadvantage to having children: ''The MCs do not see children as burdens but rather as 'blessings' for the family'' (Esparza 1977:89).

Data indicated that all of the women and most of the men had heard of family planning, and the majority (87 percent) approved of birth control utilization. Interestingly, the actual use of contraceptive measures, in terms of respondents' self-reports, reveals some unusual differences. Esparza found that MC women reported the highest use of birth control among the four groups of women. He also noted that group had the highest number of working wives, as well as the largest family size, thus providing a possible explanation for the unexpectedly large contraceptive utilization pattern.

Birth control pills were the preferred method for all four groups, and Esparza suggests that this may indicate that women are assuming more responsibility for fertility control. He also indicated that the women's educational level, rather than their income level, may be a more reliable indicator of their use of the pill.

The only group to begin contraceptive use before childbirth was the AP women, while the ACs and MACs tended to begin sometime after the birth of the first child. MCs generally began after the birth of the second child and in some instances did not begin until the family actually experienced financial pressures.

MC women indicated that contraceptive use was the result of a shared decision-making process between themselves and their husbands, in spite of Esparza's finding that MC couples had a traditional perception of marriage (that is, the husband as making many of the important decisions). While not typical of the majority of MAC couples, in some MAC marriages decisions about contraceptive use were essentially made by the wives (23 percent), while 68 percent of the MAC couples used a joint decision-making process. Esparza noted that those MAC women who were making birth control decisions by themselves tended to be more educated and more often employed than other MAC women.

He also indicated that his findings of a preferred family size of 4.3 children for MACs closely matches the 4.2 children preferred by Mexican American couples in the Austin Family Survey (Alvírez, 1973), and the finding of AP preference for 4.2 children is close to the reported figure of 4.0 children in a classic study of lower-class fertility (Rainwater 1960). He further noted that while religion does not appear to affect contraceptive use, it may influence feelings about desired or ideal family size. When the values and costs of having children are balanced, the three Catholic groups would have wanted more children than they realistically expected to have. Only the APs would have wanted a smaller family than their present one.

Esparza discusses differences between the Mexican and the Mexican American couples in terms of the different social change processes with which each group is struggling and how assimilation may affect their value preferences. He concludes that the Mexican American Catholic couples in Detroit included in his study appear to be at various stages of assimilation:

> As a group, they do not reject their traditional core valuing of children but attempt a new synthesis from a bi-cultural experience in a northern industrial state. . . . In comparison [to men], MAC women appear to make more significant value of children changes as they gain access to educational and employment opportunities. . . . As a result, some MAC women closely resemble the AC women of the study (Esparza 1977:101-102).

My own dissertation (1979), which is the most recent, focuses specifically on the question of whether a Mexican American women's cultural identity influences her feelings about family size and her contraceptive utilization pattern. I (1979) used a path analysis statistical model to survey 150 female Mexican American students at two small public universities in Texas regarding their identification with traditional Mexican American culture in relation to their attitudes about family planning issues and their use of contraceptives. The independent variable was the extent to which the women identified with Mexican American values as measured on two objective indices, one a measure of identity and the other of interaction. The dependent variables were the degree to which they accepted certain dimensions of fertility regulation (family planning, contraception, abortion, population management, and modernity) as measured on five attitudinal scales, the size of family they ideally desired, the number of children they actually expected to have, and their report of contraceptive use. I used group-administered questionnaires supplemented by a follow-up personal interview of 20 percent of the women.

In general, my findings do not support the hypothesis that cultural identification is a factor affecting the Mexican American college women's attitudes toward family planning, and there was no evidence whatsoever relating the measures of cultural identification to the women's actual use of contraceptives. The primary variable highlighted is that of male partnership. Most of the women who were sexually active were utilizing contraception. They varied in their methods, from the majority who were using the pill to one young woman and her boyfriend who had used rhythm and withdrawal for 6 years. Given the stereotypes of passivity, sexual ignorance, and virginity that exist with reference to Mexican American women in much of the social science literature, these findings are indeed provocative.

Concern about overpopulation as a social issue and the expense of a large family were the major attitudinal factors influencing the women's views of family size and contraceptive use. In addition to the cultural identification variables, it seems relevant to note others that did *not* correlate significantly with the subjects' use of contraceptives. These included age, their parents' birthplace, the location of their hometowns, religion, religious attendance, family size, their desired number of children, and their expected number of children.

As I emphasized, the question remaining to be clarified is whether the cultural background or the educational status of these Mexican American college women is the more important factor in terms of understanding their fertility regulation attitudes and practices. I pointed out that it would be inappropriate to generalize the results of my study to any other population of Mexican American women except university students. Given the fact that most Mexican American women complete less than 10 years of school, this sample is a very unique, almost privileged group. But the results also indicate the importance of sampling across socioeconomic and income lines for researchers interested in Mexican American attitudes and behaviors.

These seven recent studies—two by anthropologists, one by a sociologist, and four by psychologists—present some stimulating data with regard to Mexican American attitudes and practices of family planning. The one rural study in south Texas is complemented by the four urban studies and by two surveys of college students in an urban and in a rural setting. They conclude that Mexican American females are frequently advocates for and active seekers of contraception. Lack of education among many lower socioeconomic status Mexican Americans and limitations of the essentially middle-class, Anglo-dominated health service delivery system appear to hamper effective utilization by some low-income women, as does the group's apparent ambivalence about adolescent sexuality.

Nevertheless, several of the investigators document that a number of impoverished women in very stressful economic situations are practicing effective contraception and that as the women's education increased, their participation in family planning grew also. Esparza's work is particularly interesting, since his findings run counter to the overly simplistic interpretations of Mexican and Mexican American values that characterize much of the social science literature at present.

CONCLUSIONS

Much remains to be done in terms of gathering descriptive, baseline data about Mexican American women's attitudes and practices of birth control. Given the generally high fertility of the Mexican American population in relation to other ethnic groups, any such research must acknowledge and explore the diversity of cultural patterns exhibited by Mexican Americans, without oversimplifying or stereotyping them.

In addition to the necessity of developing theories related to reproductive and sexual behavior that include minority women, there is a need for sophisticated theoretical development of the concepts of "cultural identity" and "biculturalism." The limited theoretical and empirical work available preclude the linking of cultural factors to family planning issues at present. In addition, sex role and socioeconomic factors must be carefully investigated within studies of cultural identity to avoid confounding such variables.

Senour (1977), in a summary of research on the psychological attributes of the Chicana or Mexican American women, emphasizes that Mexican American women exist within the context of the sex-role revolution occurring within the United States. Given the dynamic process of cultural adaptation, they are inevitably going to be affected.

Clearly, there is a need for more objective information about the attitudes and practices of both Mexican American women and men and of Mexican American couples, married or partnered, with reference to fertility issues. Very little empirical research exists about how adolescents in general perceive these issues and about their decision-making processes regarding contraception. To my knowledge, there is no research on Mexican American adolescents regarding contraception. It is hoped that this chapter will stimulate an interest in additional bicultural research on family planning attitudes and practices among Mexican Americans.

NOTE

1. This article is a revised summary of some of the material presented in the author's doctoral dissertation (Andrade 1979)..

REFERENCES

Alvírez, D.
1973 "The effects of formal church affiliation and religiosity on the fertility patterns of Mexican American-Catholics." Demography X:19-36.
Alvírez, D. and F. D. Bean
1976 "The Mexican American family." In C. H. Mindel and R. W. Habenstein (eds.), Ethnic Families in America: Patterns and Variations. New York: Elsevier North-Holland, Inc.
Andrade, S. V. J.
1979 "Family planning attitudes and practices as a function of the degree of cultural identification of female Mexican-American college students." Unpublished doctoral dissertation. The University of Texas at Austin.
APA Task Force on Psychology, Family Planning and Population Policy
1972 "Report of the Task Force on Psychology, Family Planning and Population Policy." American Psychologist 27:1100-1105.
Bardwick, J. M.
1973 "Psychological factors in the acceptance and use of oral contraceptives." In J. T. Fawcett (ed.), Psychological Perspectives on Population. New York: Basic Books, Inc., Publishers.
Bean, F. D.
1973 "Components of income and expected family

size among Mexican Americans." Social Science Quarterly 54:103-116.

Blake, J.
1974 "Can we believe recent data on birth expectations in the United States?" Demography 11:24-44.

Bradshaw, B. S. and F. D. Bean
1972 "Some aspects of the fertility of Mexican Americans." In C. F. Westoff and R. Parke, Jr. (eds.), Demographic and Social Aspects of Population Growth. Vol. 1. Research Reports of the U.S. Commission on Population Growth and the American Future. Washington, D.C.: U.S. Government Printing Office.
1973 "Trends in the fertility of Mexican-Americans: 1950-1970." Social Science Quarterly 53:688-696.

Casas, J. M. and S. E. Keefe (eds.)
1978 "Family and mental health in the Mexican American community." Monograph No. 7. Los Angeles, California: Spanish-Speaking Mental Health Research Center.

Chavira, J. A.
1978 "Family organization, contraceptive effectiveness, and health among Mexican Americans of low socioeconomic status" (doctoral dissertation, The University of Texas at Austin). Dissertation Abstracts International 38:7585-A. (University Microfilms No. 7807277.)

Chilman, C. S.
1978 Adolescent Sexuality in a Changing American Society: Social and Psychological Perspectives. Washington, D.C.: U.S. Government Printing Office.

Clark, M.
1959 Health in the Mexican-American Culture. Berkeley, California: University of California Press.

Cooney, R. S.
1975 "Changing labor force participation of Mexican American wives: a comparison with Anglos and blacks." Social Science Quarterly 56:252-261.

Esparza, R.
1977 "The value of children among lower class Mexican, Mexican American and Anglo couples" (doctoral dissertation, University of Michigan). Dissertation Abstracts International 38: 1397-B. (University Microfilms No. 77-17, 991.)

Fawcett, J. T. (ed.)
1973 Psychological Perspectives on Population. New York: Basic Books, Inc., Publishers.

Gough, H. G.
1973 "Personality assessment in the study of population." In J. T. Fawcett (ed.), Psychological

Perspectives on Population. New York: Basic Books, Inc., Publishers.

Grebler, L., J. W. Moore and R. C. Guzmán
1970 The Mexican-American People: The Nation's Second Largest Minority. New York: The Free Press.

Hernández, J., L. Estrada and D. Alvírez
1973 "Census data and the problem of conceptually defining the Mexican-American population." Social Science Quarterly 53:671-687.

Hoffman, L. W.
1974 "The employment of women, education, and fertility." Merrill-Palmer Quarterly 20:99-117.

Hoffman, L. W. and M. L. Hoffman
1973 "The value of children to parents." In J. T. Fawcett (ed.), Psychological Perspectives on Population. New York: Basic Books, Inc., Publishers.

Hotvedt, M. E.
1976 "Family planning among Mexican Americans of South Texas" (doctoral dissertation, Indiana University). Dissertation Abstracts International 37:2277-A. (University Microfilms No. 76-21, 509.)

Johnson, C. A.
1970 "Fertility differentials among Mexican Americans of the five south-western states." Unpublished doctoral dissertation. The University of Texas Health Center at Houston.

Kay, M. A.
1972 "Health and illness in the barrio: women's point of view." Unpublished doctoral dissertation. University of Arizona.
1974 "The ethnosemantics of Mexican American fertility." Paper presented at the 73rd Annual Meeting of the American Anthropological Association, November, Mexico City.

Kiev, A.
1968 Curanderismo: Mexican-American Folk Psychiatry. New York: The Free Press.

Madsen, W.
1961 Society and Health in the Lower Rio Grande Valley. Austin, Texas: Hogg Foundation for Mental Health.
1964 The Mexican-Americans of South Texas. New York: Holt, Rinehart & Winston.

Moore, J. W.
1970 Mexican Americans. Englewood Cliffs, New Jersey: Prentice-Hall, Inc.

Naranjo, M. S.
1976 "Cross-cultural comparison of social psychological factors contributing to the effectiveness of genetic counseling therapy." Unpublished

master's thesis. The University of Texas at Austin.

Nies, C. M.
1974 "Social psychological variables related to family planning among Mexican-American Females" (doctoral dissertation, The University of Texas at Austin). Dissertation Abstracts International 35:2441-B. (University Microfilms No. 74-24, 914.)

O'Grady, I. P.
1973 "Childbearing behavior and attitudes of Mexican-American women in Tucson, Arizona." Paper presented at the Annual Meeting of the American Association of Applied Anthropology, April, Tucson.

Padilla, A. M.
1976 "Psychological research and the Mexican American." In C. A. Hernández, M. J. Haug and N. N. Wagner (eds.), Chicanos: Social and Psychological Perspectives, ed. 2. St. Louis, Missouri: The C. V. Mosby Co.

Pohlman, E.
1969 The Psychology of Birth Planning. Cambridge, Massachusetts: Schenkman Publishing Co., Inc.

Rainwater, L.
1960 And the Poor Get Children. Chicago, Illinois: Quadrangle Books.

Roberts, R. E. and E. S. Lee
1974 "Minority group status and fertility revisited." American Journal of Sociology 80:503-523.

Rubel, A. J.
1966 Across the Tracks: Mexican-Americans in a Texas City. Austin, Texas: The University of Texas Press.

Russo, N. F. and Y. Brackbill
1973 "Population and youth." In J. T. Fawcett (ed.), Psychological Perspectives on Population. New York: Basic Books, Inc., Publishers.

Senour, M. N.
1977 "Psychology of the Chicana." In J. L. Martínez, Jr. (ed.), Chicano Psychology. New York: Academic Press, Inc.

Uhlenberg, P.
1972 "Marital instability among Mexican Americans: following the patterns of blacks?" Social Problems 20:49-56.
1973 "Fertility patterns within the Mexican-American population." Social Biology 20:30-39.

Urdaneta, M. L.
1977 "Fertility regulation among Mexican American women in an urban setting: a comparison of indigent vs. nonindigent Chicanas in a Southwest city in the United States" (doctoral dissertation, Southern Methodist University). Dissertation Abstracts International 38:1507-A. (University Microfilms No. 77-18,607.)

U.S. Bureau of the Census
1975 A Statistical Portrait of Women in the U.S. (Current Population Reports: Special studies, Series P-23, No. 58). Washington, D.C.: U.S. Government Printing Office.
1978 Persons of Spanish Origin in the United States (Current Population Reports: Advance report, Series P-20, No. 328). Washington, D.C.: U.S. Government Printing Office.

U.S. Commission on Civil Rights
1971 The Unfinished Education: Outcomes for Minorities in the Five Southwestern States (Mexican American Educational Series, Report II). Washington, D.C.: U.S. Government Printing Office.
1974 Counting the Forgotten: The 1970 Census Count of Persons of Spanish Speaking Background in the United States. Washington, D.C.: U.S. Government Printing Office.

Chapter 3

Chicana use of abortion

The case of Alcala

Maria Luisa Urdaneta

Mexican Americans[1] are known to have the highest birthrate of any ethnic population in the United States (Bradshaw and Bean 1972:1; Moore 1970:84-85); this rate is about 50 percent higher than that of the overall United States population (U.S. Commission on Civil Rights 1968:11).

Several cultural arguments have been put forth as reasons for this exceptionally high fertility, for example: (1) The masculine need to demonstrate virility through the siring of many children—a supposed aspect of the Mexican American man's *machismo*—has frequently been cited as a cultural deterrent to fertility regulation (Stycos 1968:VII-VIII). (2) Leñero-Otero (1968:24) states that the teachings of the Roman Catholic Church have an important role in either rejection or ignorance of contraception in Mexico—a predominantly Roman Catholic country. The Chicano population continuously absorbs a steady stream of Mexican migrants. Approximately 95 percent of the Mexican American population is *nominally* Roman Catholic (Moore 1970:84-85). (3) Early anthropological analyses of social roles among this ethnic group attested to the desirability of large nuclear families by Mexican American couples (Madsen 1964:48-53; Murillo 1971:104; Rubel 1966:67-78). However, when the data are examined closely, it becomes apparent that the group is not homogeneous. Census and survey data show that it is only Mexican American women of low income and low educational levels who have the larger families, while professional Mexican American women exhibit almost exactly the same average number of children as do similarly educated whites in the United States (Bradshaw and Bean 1972:10). Since only a small proportion—24 percent—of all Chicanas have completed high school (MALDEF Newsletter 1978:8), the low fertility[2] of the better educated has little influence on the Mexican American population's overall rate (Uhlenberg 1973:35). As a group, a disproportionate number of Chicanos live well below national standards in income, education, housing, and health (Grebler, Moore, and Guzmán 1970:13-33).

Modern effective contraceptives in the United States are classified as medical care and consequently cannot be obtained without a physician's prescription. Medical care in this country is a middle-class commodity. Those who can afford the price can purchase physician services in this area, but the poor are dependent to a significant degree on charity clinic services that tend to be fragmented, insensitive, and lacking in continuity (Ehrenreich and Ehrenreich 1970:3-18).

As a direct result of governmental concern over the problems of population growth, federal provisions for modern family planning services to low-income individuals evolved during the past decade. One of these services included the legalization and (federal) funding through Title XX for nontherapeutic abortions[2] for medically indigent[3] women.

Abortion became legal everywhere in the United States as a result of the Supreme Court abortion decisions of January 22, 1973, and July 1, 1976. Prior to that time only the states of Hawaii, Alaska, California, Washington, New York, and Washington, D.C. would perform abortions on demand for a fee. In addition some of these states also imposed a residency requirement on abortion patients.

Because poor (medically indigent) women did not have the money, and/or did not know how to search out an agency that performed legal abortions, or could not afford the time from jobs or families to travel to a distant state, *legal* abortion on demand by the medically indigent—prior to the 1973 Supreme Court decision—was practically non-existent.

In 1973, the High Court declared that: (1) During the first trimester (first 3 months of pregnancy), the state cannot bar any woman from obtaining an abortion from a licensed physician. (2) After the first trimester, the state can regulate the performance of abortion only if such regulations reasonably relate to the preservation or protection of the woman's health. (3) In 1976, the Supreme Court declared that states cannot impose spousal or parental consent requirements.

Four and one-half years later, on August 1, 1977, implementation of the Hyde Amendment prohibited federal payments for nontherapeutic abortions. This restriction markedly reduced, but did not eliminate, the number of medically indigent Chicanas in Alcala[4] seeking to terminate their unplanned pregnancies.

Few people view abortion as an optimal method of family planning. However, since both contraceptives and the people using them are subject to failure, abortion is considered by many family planning agencies as a necessary backup method (Abortions and the Poor 1979:40; TARAL n.d.:2). In the United States, a much larger proportion of poor women than nonpoor women have unwanted pregnancies. The Alan Guttmacher Institute reports (1979) that in the United States mothers of reproductive age from families who are poor are three times more likely than nonpoor mothers to have had one or more unwanted births during their lives.

National fertility studies show that women who are poor have more unwanted pregnancies both because they *want* somewhat fewer children than do nonpoor women—and therefore are at risk of having an unwanted pregnancy for a longer time after they have had their last wanted child—and because they are more likely than nonpoor women to experience contraceptive failure while trying to prevent an unwanted pregnancy (Abortions and the Poor 1979:20). Thus, women of low socioeconomic status—that is, those who are not high school graduates—are 45 percent more likely to experience contraceptive failure than are those who have had more than a high school education (Abortions and the Poor 1979:20).

As part of a larger study on fertility regulation practices of two groups of Mexican American women—the poor and the nonpoor—I collected and compared data on the use of nontherapeutic abortions by medically indigent Chicanas in a city in Texas. Specifically, this chapter examines the use of nontherapeutic abortion services by medically indigent Chicanas in Alcala, pseudonym for a Texas city. The study began in 1973 when federal monies were first made available to pay for elective termination of pregnancy procedures and brings us up through May 1979—20 months after federal monies were cut off. During this period, over 46 percent of reported pregnancies (positive pregnancy tests done) at the Model Cities Family Planning Clinic in Alcala's Mexican American barrio[5] terminated in elective abortion procedures. As funding monies decreased, so did the number of nontherapeutic abortions. This suggests that contrary to widespread impressions and cultural arguments, Mexican American women do use this option when available. In this study, structural factors of the health care delivery system are examined, and their role in facilitating or inhibiting Mexican American fertility regulation is explored.

FIELD METHODOLOGY

Preliminary data for this study were gathered during a period of 18 months (April 1972 to November 1973) while I was working as a registered nurse and researcher with the Model Cities Family Planning Clinic in Alcala, a Texas city of 330,000 people of which 16 percent are Mexican American. Additional visits to the clinic were conducted intermittently from May 1974 through August 1979. The Model Cities Family Planning Clinic is a recently instituted clinic (1971) for the medically indigent. The clinic is located in the geographical center of the Model Cities area in a building that formerly housed a supermarket. Most of its clients (81 percent) are Mexican American women; 16 percent are black women, and 3 percent are Anglo women and others. By virtue of a previous arrangement with the clinic director, there was an opportunity to interview most (72 percent) of the Chicanas who attended the clinic during April 1972 through March 1976. Subsequent data have been obtained from the clinic's monthly and annual reports. In May and June 1979 data were also collected from a recently opened, low-cost abortion clinic in Alcala serving a significant number of Mexican Americans (23 percent of its clients are Chicanas). In addition to the clinic-eligibility interview required for acceptance as a client, many Chicana clients voluntarily permitted several sessions of intensive interviewing in their own homes.

The Model Cities clinic was chosen for study because it serves a higher proportion of Chicanas and at the time (1975) and today continues to have a much lower dropout rate (18 percent) than the other two service providers for the medically indigent. The other providers are Planned Parenthood, with a dropout rate of 45 percent in 1975 and 28 percent in 1978, and the Family Planning Outpatient Clinics of Alcala's City and County Hospitals, with a dropout rate of 50 and 53 percent, respectively.

In my role of participant observer, I accompanied clients throughout Alcala's City and County health care system and related agencies (for example, clinic and hospital admitting offices, social service, surgery, gynecology department, public welfare, legal aid, food stamp program headquarters, childcare center, clergy consultation services on problem pregnancy, abortion clinics, and private physician abortion services).

FINDINGS
Doctors and patients

The January 1973 United States Supreme Court ruling on abortion overturned the Texas Criminal Abortion statute and left the state with no laws regarding abortion except for those set down by the federal court (Hume 1974:55). In essence, the High Court decision allows physicians to perform abortions without fear of criminal legal reprisals and allows a woman to have an abortion up to a certain stage of pregnancy (about 24 weeks) if she can find a physician who will do it. However, by November 1973, 9 months after abortion-on-demand became legal and federal funds were available to pay doctors for their services, many Alcala physicians were opposed to performing abortions for several reasons. Some are Roman Catholic and thus forbidden by religion from performing an abortion. Others still are not clear about the law. Some fear that clients who want an abortion now will regret it later on and blame the physician. Others because of their personal sexual attitudes and upbringing have strong moral objections to it. And some fear behavioral or verbal reprisals from peers who oppose abortion (Hume 1974:55).

Even today (June 1979) private physicians who perform abortions in Alcala are reluctant to admit the fact publicly. There are several reasons for this. Today, more than ever before, physicians are under increasing pressure from the public to provide competent, inexpensive, accessible care. One of their defenses to these attacks is to band together into a medical association to protect their interests and to uphold good standards of practice. These associations make "policies" to which most doctors adhere.

The Texas Medical Association accepts that abortion may be performed at a patient's request or on a physician's recommendation but is careful to state that no doctor or other health care personnel may be required to participate in performing an abortion. The policy also states that the physician must obtain the informed consent of the patient. The Texas Medical Association policy does not specifically prohibit doctors from performing abortions in their office if emergency facilities are available.

Theoretically, physicians who perform abortions have nothing to fear from their medical peers. Practically, the situation is different. A medical doctor who scoffs at local conventions by openly doing abortions may suddenly find that his privilege to practice in a hospital is endangered or that patients are no longer referred to him by other physicians.

In December 1973 in this Texas city, no more than two or three private doctors were routinely doing abortions in their offices. But women with no private physician and women who were charity patients still could not get abortions in Alcala.

The following case study illustrates the negotiations made to obtain an abortion from a private physician by a medically indigent Mexican national. In November 1973, Berta Rosa Gil was a 38-year-old divorced mother of three boys. Berta Rosa was born in western Mexico; she completed the equivalent of a high school education and trained and worked for 8 years as a vocational nurse in a private psychiatric clinic in her hometown.

Berta had several paternal half brothers. One of these half brothers, Salvador, had resided and worked in Alcala for the past 5 years. Although he entered the United States illegally, Salvador was married to a Mexican American woman, and by virtue of his marriage to a United States citizen and the formal petition to the United States immigration office by his wife, he was a legal resident of the United States. Berta Rosa finally accepted Salvador's offer that if she came to the United States he would help her find a job.

When Berta left Mexico, she left her three sons with her aunt. Ricardo, her oldest son, was 14 years old and the twins were 10 years old. When she entered the United States, Berta had a 6 month visitor's visa. She stayed in Salvador's home for a few weeks until she found a job in an east Alcala commercial laundry earning $1.25 per hour, working from 8:00 A.M. to 4:00 P.M.

For Berta, learning English was crucial since she felt it would enhance her opportunities of finding a better job. She therefore enrolled for evening classes at a local high school and paid $30.00 per semester for her classes. Berta found it difficult, however, to study at her brother's home so she moved into the house of Ester, one of the Mexican American women that worked in the laundry with her. Ester was a very attractive 26-year-old divorcee and the mother of a 10-year-old boy. Ester had been having an affair with a married musician who traveled frequently with a band and was sometimes gone several weeks at a time, making it relatively easy for Berta to stay with her.

Berta, Ester, and her son lived in a makeshift two-floor apartment in east Alcala in a structure that was once a granary. The kitchen and a small room with no windows were located downstairs; upstairs there was a medium-sized bedroom and bathroom. Berta slept in the upstairs storage area next to the bathroom, which was barely wide enough to accommodate a twin bed. Moreover, the finances were as limited as the space. Out of her $250.00 monthly income Berta sent $125.00 to her aunt to pay for school tuition, meals, and clothes for her three sons. To Ester she paid $12.00 per week rent. The remaining funds were spent in carfare to and from work, food, tuition, and miscellaneous expenses.

Not long after Berta started to share living accommodations with Ester, she found a job baby-sitting on Saturday afternoons with the children of her English teacher who lived across town. It was while waiting for the bus that would take her to her Saturday job that she met Alfredo.

One Saturday she was running late; a new pickup truck driven by Alfredo pulled up and he asked if he could give her a ride. She declined. Some 15 minutes later Berta was still waiting. It was evident that she had missed the bus and would have to wait at least 35 minutes for the next one. Alfredo drove by and again offered her a ride. This time Berta accepted. Before they arrived at her destination, he asked if he could see her again. Berta was hesitant. But Alfredo was persistent. The following Saturday Alfredo was waiting for Berta at the bus stop and thus their relationship began. Alfredo was 12 years Berta's junior, a cheerful, outgoing, obese man, with handsome facial features.

Two months after they had been going together, Alfredo confided to Berta that he had made multiple attempts to obtain a divorce. Alfredo had been married to a Chicana for the past 4 years, and they had no children. Even before he met Berta, he had asked his wife for a divorce, but she refused to grant him one.

Berta found Alfredo affectionate, naive, disarmingly charming, easy to get along with, and a gentle man who added a pleasant, although in her mind, temporary change to her otherwise austere routine. Yet, Berta was surprised that Alfredo was unaware of their age difference, appreciating that he, unlike her ex-husband Carlos, treated her as his confidante and equal.

Three months after Berta and Alfredo met they began living together. Berta tried to buy some birth control pills but was informed by the pharmacist that she needed a doctor's prescription before she could dispense them. This took Berta by surprise. Back home in Mexico a woman, if she had the money, could obtain oral contraceptives without prescription.

Therefore, Berta suggested that Alfredo use condoms, but he was reluctant to do so. He rationalized that if Berta had his child his wife would grant him a divorce and then he and Berta could be married.

According to Berta, the last thing she wanted was another child. She was fond of Alfredo but did not want to marry him, even if he were free to do so. In her opinion he was too young, somewhat immature and hedonistic, and did not understand how deeply committed she was to her sons in Mexico.

Obviously, Berta became quite concerned when her menses was 3 weeks late. Since Ester had been a client of the Family Planning Clinic in the barrio for several years, one of the clinic's first gynecologists prescribed sequential birth control pills for her, which she tolerated quite well. For a while Berta tried using Ester's oral contraceptives but discovered she could not tolerate them; they made her extremely nervous, dizzy, and nauseous.

Berta came to the Family Planning Clinic one evening directly from work. Since she did not speak English, she was assigned to one of the bilingual staff workers. During the interview, Berta expressed her fear that she might be pregnant; she had been feeling unusually sleepy and tired and had been experiencing marked urinary frequency.

The counselor asked Berta to bring her first voided urine specimen the following morning for a pregnancy test. The test was positive. She was then asked to return that afternoon to see the doctor for a medical examination. After the clinic doctor finished the examination, he informed Berta that she was 10 to 11 weeks pregnant. Berta was visibly upset. When she tried to talk, her voice quivered and she could not stop the tremors in her hands. Since Family Planning Clinic counselors were expected to discuss available options with a patient, the following session with Berta took place (these excerpts from the session have been translated from Spanish to English).

Nurse: How do you feel about the baby you are expecting?
Berta: I do not know. All I can think about is *what* am I going to tell my aunt?
Nurse: (noting from the chart that Berta is [1] divorced, [2] not eligible for Title XX benefits, and [3] has three other dependents) Why is this? Do you live in your aunt's home?

Berta: Oh no, she is in Mexico and she takes care of my children while I try to earn a living for us here.

Nurse: How does your partner feel about it?

Berta: It does not matter. He is married to someone else, and I am the one who will have to give birth and care for the new being.

Nurse: Here at the clinic you can receive prepartum care all during your pregnancy if you decide you want to keep your baby. If you want to discontinue your pregnancy, we can also help you with that; but we like for our patients to think it over well before a decision is made.

Berta: You mean there is a way I can get an abortion?

Nurse: Yes, in this state now (fall 1973) you can get an abortion safely and legally if you are less than 5 months pregnant.

Berta: I can get it done here?

Nurse: No, not here but we can refer you to a private clinic in Springdale.

Berta: What do I have to do? How much do I have to pay? How long will I have to be off from work? Will I. . . .

Nurse: Wait. Wait. Let me explain several things first and then let's see if I have answered all that you want to know. Then, we shall pick up from there. Is that all right?

Berta: (manages a brief smile) Yes, that is fine. It's just that I am so relieved that someone will talk to me about these things.

Nurse: In Alcala we do not yet have facilities to do pregnancy termination but we are working on it. The closest place to us now is Springdale—a city about 80 miles from here. They are very nice there. Unfortunately, since you are not eligible for free services, they charge $150.00 if you are up to 10 weeks pregnant. No overnight stay is required and you will be at their clinic for approximately 3 hours. When one is less than 10 weeks pregnant, the termination is a one-stage procedure. Have you ever had one done before? Or would you like for me to tell you about it?

Berta: Yes, I would like to know what they do. I have not had an abortion before, but several of my friends back home have.

Nurse: Oh really. Is it difficult to have one done in Mexico?

Berta: Well . . . no but you see . . . you just get a *comadrona* (a lay midwife) or a nurse who does these things. And she tells you "I am going to do the job but if you start bleeding or feel a fever *don't wait,* just go straight to the hospital's emergency service and tell them that you were pregnant and that you suddenly started bleeding. Don't tell them anything at all about having come to me because if you do they will put *both* of us in jail." Back home, I have accompanied one or two of my friends to the hospital after they have been to a *comadrona*. One friend was very sick for several weeks with red spots all over her body but she got all right.

Nurse: Well, over here we try to prevent the patient from getting sick at all. The clinic in Springdale has been open for about 6 months now. They have done about 800 abortions on women up to 14 weeks pregnant without a single complication. Here is what they do (picks up a plastic mannequin of the reproductive system): This is the way that female organs are shaped (points out the various structures and gives them the lay Spanish term and the medical name; for example, this is the womb or what the doctor calls the uterus. There are several components or parts to the womb. This part is called the fundus or the body of the womb; pregnancy terminations in the first three months of pregnancy. . . .)

Berta: (interrupts) By pregnancy termination do you mean abortion?

Nurse: Yes. Abortions in the first 3 months of pregnancy involve the insertion of a plastic tube (a cannula) into the womb (uterus) and removal of the womb contents by suction.

In order for the tube to be placed in the womb, the cervix (that portion of the womb that opens into this area here that is called the vagina) must be widened (dilated). Cervical or mouth-of-the-womb dilation is usually accomplished by inserting metal rods of increasing size (diameter) into the cervical opening. As each rod (dilator) is introduced and withdrawn, the cervical opening widens, until the correct width necessary for placement of the cannula is attained.

Berta: Uuy . . . is that painful? Will I be able to stand it?

Nurse: Most of the time it is not painful at all and they do use a local anesthetic. But I will get into that in a minute. Let's see . . . after the cervix has been widened, a cannula whose length and width correspond to the size of the uterus is inserted. The cannula is connected to a vacuum aspiration machine by plastic tubing. When the cannula is in place, the machine is turned on, and the contents of the womb are drawn out and into a container on the machine. The actual abortion process takes from 5 to 10 minutes.

Berta: Will I be conscious while this is going on?

Nurse: Most doctors prefer that the patient remain awake during the procedure. Local anesthesia and a "deadener" similar to that dentists use, are usually injected in the cervical area to lessen discomfort. Relaxation by the patient can greatly aid in reducing pain. Slow, deep breaths are very helpful in obtaining and maintaining relaxation.

On the day the abortion is scheduled, you should have a bowel movement. If you do not have a bowel movement, you should take an enema. An empty lower intestine will allow the vaginal passage to be opened widely during the abortion, giving the doctor more room in which to work.

You should arrange for someone to drive you home after the abortion, in case you are not feeling well. By the way there are several laboratory tests that need to be done before arranging an abortion. We have already done them here for you and will include a copy of them in the letter of referral to the Springdale clinic, which we will give you when you go. One of them is the positive pregnancy test; another is a blood test to determine if you are anemic. A third test is a blood typing and what is called an Rh factor determination in case a transfusion is needed. Another test is for vaginal infections (venereal disease). In your case the vaginal infection test was negative.

Some doctors and clinics include the necessary laboratory work in the price of the abortion. One should find out in advance what is included in the price. No woman should have an abortion without these laboratory tests. They provide information that the doctor should know in case complications arise during the procedure.

Berta: If the procedure takes only 5 to 10 minutes, why do I have to stay there 3 hours or more?

Nurse: Most doctors have the patient remain 1 to 2 hours after the abortion for observation. During this time, temperature, blood pressure, and pulse are checked, and the patient is watched for any signs of bleeding. If no problems are detected, you are free to leave. Most women experience some vaginal bleeding following an abortion, although some women do not bleed at all. The bleeding may last from 2 to 6 days. If the bleeding lasts more than 10 days, or if it is more than . . . half a cup, and/or accompanied by large blood clots or cramping, the doctor or the clinic should be contacted immediately.

Berta: If I have the abortion on a Friday, can I be back at work on Monday?

Nurse: What do you do at work?

Berta: I fold linen.

Nurse: Is it hot or air-conditioned where you work? And do you stand up all day long or do you have a chance to work sitting down?

Berta: Now I work in an air-conditioned room and I can either sit or stand to do the work.

Nurse: Well, it would be better if you waited a few days before going back to work, but since they won't hold your job open you can go back to work on Monday. But be sure to call us and let us know how you are feeling. You should take your temperature each day for 1 week following the abortion. Do you know how to read a thermometer? Good! If the temperature rises above 100 degrees, you should contact us. This may mean an infection has occurred. We will keep an eye on you to see how you are getting along. And if you need us at any time, call us. Here is a card with our name, address, and telephone number. If they answer you in English at the switchboard, keep talking in Spanish . . . they will get someone that speaks Spanish for you. Two weeks after the abortion come back and see us for a checkup. This is important to ensure that you are completely recovered as well as to make sure that a good method of birth control is made available to you.

Berta: Ay Dios Mio, if I get through this alive I am not going to need contraceptives because I don't plan to see him again, ever!

Nurse: I know how you must feel. But we are creatures with feelings and needs and you have the right to change your mind. If, later on, you do change your mind, I want you to remember that we can help you choose a method of contraception that you are comfortable with, OK?

Berta: Thank you. But I don't think so.

Nurse: OK. Let's see where we are . . . oh yes, unfortunately we do not have any pamphlets that I can give you on this that are written in Spanish. I would like for you to think over what you and I have discussed; that is, you can go ahead and have your baby and we will help you throughout your pregnancy. Or you could have the baby and put it up for adoption—an alternative I had not mentioned before. Or you could go ahead with the abortion.

Berta: Oh, I want to have the abortion and may God forgive me.

Nurse: Why don't you go home and talk it over with your partner or someone you trust and then let us know. I would advise though that you don't take longer than 2 or 3 days because the further along you are in your pregnancy the more the health risk involved, the more it will cost, and the longer you will have to stay in the clinic.

Berta: I know he will not consent to it. Besides this is my problem, not his. I have to fend for myself. I cannot afford to have a baby. I am having a hard enough time trying to make ends meet with my three sons. To say nothing of the hell I would have to go through with my Aunt. . . . She probably will throw my sons out of her house and where will they go since I don't have the legal papers or money to send for them. No, I want the abortion. Tell me what I need to do.

Nurse: I want to make sure you are comfortable with your decision, and that you are not doing something you will regret later.

Berta: No, I am sure this is what I want to do.

Nurse: Fine. Just remember that if you want to talk about your feelings we will be glad to listen and try to be of help.

Berta: Thank you.

Nurse: The next thing you need to do is raise the $150.00 that Springdale is going to charge you for the procedure. How soon do you think you could get the money?

Berta: I don't know, but I will try. I know I might be able to borrow part of it. Will they (clinic at Springdale) let me pay some money now, and then I will pay some of it weekly?

Nurse: Usually they don't like to do that particularly if you are from out of town, but I could ask them when I call to make the appointment. Also, who do you know that has a car and would be willing to accompany you to Springdale?

Berta: My friend Ester could accompany me but she does not have a car.

Nurse: I tell you what . . . why don't you go home and see what you can arrange regarding this, between now and tomorrow morning. I will do the same. Just remember you should not delay too much longer.

Berta: Nurse, is there no place in Alcala that will do abortions?

Nurse: There is a slim possibility and that is what I want to check out.

Early the following morning, Berta Rosa returned to the clinic with $50.00 she had been able to borrow from her stepbrother. However, Ester, the only friend Berta would confide in, could not accompany her until the weekend. Meanwhile the counselor had contacted one of the three physicians in Alcala who would do abortions. One of the bilingual vocational nurses from the clinic, Alicia, provided transportation and served as Berta's interpreter. When Alicia and Berta arrived, they were ushered directly into the doctor's office. This particular doctor required a personal interview with the prospective patient so he could determine if the woman was psychologically ready and emotionally stable enough to go through with the abortion. After about a 20-minute session with Berta and Alicia, he agreed to perform the procedure. He also charged $150.00 for the abortion and accepted the $50.00 down payment, with the assurance that Berta would pay the balance in monthly installments.

Alicia had brought Berta's reports on the required laboratory tests to the interview. After briefly studying the laboratory reports, the doctor asked Berta to sign a release form (written in English) testifying that the procedure had been thoroughly explained and that she had been fully informed of the risks involved. Berta and Alicia were then taken to one of the examining rooms where the physician's office nurse assisted him during the 10-minute procedure. Following the abortion, Berta remained resting on the table for about 15 minutes. Before they left the office, Berta was given a prescription for a week's supply of antibiotic capsules. The neighborhood pharmacist was going to charge $15.60 for the capsules, but Berta did not have the money. At Alicia's suggestion, they stopped by the clinic. The R.N. gave Berta the capsules from a small drug supply stock that remained after pharmacy services were switched from the clinic to a private contract pharmacist, a few months after the Family Planning Clinic first opened. Berta was started on the antibiotic capsules less than an hour after the abortion was performed—an important precautionary step that is often omitted by indigent patients because they lack financial resources, and medications are not included in health care coverage.

Twice during the weekend Alicia visited and monitored Berta's vital signs. The following Tuesday after work, Berta stopped by the clinic where, in addition to a brief physical checkup, she was provided with a 3-month supply of oral contraceptives that she reluctantly accepted.

Nothing was seen or heard of Berta Rosa until 8 months later when she arrived at the clinic and asked to talk to her counselor. Many changes in her life had transpired during this time interval. The week following the abortion, in an attempt to sever her relationship with Alfredo, she purposely accepted a job offer as janitor in a private college—with a large foreign student enrollment—in the southernmost sector of Alcala. The offer was extended by a friend of her English teacher. Berta had moved into the home of one of her sister-in-law's friends within walking distance of the college. The job not only paid better but Berta was able to attend an English class, free of charge, for foreign students. This seemingly ideal arrangement lasted for 4 months until anticipated federal funds failed to materialize, forcing the college into an economy drive and leaving Berta without a job.

In the interim, Alfredo had traced Berta's whereabouts. Now working as a welder for a local steel welding company, Alfredo and a co-worker had rented a modern two-bedroom furnished apartment in the southwest section of Alcala. As explanation for her estrangement from him, Berta told Alfredo she had miscarried his child and had to undergo medical treatment. Knowing his situation, she had not wanted to burden him. According to Berta, Alfredo lamented the loss of the child but was pleased to learn he could father a child—a doubt that had nagged him since he married.

For several months Berta had been unsuccessfully trying to find a job. The task was made more difficult by her lack of mobility and of bus fare money for the long rides to and from east and downtown Alcala where her chances of finding employment were greater. Therefore given the financial destitution she faced, Berta decided to accept Alfredo's offer to move in with him. He also provided some money to mail to her sons and to pay part of the Alcala physician's bill. Moreover, he offered to help her find a job by driving her to employment agencies and filling out, in English, job application forms.

The purpose of Berta's clinic trip had been to obtain a pill prescription refill because she still did not want to have another child. She was down to her last week's supply of oral contraceptives. She had hidden the envelope with the individually foil-wrapped contraceptives in the inside lining of a zippered compartment in her purse, so Alfredo would not know she was taking the pills.

Meanwhile, the man sharing the apartment and expenses with Alfredo had reconciled with his wife and moved back home. Beginning the following month, Alfredo was responsible for all the apartment expenses. Consequently, he and Berta were thinking of moving into a one-bedroom apartment in the same complex or of finding less expensive accommodations. As one can see, Berta's socioeconomic situation continued to be a most inauspicious one, and this in many ways affected her precarious access to the effective contraceptives.

The last field note entry on Berta Rosa is dated August 1976, at which time she was still a successful oral contraceptive user.

Hospitals

Hospitals are governed by a board of trustees in conjunction with a medical staff. The medical staff of a hospital is composed of private physicians who have the "privilege" to admit and treat their patients at that hospital. The internal policies of a hospital are a matter of individual choice. No *private* hospital is required to allow abortions to be performed within its walls.

If the governing board of a private hospital decides to perform abortions in its institution, guidelines are set up that dictate what kinds of procedures will be allowed, what kinds of consent and consultation are needed, who will perform the procedure, and where (Hume 1974:58). Hospitals can discourage abortions by requiring patients to stay overnight for what can be an outpatient procedure, thus making it more inconvenient and more expensive; by requiring consultation with several other physicians; by allowing only "therapeutic" abortions; by requiring consent forms from several persons other than the woman herself; or by scheduling the procedure at a time auxiliary personnel such as anesthesiologists or scrub nurses are unwilling to cooperate.

In Alcala there has been controversy over the abortion policies of the only publicly supported *(nonprivate)* hospital—the *only* local hospital that provides services to the medically indigent and that reluctantly allows abortions to be performed within its walls. This City-County Memorial hospital is financed by tax money for the health care of all the people of the area, especially the medically indigent. Many who are on Medicaid or who are just above the poverty line use the public hospital as their sole source of health care. The City-County Memorial Hospital has outpatient clinics where patients can receive treatment for ailments that do not require hospitalization; however, public outpatient facilities for abortion to this date (June 1979) are nonexistent.

Alcala's city manager has refused to allocate money for abortion equipment such as the vacuum suction machine, tubing, and cannula aspirator despite endorsement of the request by the obstetrics and gynecology staff. In the winter of 1973 a private donor loaned the equipment; with it, two of the private gynecologists began doing abortions without compensation for medically indigent patients who did not qualify for Title XX funds. Since that time, other local physicians have learned the procedure.

In October 1973 the City-County Memorial Hospital, pressured by a local feminist group and the recent federal ruling, reluctantly allowed private physicians to perform abortions in the hospital. Operating room personnel were not required to participate in surgical procedures that were contrary to their personal moral values. Some personnel however did not object to participating in abortion procedures, as the following case study illustrates.

María Gómez is a 30-year-old Mexican American woman with marked Indian facial features who has five living children. Her husband is a construction worker who, according to María, has been having extramarital affairs on and off throughout their married life.

When María made her initial visit to the Family Planning Clinic (FPC), she was 3 months pregnant and wanted an abortion. Six weeks earlier María's husband had gone to live with another woman, leaving María with no financial resources other than welfare. Fortunately, she was offered an evening shift job at a 7-Eleven store close to her home. However, before she could qualify for the job María had to submit to a medical history and physical examination. At that time (December 1973), the store manager did not hire pregnant women since he did not want to train temporary employees. Obviously María's desire for an abortion was justified by the financial hardship she would face if she gave birth to another child, not to mention the emotional stress caused by her husband's desertion. Therefore, the staff at the FPC complied with María's request and initiated the process necessary to begin abortion procedures. First, the Model Cities Family Planning Clinic nurse got María a staff (charity) card at the City-County Hospital, and the private gynecologist whose services would be paid by Medicaid was able to post Mrs. Gómez's procedure on the following day's hospital surgical schedule.

The anesthetist who administered María's general anesthetic stated candidly, "If a woman wants an abortion, she ought to be able to get one." The R.N. who circulated during the surgical procedure expressed that:

> Anyone who makes a decision of that magnitude ought to have all the medical and nursing help that she needs. These women are desperate, and if we do not do them (the abortions), they are going to find someone in a dark alley who will do it for them.

The scrub nurse on the case, a licensed vocational nurse, summed up María's situation aptly:

> There are times in a woman's life when everything backfires. I know it. . . . I am going through a divorce myself . . . we have hesitated and postponed the divorce decision so many times that if, during one of our reconciliations, I had turned up pregnant, I know I would have terminated that pregnancy so fast it would make your head swim.

Finally, the gynecologist who performed María's abortion commented:

> I don't want an abortion to become a pleasant, easily accessible service. On the other hand, I have to be realistic and human. I do not perform abortions on demand. I have to have a long chat with the patient to assess her emotional stability and to convince myself that it is needed. This patient, for example, is in no position economically or emotionally to bring another child into this world. From my conversations with her I can see this is not a decision she has made lightly. Furthermore, if she gives birth to another child, all we are helping to promote is dependency on welfare and eliminating, however small, her chances of becoming employed and self-supporting. Of course, the ideal would be to insert an I.U.D. in her right away, but that is a topic that you all (Family Planning Clinic nurses), will have to bring up in your counseling with Mrs. Gómez.

The last field note entry on Mrs. Gómez was dated July 1975. For contraceptive use, she had chosen the foam and condom. María had left the 7-Eleven store job and was employed as a teacher's aide at a nearby grammar school.

Clinics

Despite the 1977 withdrawal of federal funds to pay for abortions for medically indigent women, abortion services for women in Alcala are slowly but steadily improving. For example, in October 1973, some private patients were able to obtain abortions from their doctors, but women who were charity patients could not get abortions in the city. Today (June 1979) three Alcala Womens' Health Centers—privately owned by board-certified gynecologists, the City-County Memorial Hospital, and one nonprofit, free-standing[6] abortion clinic—provide nontherapeutic abortion services.

The three privately owned Womens' Health Centers take only private (paying) patients. The centers' sliding fee scale charges a minimum of $175.00 for first trimester and $350.00 for second trimester abortions. Both procedures are done at the center. First trimester procedures take only 4 hours, second trimester abortions have to be two-stage procedures: during the initial visit a medical history and physical examination, laboratory tests, financial intake, counseling, and insertion of *Laminaria*[7] to dilate the cervix are done. The woman is then sent home to return the following morning for the vacuum aspiration of uterine contents under local anesthetic.

Since the implementation of the Hyde Amendment prohibiting use of federal funds to pay for nontherapeutic abortions for Medicaid-eligible women, the City-County Memorial Hospital has restricted the number from 20 to 6 abortions per week. It still continues to discourage abortion patients by requiring that: (1) all abortions be performed by a private physician (instead of a resident or intern); (2) *all* abortions be performed as two-stage procedures—*Laminaria* is inserted the evening before, then the patient returns the following day for the vacuum aspiration; (3) no professional counseling is provided, thus the patient seldom has the opportunity to discuss with a counselor her feelings concerning abortion, birth control, and possible alternatives to pregnancy termination—an important aspect in educating and preventing another unwanted pregnancy; and (4) the number of abortions is restricted to six per week, thereby placing a hardship on the borderline client who may be 11 to 12 weeks pregnant and insidiously forcing her into a second trimester abortion that markedly increases complication risks and the price of procedure.

The emergence of free-standing abortion clinics in the state is a response to the fact that private doctors do not perform significant numbers of abortions and hospitals do not accommodate significant numbers of abortion patients (Hume 1974:58). To fill the need, ''Reproductive Services'' clinics, a nonprofit association that provides legal, reasonably safe abortions for large numbers of women, have begun to take hold in Texas.

In February 1978, 6 months after implementation of the Hyde Amendment, a Reproductive Services clinic opened in Alcala. The essential difference between this and three private Women's Health Centers clinics is that Reproductive Services has a *federal* contract to provide family planning services to women who qualify; the others do not. Prices for abortions here range from an average of $160.00 for a vacuum aspiration to $295.00 for an 18- to 20-week second trimester abortion. Owing to an unexpected withdrawal of insurance coverage by the insurer, as of April 1979, the clinic discontinued second trimester abortions. Today these are being referred to sister clinics in other Texas cities. The facility—like all outpatient abortion clinics—offers several advantages to women seeking termination of their pregnancies; for example: (1) the stay is rarely more than 4 hours; (2) a woman can usually get an appointment within 24 hours; (3) patients seldom, if ever, encounter hostile staff attitudes; and (4) the small amount of equipment required makes this clinic homelike and intimate, geared exclusively to the needs of the abortion patients.

The hospital mood has been toned down to ease patients' fears, for example, the decor is colorful. Few staff personnel wear white coats. The abortion is called a ''procedure''; it is performed in the ''procedure room.'' These three rooms resemble regular operating rooms in that they have an operating table and bright lights. But there is far less equipment—a tray of sterile instruments and a suction machine.

In most cases the client first contacts the clinic by telephone. At that time information is given, an appointment is made, and the patient is requested to bring her first voided urine specimen of the following morning and payment in cash or money order. When a client arrives, a receptionist fills out a basic fact sheet. The client then goes to another room for laboratory tests such as urinalyses, hematocrit (for anemia), and blood typing. A pelvic examination is done by a licensed family nurse practitioner to make sure that pregnancy is not too advanced for a clinic abortion, and the patient is given counseling by professionally trained individuals. The counselor is usually a young woman, wearing informal clothes, who counsels patients on an individual basis in a small private room. The counselor discusses various options, encourages questions, and discusses the many different methods of birth control and how reliable they are. She also displays samples and information pamphlets on the various available contraceptive methods. The patient then goes to one of the procedure rooms where a family nurse practitioner prepares the patient by explaining the procedure in simple language. The abortion is then performed under local anesthesia by one of the gynecologists. The patient then is accompanied to the "recovery room" where another nurse practitioner will periodically check the patient's vital signs for the following 3 hours. The recovery room is gaily decorated in yellow, orange, and brown colors. It has two couches and several stuffed chairs. There patients can obtain free soft drinks and a variety of pamphlets and information on birth control methods.

On discharge the patient is given printed instructions on aftercare. A counselor explains the "hot line" available—a free 24-hour telephone service to one of the family nurse practitioners or gynecologists—and an appointment is scheduled for a 2-week medical checkup.

The clinic is open from 8 A.M. to 5 P.M. Monday through Saturday. It is closed on Sunday. It is staffed with three bilingual counselors and a receptionist. Its executive director is a young woman with a B.A. in social work. It has three family nurse practitioners and two board-certified gynecologists on its staff.

By virtue of its federal contract for Title XX family planning services, this clinic is able to provide abortions for as low as $95 to medically indigent women. The remaining $65 paid by Title XX funds covers laboratory tests, physical examination, professional counseling, and contraceptives—all family planning services rendered to the client before and after the abortion *procedure* (for which the client pays out of her pocket).

In its 15 months of operation, the clinic has averaged approximately 130 procedures per month. Fifty-six percent of its clients are Anglo; 23 percent are Mexican American; 13 percent are black; and 8 percent are of other racial and ethnic backgrounds.

Eighty-seven percent of all abortions performed at this clinic have been first trimester procedures. The youngest patient was 14 years old and the oldest 51 years old.

Fifty-four percent of the women were single; 33 percent were married; and 2 percent were separated or divorced. For 28 percent of the clients this was not their first abortion. *Twenty-two percent of its clients were referred from the Model Cities Clinic.*

Before funding cutoffs, more than 1,200 Texas women applied for and received federal and state monies for abortions. In 1978, 34 abortions were paid for with federal funds (Records: Alcala Department of Human Resources).

What happens to all those women who once qualified for and received funds that are no longer available?

A check of Alcala Abortion Clinics shows that, despite cutbacks, women are still seeking and getting abortions. *Not* including those done by private physicians in their offices, more than 400 abortions are performed in Alcala each month (Records: Alcala Department of Human Resources).

"The majority of women manage to come up with the money. Most of them are getting it, one way or another," said the director of Alcala's Department of Human Resources. Some clinics, but not many, will give reduced rates to medically indigent women. That they are able to do so is in part a result of receiving Title XX family planning funds. As it has been explained before, the woman pays for the abortion, while Title XX money is used for her laboratory workup and professional counseling. Long-term payment arrangements can also be made at this clinic.

SUMMARY AND CONCLUSIONS

Data obtained from the active membership file (those with paid 1976 membership dues) of Alcala's Mexican American Business and Professional Women Association (MABPWA) reveal in Table 3-1 that the average number of children of an Alcala college graduate MABPWA member is 1.017—a rate considerably lower than that of the national average.

Table 3-2 shows the eventual outcome and disposition of pregnancy tests done at Alcala's Model Cities Family Planning Clinic from April 1975 to March 1976—a time when federal funds were available to pay for nontherapeutic abortions for medically indigent women. During those 12 months at this clinic where 81 percent of its clients are Chicanas, 219 (46 percent) out of a total of 471 women terminated their pregnancies with

Table 3-1. Education and fertility of college graduate MABPWA members, 1976

| Education | Number of children | | | | | | | | | | | |
| | 0 | | 1 | | 2 | | 3 | | 4 | | 5 | |
	No.	%	No.	%	No.	%	No.	%	No.	%	No.	%
BA (N = 33)	21	63.6	5	15.1	5	15.1	1	3	—		1	3
MA (N = 20)	14	70	1	5	3	15	2	10	—		—	
PhD (N = 4)	4	100	—		—		—		—		—	
N = 57	39	68	6	12.2	8	14.0	3	5.2	0		1	1.6
		68		12.2		14.0		5.2	—			1.6

$$\frac{\text{Total number of women} = 57}{\text{Total number of offspring} = 58} = 1.017 \quad \begin{array}{l}\text{Average number of children of}\\ \text{college educated MABPWA member}\end{array}$$

elective abortions. In December 1978 (Table 3-3) 6 months after federal funds were no longer available, only 100 (23.5 percent) out of a total of 420 obtained abortions.

According to the Texas Department of Human Resources, prior to the implementation of the Hyde Amendment, the birthrate of Medicaid mothers was dropping at the rate of 10 percent annually. Since the implementation of the Hyde Amendment, the first year indi-

Table 3-2. Eventual outcome and disposition of 663 pregnancy tests done at Alcala's Model Cities Family Planning Clinic from April 1975 to March 1976

	Positive results		Negative results	
	No.	%	No.	%
Family planning record				
Yes	171	36	111	57
No	300	64	81	42
Number of children				
0	165	35	69	35
1-3	243	51	99	51
Over 3	63	13	27	14
Age				
11-14	12	2	0	0
15-19	180	38	63	32
20-24	168	35	78	40
25-29	84	17	12	6
30-34	6	1	24	12
Over 34	21	4	15	7
Previous abortions	36	7	24	12
Planned pregnancy	108	22	36	18
Unplanned pregnancy	345	73	156	81
Using birth control pills	204	43	102	53
Ran out of pills	36	17	9	8
Stopped using pills	47	72	39	38
Missed pills	21	10	9	7
Using other method	30	6	9	4
Using no method	213	45	75	39
Referred to prenatal clinic				
MCOB*	186	39		
Other OB	21	4		
Abortion	219	46		
Unknown	45	9		
If positive, desired				
Obstetrics			72	37
Abortion			63	32
Unsure			57	29
TOTAL	471		192	

*MCOB = Model Cities Obstetrical Clinic.

Table 3-3. Eventual outcome and disposition of pregnancy tests done at Alcala's Model Cities Family Planning Clinic

	From April 1975 to March 1976	From January* to December 1978
Total pregnancy tests done	663	705
Negative results	192	285
Referred to family planning clinic	168	285
Positive results	471	420
Carried pregnancy to full term	207 (43%)	320 (76.5%)
Nontherapeutic abortion	219 (46%)	100 (23.5%)
Unknown	45 (11%)	0 (0%)

*Six months after implementation of Hyde Amendment prohibiting use of federal funds to pay for nontherapeutic abortions for Medicaid-eligible women.

cated no drop of the previously noted 10 percent but an increase of 6 percent. These combined figures indicate a 16 percent increase in births to Medicaid mothers.

These findings suggest that Mexican American Women—regardless of apparent resistances to fertility regulation attributed to Mexican American culture—are eager to regulate their fertility particularly when the regime to be followed is sensitively presented and consonant with their economic reality.

NOTES

1. The terms "Mexican American" and "Chicano" will be used interchangeably in this work. "Mexican American" is used because it reflects that most Americans of Spanish surname in the southwest United States are of Mexican descent or birth and that they retain and acknowledge some cultural and biological characteristics of this Indo-Hispanic heritage. In addition, the term differentiates them from other Spanish-surnamed groups in the United States such as Puerto Ricans or Cubans. Most importantly, the term is used because the people with whom I worked do not find it objectionable.

    The word "Chicano" is used as an alternate in this study because its use among Mexican American youth, among politicized Mexican Americans, by the mass media, and by the majority of the health care agents in Alcala is increasing notably.

2. In this study nontherapeutic abortion is defined as the termination of a pregnancy by medical means at the voluntary request of the woman. Other alternates used will be "abortion," "abortion on demand," and "legal abortion." These four terms contrast with "therapeutic abortion," which in Hyde Amendment language means termination of a pregnancy by medical means when a pregnant woman's life is endangered, or if pregnancy is the result of reported rape or incest.

3. People officially recognized by the government as unable to afford medical services.

4. All persons and places mentioned will be provided fictitious names to protect those who aided so graciously and willingly in this research endeavor.

5. A section of a city where most Mexican Americans of low socioeconomic status live.

6. Facilities separate from hospitals but dependent on them for emergency services.

7. Sterile *Laminaria digitata* is used to cause some dilation of the cervix in advance. The dried, rounded stems of seaweed 5 to 7 cm. long and 1 mm. or more in diameter are inserted into the cervix 12 hours before instillation. The seaweed stems gradually expand as they absorb moisture, dilating the cervix in a gentle and painless way. They must not be left in longer than 12 hours because of risk of infection.

REFERENCES

Abortions and the Poor
  1979 Private Morality, Public Responsibility. New York: The Alan Guttmacher Institute.
Bradshaw, Benjamin S. and Frank D. Bean
  1972 "Some aspects of the fertility of Mexican Americans." Pp. 139-164 in C. F. Westhoff and R. Parks, Jr. (eds.), Demographic and Social Aspects of Population Growth. Washington, D.C.: U.S. Government Printing Office.
Clark, Margaret
  1959 Health in the Mexican American Culture. Berkeley, California: University of California Press.
Ehrenreich, John and Barbara Ehrenreich
  1970 The American Health Empire. New York: Random House.
Grebler, Leo, Joan W. Moore and Ralph C. Guzmán
  1970 The Mexican American People: The Nations Second Largest Minority. New York: The Free Press.
Hume, Martha
  1974 "Abortion in Texas." Texas Monthly Magazine, March.
Leñero-Otero, Luis
  1968 Investigacion de la Familia en Mexico. Mexico: Instituto Mexicano de Estudios Sociales.
Madsen, William
  1964 The Mexican American of South Texas. New York: Holt, Rinehart & Winston.

MALDEF (Mexican American Legal Defense and Educational Fund) Newsletter
  1978 "Profile of the Chicana: a statistical fact sheet." March. San Francisco, California.
Moore, Joan W.
  1970 Mexican Americans. Englewood Cliffs, New Jersey: Prentice-Hall, Inc.
Murillo, Nathan
  1971 "The Mexican American family." Pp. 77-108 in N. W. Wagner and M. J. Huags (eds.), Chicanos: Social and Psychological Perspectives, ed. 1. St. Louis, Missouri: The C. V. Mosby Co.
Rubel, Arthur J.
  1966 Across the Tracks. Mexican Americans in a Texas City. Austin, Texas: University of Texas Press.
Stycos, J. Mayone
  1968 Human Fertility in Latin American. Ithaca, New York: Cornell University Press.
TARAL (Texas Abortion Rights Action League)
  n.d. "Choice: a woman's right to choose; a child's right to be wanted." Austin, Texas.
Uhlenberg, Peter
  1973 "Fertility patterns within the mexican american population." Social Biology 20:30-39.
U.S. Commission on Civil Rights
  1968 The Mexican American. Washington, D.C.: U.S. Government Printing Office.

Chapter 4

Mexican, Mexican American, and Chicana childbirth

Margarita A. Kay

"Resuella hondo, puja fuerte cada vez que te venga el dolor . . . Más fuerte, más . . . ¡grita, hija!"

Francisco Rojas Gonzalez[1]

These are the words of a *comadrona* (empiric midwife) delivering a young Mexican Indian girl, but they are the same words repeated everywhere to the woman who is being delivered of a baby, "take a deep breath and push." They are words that the Mexican American woman may have heard more often than others, for the stereotype emphasizes her status as mother.

This chapter describes the Mexican American culture of childbirth. It takes a degree of temerity to discuss "the" Mexican American woman. Differences come from individual personality, position in a family constellation such as oldest or youngest daughter, sexual preference, economic class, educational attainment, place of enculturation, and education. My conceptual orientation is that of Wallace's (1970) organization of diversity, and Goodenough's (1963:258-259) definition of culture as "standards for deciding what can be, standards for deciding how one feels about it, standards for deciding what to do about it, and standards for deciding how to go about doing it."

Each childbirth is a unique event that reflects the individual experiences as well as the social norms and cultural theory of the participants. Nonetheless, the childbirth beliefs and rules for behavior that may be expected to occur at a birth can be described with reasonable accuracy if the generation removed from Mexico and the historical time of childbirth are considered. One way to adjust for differences in order to predict behavior is to learn the ethnic identity label that the childbearing woman chooses.[2] Herein are related the childbirth practices of four groups of women, three generations of Mexican Americans and one group of Mexicans in southern Arizona. The home childbirth of women who are now grandmothers, delivery in the hospital of their daughters, return to home birth by a few of their granddaughters, and the attainment of hospital birth by newly arrived Mexican relatives will be depicted. Women in one group call themselves Mexicans. These women are likely to be past childbearing age. They used to give birth at home attended by a traditional midwife, either a *partera* or a *comadrona*. Their childbirth culture was an elaborate system of rules that was learned from their mothers and other conjugal, affinal, and ritual kinswomen as well as the midwife. The rules functioned to assure normal fetal development, safe delivery, transition to the role of mother, and a healthy child. Reintegration into society followed a long convalescence, called *la dieta*. The mother was an active recipient of care during each stage of the reproductive cycle.

The material reported in this chapter has appeared in other publications. Much of it derives from "The Mexican American" in *Culture/Childbearing/Health Professionals*, edited by Ann Clark, published by F. A. Davis Company, and copyrighted in 1978; it appears here with their permission. Data for the chapter were obtained in the course of various studies. The first was "Mexican and Mexican-American Mothers," USPHS Grant CH00-132. The second was a study of "Determinants of Prenatal Care," conducted for the Maternal Health Care Project of the Tucson Committee for Economic Opportunity. The third study was dissertation research, funded by a special predoctoral fellowship 4F04-NU-27, 134-05. The title of the dissertation is "Health and Illness in the Barrio: Women's Point of View." An abbreviated version, "Health and Illness in a Mexican American Barrio," (Kay 1977b) is one of four cultures described in *Ethnic Medicine in the Southwest*. A fourth study (Kay 1977a) was entitled "The Ethnosemantics of Mexican American Fertility," funded by Grant HD 0748-01 of the National Institute of Child Health and Human Development. A fifth study (Anderson, Kay, and Shaw 1978) compared home and hospital birth and was supported by the College of Nursing, University of Arizona. Data for a sixth study, concerned with Mexican nationals who cross the border to give birth, are presently being collected by Sergio Bustamante and Margarita Kay, principal investigators.

At this writing, some of the daughters of the women interviewed and observed in the early pilot study that preceded the first funded research in 1965 are now giving birth themselves. The practices of these young women are not the same as those followed by their mothers. This is not simply because of the general gap between generations. As a matter of fact, the practices of their accoucheurs, their obstetricians and midwives, have also changed in the intervening years.

MEXICAN AMERICAN KINSHIP

The women who support each other through the childbirth cycle are most commonly *familia* (family). That is, they are related by blood, marriage, or choice through religious ceremony. No discussion of Mexican American women is complete without explaining the kinship system and the terms that label each kind of kin. If a particular relationship has a label, it indicates a group of people considered to be significant because there are critical responsibilities as well as rights toward them. If a kinship status has a label, this suggests a category of persons with whom social interaction is expected.

In Fig. 1, 33 terms for each sex are illustrated. Since this is a discussion of women, the kinship chart departs from custom with *ego,* a woman. In ego's own lines there are kin terms for each of nine generations. Her parent's sister is *tia*. After her *madre* (mother) is

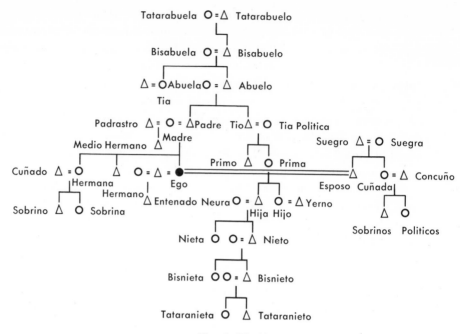

Fig. 1. Kinship.

her *abuela* (grandmother), then *bisabuela* (great-grandmother), and then finally *tatar-abuela* (great-great-grandmother). After her *hija* (daughter) is her *nieta* (granddaughter), then her *bisnieta* (great-granddaughter), and her *tataranieta* (great-great granddaughter).

An entire terminological group is added to encompass relations resulting from re-marriage. Thus, ego's stepfather is her *padastro;* her stepmother is her *madrastra;* her stepdaughter is her *hijastra* or *entenada;* her stepsister is her *media hermana.*

Relations by marriage, "in-laws," are quite explicit. There are terms to designate not only ego's spouse, *marido* or *esposo,* his parents, *suegros,* and ego's child's spouse, *yerno (nuera,* f.), but also ego's spouse's sibling, *cuñado,* and ego's spouse's sibling's spouse, *concuño.* There are also terms for ego's parent's sibling's spouse, *tío político,* and ego's spouse's sibling's child, *sobrino político.*

Collateral relatives are differentiated only by generation according to most informants. A few differentiate between first, second, and third cousins as *primos carnales, primos secundarios,* and *primos terceros. Prima,* cousin, covers women who are of one's own generation who have not attained the relationship of *comadre.*

Compadrasgo, the so-called fictive kinship relationship, is a system of designating certain persons as sponsors in ritual relationships for life-crisis and life-passage events. When a woman in southern Arizona faces a major turning point in her life, she looks to those closest to her for support. This strengthens already existing bonds of friendship or kinship. When a woman gets married, baptizes her baby, confirms it to the church, or dedicates it to a saint in gratitude for the child's recovery from illness, she turns to people who are closest to her, relatives who are also friends. The *comadre* relationship then supersedes kinship, so that the sister, sister-in-law, or aunt is now called *comadre*.

PREGNANCY

Pregnancy is desired as soon after marriage as possible. If it does not occur in a year, a *novena* may be offered. This is a series of 9 days of prayers. One of several spiritual advocates may be invoked. The Mother of God may be prayed to or her cousin, St. Elizabeth, who was pregnant with St. John at the same time that Mary expected Jesus Christ. A shrine in the barrio erected to San Ramon Nonato may be visited.

Physical measures are also undertaken. Certain herbs are reputed to ''heat'' the womb. Damiana *(Turnera diffusa)* and mariola *(Artemisia* or *Parthenium incanum)* are used, either as teas or as steam baths. In the latter case, the woman sits over a pot of boiling water that has these herbs laid on the top.

Once pregnancy is achieved, the life of the young woman is directed by her mother or mother-in-law. She is presented with the childbearing rules, which vary according to whether the woman is expecting her first child and is in close communication with traditional people.

Pregnancy rules

For the woman who is pregnant many times, her daily life is not affected a great deal when she is ''ill with child,'' ''fat,'' ''with family.'' However, she does attempt to control the environment as much as possible. Cool air that is in motion is considered dangerous at such times. Mexican American women therefore avoid sitting near evaporative coolers or breezes. Sun rays heat as they are passed through glass; thus, sitting by a closed windowpane is also dangerous. Night air is not desirable, moonlight is alarming, and the moon in eclipse is perilous. One informant told me about the precautions:

> Poor people use something of steel to protect from the eclipse. Scissors, pins. It is important to use it at the beginning when the fetus is forming. Afterwards it doesn't matter. Sometimes they are born with six fingers or toes, I've seen them, and they say it is caused so. Also the split lip. I don't know about that myself but so they say.

Bathing, forbidden during the menstrual period, is encouraged during pregnancy. My same informant went on:

> Many poor people don't bathe. And they spend too much time sleeping all day. Well, lots of times the baby has a hard time being born. Or the placenta won't come. Many are accustomed to eating dirt, and that is very bad. This also makes the placenta stick. My sister ate a lot, and after the baby was born, two hours and the placenta did not come. She bathed, but she also ate dirt.

Certain foods must be taken and others must be avoided. Food taboos function to call attention to the status of pregnancy. But they are believed to have physiological bases by the people who follow them. To the Mexican American woman *antojos,* or cravings, must be satisfied or the infant may be marked by whatever food was craved. *Pica,* the habit of eating substances not recognized as food, usually takes the form of eating ashes or dirt with Mexican Americans. It is not common.

Milk is avoided by many who believe that it will make their babies grow large and difficult to deliver. Otherwise, nutritious food is recommended. Flour (wheat) tortillas are believed to be better than bread.

Certain complications are known to accompany pregnancy. Nausea and vomiting are treated by drinking flour and water, flour and lemon juice, or chamomile tea. Heartburn, believed by some to be caused by eating chili and by others to be a predictor of much hair on the baby's head, is treated by Alka-Seltzer, Pepto-Bismol, and baking soda. Constipation is treated by a variety of proprietary medicines from the drug store as well as herbal tea. Among the herbs used are epazote, wormseed *(Chenopodium ambrosoides),* wormwood *(Artemisia mexicana),* and bluing *(Indigofera suffruticosa).* All three are known to be violent purges. "If you use epazote, be careful to use just a little of the leaf." Milder laxatives are made from rose petals or *granada,* the shell of the pomegranate.

Mexican American mothers have great faith in vitamin and iron preparations and take them in preference to herbal remedies formerly believed to enrich the blood. These include the desert limberbush *(Jatopha cardiophylla)* called *sangre de drago,* or dragon's blood, because it makes a bright red tea. It also includes what is called Mormon tea by Anglos and *canutillo (Ephedra trifurca)* by Mexicans.

Recognizing a desire to sleep, the pregnant Mexican American woman tries to keep active, again to assure easy delivery. Women are supposed to sleep flat on their backs in order to protect the fetus.

Mexican American women believe that they should keep working and moving about so that the baby will not grow big. If they have many household duties, they are excused from only the heaviest activities. They do not undertake special active exercises, but passive movement, that is, massage, is an important part of prenatal care. The massage is given in order to fix the fetus in a position favorable for delivery. Treatments are given monthly to pregnant women by their midwives or by an older female relative.

> You go to be adjusted. It is a kind of massage. Sometimes you go because the baby sticks to one part, so that you can't walk. Almost all women are accustomed to go.

There are certain activities that must be avoided. Women shouldn't hang laundry or reach high, for such actions can cause knots in the umbilical cord. They shouldn't sit tailor fashion or even cross their legs.

Baby showers are not planned until the delivery time is near. To have a celebration earlier is to invite bad luck, even the evil eye. The baby shower is a female solidarity rite. The usual hostess is the mother of the expectant woman. The living room is decorated for the event with items used for games. Balloons and a stork dominate the table on which guests place gifts for the baby. The shower is supposed to be a surprise. Since the young woman's presence has to be assured, it seems unlikely that she does not know of the party, but the pretense is not challenged. The games follow simple formulas—there are guessing games and races with the theme taken from the occasion of the birth of a baby. The games may be primly obscene or scatological and attended by much laughter. Mexican hot chocolate, cookies, *pan dulce,* and guacamole dip are common refreshments.

Many women will undertake the prediction of the sex of the unborn baby. "A girl is conceived from the right ovary and will occupy the right side of the uterus, where it can be felt." Also, ". . . a woman carrying a female baby will have no depression between the two muscles that lie along either side of the spine and insert into the crown of the head." It is "known" that girl children are stronger than boy children and less vulnerable to disease.

The relationship between body and mind are given close attention by Mexican Americans. Serenity is cultivated by thinking pleasant thoughts and avoiding quarrels. Simple nervousness is soothed by *azahar,* orange blossom tea, an old world remedy prescribed by Arab and Spanish physicians. It is believed that the pregnant woman is particularly prone to great anger, *coraje.* If this rage is allowed, the consequences can be fearsome—spontaneous abortion, premature labor, or knots in the umbilical cord. If she experiences a sudden fright, this emotion may cause the same complications that anger brings on. The consequences may not be observed until much later. Future lactation may be affected by an untoward event in pregnancy.

One experience that may be very frightening to the pregnant woman is the pelvic examination. Most traditional cultures reject the idea of a man viewing the genitals of someone not his mate. Physicians in Mexico have learned how to do a physical examination through cloth gowns that extend from the neck to the ankles. Pelvic examination was not acceptable to the women or their mates, so it was not done without strong indication. Women physicians, more common in Mexico, and women midwives may examine the pelvis internally without fear of censure.

Sexual activity is supposed to be continued throughout pregnancy in order to assure that the birth canal is kept well lubricated. Thus, when a mate must be absent for a long period of time, such as a prison sentence, it is feared that his pregnant wife will have a difficult "dry" labor.

In traditional society, sex is supposed to be a man's pleasure and his wife's duty. Mexican American women report that their responses fluctuate during pregnancy. They are more likely to experience orgasm during pregnancy. But they are worried about the putative dangers of the standard position to the fetus and are "too ashamed" to experiment with others.

MEXICAN GRANDMOTHER'S LABOR

Until 1950, most Mexican Americans delivered at home, attended by a folk midwife called a *partera.* The calling of *partera* was a sacred one that required hard work. Training was given by apprenticeship, with the novice helping more and more with childbirth until she was able to work by herself. In the adjoining state of Sonora, delivery by midwife continued to be the rule. But in Arizona in 1952, the Midwifery Practice Act was passed, requiring literacy in English or Spanish so that a birth certificate could be filed. This law reduced the number of legally practicing midwives to two.

When the probable time of confinement grew near, the patient was visited by the midwife to see if everything was ready for the birth. She first examined the mother to learn where the fetus was located, using palpation and a stethoscope. Then she would check the bed, seeing where it was located, how high it was, and if it were located near the bathroom or another source of water, since toilet facilities were often outside the house. She would tell the family how to arrange the bed so that she could work with her right hand.

The patient was expected to have a big box of sanitary pads and six 100-pound empty cloth flour sacks. These were washed and opened and filled with a thick layer of newspaper to make pads. Clean sheets and a rubber protection for the bed were to be made ready.

As the day approached, the bed was moved and a spread or heavy blanket was hung across the door so that cold air could not get in. Arrangements were made for any small children to be cared for because their presence during delivery was not allowed by the culture. The midwife brought her own bedpan and pans for washing her hands and the instruments; she also brought alcohol, gauze, and ties for the cord, obtained from the health department, as well as silver nitrate eyedrops.

During the eighth month, the expectant mother began drinking chamomile tea to assure effective labor and uncomplicated separation of the placenta. With the first contractions, the mother began to take more chamomile tea. She was told that if it were false labor, the tea would soothe the pains away. But if it were true labor, the contractions would start coming stronger and harder.

The *partera* was called. She came when the pains were 5 minutes apart. If she missed the delivery, she would not be paid. The traditional massage of the abdomen was performed for diagnosis and adjustment of fetal position. Also, the lower back and the crests of the pelvic bones were rubbed for comfort whenever the mother was in bed. Mothers were instructed to walk until the moment of birth. "You have to walk until you feel the baby coming. Then you climb in bed."

The *parteras* discouraged voluntary bearing down with pains until the time was right. But they were sometimes sabotaged by the young parturient's mother, who would tell her daughter that pushing would hasten delivery. When dilation was 1½ inches across, the midwife would let patients turn to the side in order to have harder pains.

The midwives took pride in avoiding tears. Some got the mother up on her knees when the baby was crowning and this prevented tearing. If the baby was slow in coming, the husband or the patient's mother applied pressure at the fundus while the midwife dilated the birth canal with a finger lubricated with olive oil.

Delivery was usually not hastened. Women who preferred the midwife's attentions said that she was not in such a hurry as doctors were. She would not cut you or use forceps but went with nature. Pain was endured with patience not blotted out with medicine. Women were instructed to close their mouths, for opening them to scream would cause the uterus to rise. If they yelled an /ai/ or /ai-yai/, it was uttered during exhalation. If necessary, the parturient's mother or mother-in-law exerted pressure on the fundus.

> All my babies come fast, only with Laura I labored long, because I was so worried about my
> son in the hospital. Laura was born purely from the strength of the doctor. She pressed so
> from below, and my mother from above, at the waist.

As soon as the baby was born, the mother's legs were placed together to prevent air entering the womb, which would "chill" it. The cord was cut with scissors that had been boiled and then "sterilized" with alcohol, with a remaining stump of three fingerwidths whether a boy or a girl. The baby was washed and drops, ranging from silver nitrate to lemon juice, were put in the baby's eyes. The midwife dipped her thumb in olive oil and then pressed on the palate to prevent "falling of the fontanel." The breast was offered immediately and "everytime the baby cries." After the baby was dressed, the midwife returned to the mother to deliver the placenta. Retained placenta with hemorrhage was the single most feared complication. In Mexico, most midwives treated such conditions with ergotrate injections or tea of zoapatle. In Arizona, the patient was given a bottle to blow on or stimulated to vomit. In an emergency, the doctor would be called to give oxytocin (Pitocin).

The mother stayed in bed for at least 3 days. Before she could get up, a wide binder of coarse cotton cloth was applied, a *faja* made of *manta*. It was pinned on with a dozen safety pins. Mothers could walk about the house after the eighth day when the spread in front of the door could be removed. They did not go outside for 15 days or until the first bath had been taken. The midwife returned to care for the mother until the cord stump dropped.

> If it falls at three days, she doesn't return. If it stays eight days, she comes until then. I don't
> pay her until she brings the umbilical cord.

Some of the mothers saved the stump, some for the same reason that other mothers save baby curls, just a souvenir, while other mothers saved it for magical use.

The placenta itself was usually burned or buried. It was believed that the placenta should be buried deeply so that animals could not get at it. If the placenta was eaten by an animal, that would cause afterpains, *entuertos*.

Afterpains were treated with 1 teaspoon of olive oil and warm Manzanilla tea at 3 hours. Calcium lactate given in two 5-grain tablets every hour was considered to work marvelously. Aspirin was not given "because it liquified the blood." Milk of magnesia was taken on the third day after birth.

POSTPARTUM AND LA DIETA

The postpartum diet was quite restricted. Immediately after birth, the mother might be given chamomile tea. For the first 2 days, "purely" toasted tortillas and boiled milk or *atole* was taken. Atole is a corn gruel, thin enough in consistency to be drunk. For the next 2 to 3 days, the diet was increased to chicken as pieces or in soup. No vegetables or fruit were allowed; some excepted oranges, but others felt they were dangerously acid or cold. Pork, chili, and tomatoes must always be avoided for the full 40 days because these were believed to harm the breast milk.

If possible, the parturient went to the home of her mother. If not, her mother came to her house. The parturient could not sweep, sew, or do heavy work. Depending on economics and the availability of her mother's help, convalescence may end at 40 days when she had her bath. She was careful to cover her feet, head (including ears), and body from cold air. The infant was similarly protected.

Why the delayed bath and restricted activity? For the primipara, the restrictions were an unwelcome surprise. "My mother told me so," said one. A physician teaching preventive medicine told me that his wife was instructed by his mother as follows: "Never mind what my son says, this is what you are to do after childbirth," and she outlined the restrictions. A nurse who is a neonatal nurse practitioner is now pregnant for the first time. Her mother, too, has instructed her daughter and will come to stay after the birth in order to see that her instructions are carried out.

Mothers spoke of *aire* (air). Currents of air are always thought to be dangerous but especially so after delivery. Air can harm the eyes causing *punzadas* (stitches, a kind of pain), which may lead to blindness. It may harm the ears as well. If it is necessary for the mother to leave the house before the prescribed time is over, she must be very careful to cover her head with a cloth that conforms to the shape of the head and thus completely protects it. She must always keep her feet covered, for air can enter through the feet. The shoulders must be covered or a breast infection may develop.

In the case of mastitis, the infection may also be caused by eating cold or sour things. Poultices of *alcanfor* (camphor—probably Vick's) and other forms of local heat are considered to be the most efficacious treatment.

Pasmo (sudden infection) is the condition that is the result of carelessness in the postpartum period. "What happens is that the blood gets cold," from the air or from chilling the body too rapidly as with a bath. There are two prescribed treatments. The most common is sulfur flowers. Sulfur is not soluble in water; it must first be dissolved in liquor, then put in water and drunk. It may also be taken preventatively, as when the mother has to go out of the house before convalescence has ended. Another treatment is *hierba del pasmo (Bacchans pteronoides)* brewed in tea and applied in a fomentation or prepared for inhalation.

Carelessness in the puerperium, not using a binder, disregarding the rules for inactivity, and eating the wrong foods result in coldness of the uterus. This condition, externally visible by a fat belly, causes frigidity and sterility.

Chloasma, or mask of pregnancy *(paño)* is considered a "natural" consequence of pregnancy. It was bleached by applying wet diapers from the infant to the mother's face.

MEXICAN AMERICANS

Now let us discuss the second generation of mothers, who also call themselves Mexicans when they are with each other but use the label Mexican American elsewhere. It is a label that reflects two worlds. Their childbearing practices were changed abruptly when they began to deliver in the hospital. The change began with World War II, when wives of servicemen were eligible for hospital birth and continued with trade union benefits providing hospitalization for family members. Suddenly, their mother's knowledge and support were irrelevant, useless in a technological site where women were delivered by an obstetrician who represented a different system of practice and belief. The Mexican childbirth culture was seen as superstition and was forgotten. The women became passive recipients of an obstetrical care system whose rules they did not understand.

The alienation from traditional knowledge was acute in the hospital where personnel found the young Mexican American mother to be a difficult patient in labor. "They're so emotional. They can't stand the pain. They don't know when or how to push. And they keep asking for all those relatives to stay with them. We can't have the confusion of all those people."

Left alone, or attended by unknown people, with supportive women barred from the labor room, the laboring woman panicked. There was no one to tell her the rules of behavior in labor. Scopolamine and meperidine (Demerol) analgesia were the medical solution—then oblivion, which was extended through delivery. "Do you remember the last shot?" queried the doctor. "No, well that's as it should be."

The delivered mother would waken from anesthesia to hear someone telling her to get out of bed and walk to the bathroom. The expected *faja* (binder) was not applied to her abdomen. No one placed slippers on her feet to protect them from the dangerous cold. She was told to sit in water to treat her unexpected stitches, and then a heat lamp was applied for further healing. That felt good, but the patient worried about the rapid temperature change. The next instructions were to take a shower! A mother with no previous experience in a hospital would protest that she could not bathe because the water would cause *pasmo*. The sophisticated mother would walk to the bathroom, close the door, turn on the shower briefly, and then return to bed, still dry and safe.

Gradually, Mexican American mothers learned that the restrictions of the immediate postpartum were not necessary. Eating an "American" diet did not result in calamity. Many reported their relief in being able to bathe immediately. "What a penance" it was to wait 40 days! But at the same time they could no longer have the privileged status of convalescence, surrounded by protecting, helpful women. "My mother's weeds" were disparaged for colics and infections. The doctor prescribed a formula, and so the art of breast-feeding was lost.

CHICANAS

Today some mothers have come full circle around to their grandmothers' practices. Rebecca Madero was born in a hospital 23 years ago. A recent college graduate in nursing, she is excited by the feminist and Chicano movements. The perspectives of both suggested to her that a home birth would be more fulfilling to her than a hospital birth. She talked to her mother about her plans, but her mother was opposed because the hospital was safer "in case anything would happen." Her grandmother, however, was enthusiastic about the idea of home birth. Childbirth, she told Rebecca, is a very natural thing and can be accomplished at home as long as you have a reliable *partera* (midwife). Lay midwives, all Anglos, are available in her community, so Rebecca began early to attend the clinic organized to give prenatal care to mothers planning home birth.

During the last month of pregnancy, Rebecca began drinking *te de Manzanilla* (chamomile tea) to facilitate birth. After a day of latent labor contractions, she took more Manzanilla, which she believes stimulated the labor to an active phase. Delivery occurred a few hours later, not in bed like her grandmother, but in an obstetrical chair built like the thirteenth century stools that were used by the Arabic physicians of Spain.

In the postpartum period, Rebecca followed a few of the restrictions of *la dieta*. She does not sweep or lift heavy things. Rebecca did take a bath and washed her hair but hid the evidence when her mother was visiting. Even though her mother delivered in a hospital, she was one of the women who believed that bathing was dangerous. Her mother's practice had been to stay indoors for the full 40 days. Rebecca did not follow this custom either.

Rebecca is accustomed to drinking a lot of citrus juices but stopped in the postpartum period when her baby was having runny stools. Her grandmother said that orange juice was too cold for the baby. She also made belly bands for her grandchild and is pleased that they are used, as well as socks, to keep out cold.

The Chicana who is taking on the medical system by reverting to home birth is selecting those elements that she considers essential to her self-determination as a woman. She is not interested in those practices that she believes are likely to be injurious to her health. Ignorance about the body is not a cultural requirement, and so she participates in women's health groups. Not all women are Chicanas. Some will continue to call themselves Mexican American, assimilating into the dominant health culture. For others there will be a gap between generations of women new to that society.

Another reason for the college-educated, feminist Chicanas to give birth at home is to return to the family the functions that the dominant society has delegated to official medicine. The doctor's advice has formed the present rules for acceptability of pregnancy and the timing and spacing of pregnancy through genetic counseling and physical examination. Official medicine suggests the location of birth: a hospital approved by a National Commission for Accreditation of a technological level assigned according to diagnosed maternal risk. Formerly these and other decisions about childbearing belonged to *la familia*.

Such technological advances are greatly appreciated by Mexican women, those who are not citizens and may be undocumented. It has been believed that uncountable numbers of women cross the border ostensibly to visit or to shop in the United States but actually in order to give birth to an American citizen. This does not seem to be the case, according to preliminary analyses of interviews with Mexican nationals who deliver in Tucson. For one thing, the infant, even though a citizen, cannot help his parents emigrate legally until he reaches age 21. The stated reasons for delivery in the United States seem to be the same given by other mothers who go away from their home communities. Some leave because they are not married and want to conceal their condition. Others come because the help of mother, sister, or *comadre* is available in one place and not another. Many others come for specific obstetrical care. The medical centers of Mexico in Mexico City or Guadalajara are a great deal farther than the few miles across the border for the Sonoran woman. However, care is very expensive. Many allegedly new arrivals are in fact residents of several years but wives or partners of undocumented workers whose presence is illegal. For such women, it is safer to say that they "just came for vacation, but the baby was born early."

The woman whose partner is an underemployed laborer, or who is a migrant, or who is not married to an American is not eligible for financial assistance for prenatal care and delivery. In Mexico she is similarly denied care from the Instituto Mexicano de Seguro Social when her husband is unemployed and then she cannot afford private care. Lay care is disparaged as crude, dangerous, or superstitious. But for the Mexican woman who does not have resources for scientific medical care, there is a long tradition of women's mutual help and lore that is being revitalized.

The following tables summarize herbs that are used in place of medical care by the Chicana whose consciousness of her heritage has been raised and by the Mexican woman who is unable to get official scientific medical care. Table 4-1 summarizes plants used before pregnancy occurs; Table 4-2 lists plants used during the reproductive cycle. Plants are listed according to use, Spanish lay name, botanical name, and preparation. In

Table 4-1. Medicinal substances used in childbearing

Use	Spanish name	Botanical name	Preparation
Facilitate conception	Damiana	*Turnera diffusa*	Tea
	Mariola	*Artemesia rhizomata*	Tea
		Parthenium incanum	
Prevent conception	Escorzonera	*Eryngium carlinae*	
		Eryngium conosum	
	Aceite de oliva	*Olea europaea*	Vaginal suppository
Promote menstruation	Oregano	*Lippia berlandieri*	Tea
	Romero	*Rosmarinus officinalis*	Tea
	Ruda	*Ruta graveolens*	Tea
	Cilantro	*Coriandrum sativum*	Tea
	Canafistula	*Cassia fistula*	Tea
Clean out uterus	Tlachichinole	*Kohleria deppeana*	Vaginal douche
			Solution of boiled leaves
	Chicura	*Ambrosia ambrocoides*	Vaginal douche
			Solution of boiled leaves
Treat heavy bleeding	Hierba del manso	*Anemopsis californica*	Douche of boiled root
	Nogal	*Juglans* sp.	Douche of solution of boiled shells
Menstrual cramps	Manzanilla	*Matricaria chamomilla*	Tea
	Hierba buena	*Mentha spicata*	Tea

Table 4-2. Medicinal substances used in pregnancy

Use	Spanish name	Botonical name	Preparation
Urinary tract disease	Barbe de elote	*Zea mays*	Tea of corn silk
Anemia	Canutillo	*Ephedra trifurca* *Equisetum*	Tea
	Sangre de drago	*Jatropha cardiophylla*	Tea
Hemorrhoids	Pitahaya	*Opuntia*	Apply pulp of pad
	Tuna	*Echinerocereus*	Apply fruit
Strengthen perineum	(Frambueso)	*Rubus*	Tea of leaves. (NOTE: not traditional—learned from Anglo midwives.)
Induce labor	Manzanilla	*Matricaria chamomilla*	Tea and enema
	Higuerilla	*Ricinus communis*	Buy castor oil and take orally
	Aceite de comer	*Olea*	Olive oil orally
Prevent afterpains	Hierba buena	*Mentha spicata*	Tea
Promote lactation	Albaca	*Ocimum basilicum*	Tea
Treat mastitis	Alcanfor	*Cinnamomum camphora*	Apply ointment
Treat constipation	Epazote	*Chenopodium ambrosoides*	
	Estafiate	*Artemisia mexicana*	
	Añil	*Indigofera suffruticosa*	
Treat nerves	Azahar	*Citrus aurantium*	Tea of blossoms
Prevent puerperal fever	Hierba del pasmo	*Bacchans pteronoides*	Tea or inhalations
Induce labor	Zoapatle	*Montanao tormentosa*	Tea (dangerous, rarely used today)

almost all cases, the plant has a long history of use by Mexican women. The one exception is raspberry leaf tea, promoted by the Anglo lay midwifes who deliver the Chicana women.

NOTES

1. F. Rojas Gonzalez, "La Tona" in *El Diosero,* 1964, Mexico and Buenos Aires Fondo de Cultura Economica, pp. 9 to 10.
2. See E. H. Spicer, "Plural Society in the Southwest," in E. H. Spicer and R. A. Thompson, *Plural Society in the Southwest,* New York, Weatherhead Foundation, pp. 22 to 25, for comments on the meaning of ethnic terminology employed by Spanish-speaking people of the United States.

REFERENCES

Anderson, S., M. Kay and E. Shaw
    1978 "Childbirth as they like it." Arizona Nurse 31 (3), May-June.
Goodenough, W.
    1963 Cooperation in Change. New York: Russell Sage Foundation.
Kay, M. A.
    1977a "Mexican American fertility regulation." Pp. 278-295 in M. Batey (ed.), Communicating

Nursing Research, Vol. 10. Boulder, Colorado: Western Interstate Commission for Higher Education.

1977b "Health and illness in a Mexican American barrio." In E. H. Spicer (ed.), Ethnic Medicine in the Southwest. Tucson, Arizona: University of Arizona Press.

1978 "The Mexican American." In Culture/Childbearing/Health Professionals. Philadelphia: F. A. Davis Co.

Spicer, E. H.
1972 "Plural society in the Southwest." In E. H. Spicer and R. A. Thompson (eds.). Plural Society in the Southwest. New York: Weatherhead Foundation.

Wallace, A. F. C.
1970 Culture and Personality, ed. 2. New York: Random House.

Chapter 5

Breast-feeding and social class mobility

The case of Mexican migrant mothers in Houston, Texas

Carmen Acosta Johnson

Food policy analysts (Jelliffe 1968) have recognized for 15 years that breast milk is a valuable natural resource constituting an important part of the food supply of any nation. In high birthrate countries, it is both culturally and politically acceptable to point out that a higher proportion of the food budget must be spent to satisfy the nutritional needs of infants. Matters such as self-sufficiency in food production; low wastage; no industrial processing, storage, or transport; and reduced need for milk cow forage are important economic advantages to the practice of lactation.

In low birthrate nations, health considerations outweigh those of economics in decisions to promote breast-feeding. This is partly because a smaller proportion of the food supply is needed for infants. But a more powerful reason is that such countries are approaching a situation in which a very high social investment in each pregnancy is expected to pay off in a live and healthy baby. Reproductive wastage is becoming less and less tolerable; optimal, robust health for mothers and babies is more efficient than the treatment of illness or disability that might have been ameliorated by the nutritional advantages of breast-feeding, and there may be certain psychological advantages as well.

The problem is not overt opposition to breast-feeding on the part of either policymakers or scientists. Rather women themselves in greater and greater numbers have refused to produce breast milk. Neither economic analyses, biochemical studies, nor psychological measures have provided an explanation of those elements in modern society that discourage and prevent women from nursing their newborn infants.

A comparison of differentials within and between nations provides one consistent clue: a relation exists between successful breast-feeding and social class. The particular classes where breast-feeding is most prevalent vary according to the degree of demographic advancement of the population.

This study presents a series of interviews with mothers who had recently left an agrarian village setting in Mexico, a high birth–high death nation, and entered the urban industrial setting of Houston, an intermediate birth and death setting. The manner in which this migration affected their infant feeding practices is traced, and the implications for explaining the social class patterning of breast-feeding behavior are developed.

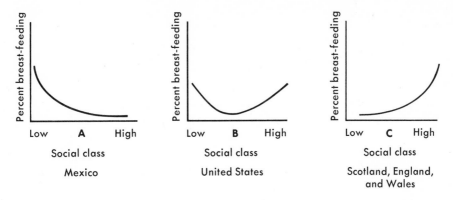

Fig. 2. Patterns of breast-feeding according to demographic advance and social class.

THE MACRO PATTERN

Observations from Mexico, the United States, and the British Isles have been selected to illustrate the range of variation in breast-feeding behavior according to social class, in nations with greatly contrasting levels of demographic advancement.

In Mexico (Fig. 2, *A*), with a high birthrate and relatively high infant mortality, the incidence of breast-feeding varies indirectly with social class; that is, the higher the class the less likely is a mother to choose breast-feeding (see, for example, Bleek 1976; Monckeberg 1970; Sanjur 1970). In the United States (Fig. 2, *B*), with intermediate birth and death regimes, a U-shaped relation obtains, with more women in rural areas (see Jones [1972] on Appalachia) or inner-city ethnic neighborhoods (Acosta 1972, 1974; Clark 1959) choosing to breast-feed; more college-educated women also choosing to breast feed; but relatively few middle-class women opting for breast-feeding over commercial milks (Hirshman and Sweet 1974; Robertson 1961).

Breast milk under advanced demographic conditions (Fig. 2, *A*) appears to have high prestige value, since it is the method of choice of the upper class. Under lesser developed demographic conditions, breast milk has low prestige value and is associated with poverty, unfavorable reproductive histories, and low education. In the United States, both demographic patterns can be readily identified.

MEXICAN WOMEN AND SOCIAL CLASS MOBILITY

All societies have systems of inequality, but some systems are more open to movement between levels than others, some have more identifiable levels than other systems; all societies differ with respect to the proportion of the population that occurs at each level, as well as the criteria by which an individual is identified with one level instead of another. Class distinctions in Mexico and the United States are useful in explaining a wide spectrum of social behaviors in each society, in particular for present purposes, infant feeding customs.

In general, the class system of the United States includes a large middle class, a small

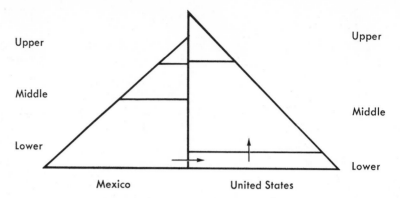

Fig. 3. Migrant flow and social class patterns in Mexico and the United States.

lower class, and a small upper class of wealthy persons, some of whom acquired wealth in their lifetimes and some of whom inherited wealth through kinship.

By contrast, the social system of Mexico includes prominently a large lower class composed of agricultural workers and of persons who have migrated into urban areas of Mexico in the hope of securing work; a small middle class composed primarily of the descendants of middle-class families but also a few persons who have moved up from lower class status; and an even smaller upper class composed almost exclusively of persons with inherited lands and wealth. The relation of the two neighboring systems can be diagrammed as in Fig. 3. Mobility upward in the class structure is not a strong feature of the Mexican system, while it is seen as a basic American ethic to be able to move up in the class structure by individual achievement alone, without the requirement of inherited position.

From the point of view of the Mexican lower-class woman living in the northern border area, three possible opportunities exist for upward mobility in the social class system. She can marry a man with higher class characteristics than her own, she can acquire a higher education and become a white collar worker, or she can migrate to the United States and use her earnings as an unskilled worker to buy a middle-class life-style. Marrying up occurs rather infrequently because of segregation of the classes; educational achievement is virtually blocked in Mexico for women who lack financial means. Therefore, the option of migrating has been seized by large numbers of Mexican women as virtually the only viable opportunity for improving their living conditions.

Although lack of industrial work skills and English language facility preclude immediate access to certain benefits, changes in style of dress, choice of food, and childrearing behavior indicate the entry of women into the modern industrial setting. With respect to breast-feeding, the process is traced in the following discussion.

Materials and methods

Fifty-one mothers and grandmothers and two grandfathers were interviewed for this project. Interviews were held in small groups with participants speaking to each other

more often than to the investigator. Each group was gathered casually by entering the waiting room of an inner-city clinic about mid-morning and asking a conversation group if they would like to discuss infant feeding customs in Mexico and Houston. Any mothers seated nearby who showed an interest were invited to join the group. Spirited discussions were quick to develop; each group continued for several hours. Thus, information was entirely public, not at all privileged, and represents a concensus of the particular small group that produced it.

The clinic was a Catholic-sponsored medical service located on the edge of an area of heavy Mexican American population concentration. It was utilized primarily because proof of citizenship was not required for service. All families had incomes well below poverty level; most mothers had attended 3 years of formal school in Mexico; none of the mothers were employed.

Access to the doctor was on a first come, first served basis. Women usually obtained a ride from a relative or neighbor, arriving at the clinic around 7:30 A.M. The physicians arrived and began seeing patients around 9:30 A.M., so that a total of 4 hours waiting time was the general rule. Some families brought picnic lunches to ease the strain of requiring young children, some of them ill, to sit in straight chairs in a noisy, enclosed room for so many hours. The attitude of the women to the discussion situation was one of relief for the distraction during the long wait.

Discussions were held in border Spanish; no payment of any sort was offered. Comments were recorded by hand in full view of the respondents, with feedback and corrections offered and requested as the session progressed. Two extended families were interviewed at home to ascertain whether the clinic setting blocked discussion of pertinent topics. This did not seem to be the case as the infant feeding customs did not constitute esoteric knowledge or elicit defensive reactions among respondents.

In order to reduce selective bias, days and hours of interviewing were randomly selected. Specific topics for discussion were largely determined by group process; however, most information was cross-checked between groups to establish the existing range of variation in behaviors and opinion. Respondents were self-selected, and to this extent the generalizability of results was compromised. Furthermore data were retrospective, dealing with experiences early in childbearing careers in Mexico, as well as more recent experiences in Houston. No doubt memories were shaped by group opinion. Group atmosphere was entirely cooperative; women tended to agree or to enhance the topic under discussion rather than to disagree. Comparison with other cultural materials pertaining to persons of Mexican heritage in the southwest suggests that respondents did not differ in ways that would significantly affect their infant feeding behavior.

Results

All but two mothers had been born in small towns or ranches in northern Mexico and had moved to Houston within the past 5 years. The remaining two women had been born in Texas border towns with a predominantly Mexican population. All were married and living with their husbands. All had been either married or betrothed in Mexico to Mexican men.

Sixty percent of Mexican women delivering infants in Houston chose not to breast-feed but allowed their infants to be fed commercial milks at first feed. Thus, 40 percent chose to lactate for varying lengths of time. While this proportion is high in comparison with American middle-class norms, it is approximately the same as the proportion expected among American lower-class mothers of rural, traditional backgrounds. It is a low proportion in comparison to Mexican lower-class norms. Both cultural continuities and situational determinants can be distinguished in the behavior patterns that are described in the following. Both sets of variables appear to function to inhibit breast-feeding in the urban setting.

Preparation for motherhood. There were 196 deliveries included in the analysis of the materials. The number of pregnancies per woman ranged from two to eleven, with an average of four. Losses were reported in fertility histories of all but six mothers. Among all reported deliveries, 14 percent had been lost. Half of the losses had been delivered by midwives on either side of the border; the other half of the losses were delivered in various hospitals in Texas. According to the mother's reports, all but two losses had occurred during labor and delivery after a normal pregnancy.

The midwife's role was a technical one, not a nurturant one. Breast-feeding was not more frequent among midwife-delivered births when the birth occurred in Houston. There was a suggestion that some midwives might have potentially harmful esoteric knowledge, so that a certain distrust permeated discussions of midwifery. For example, in a number of deliveries the midwife had declared the baby to be premature, but in each of these cases the mother had disbelieved her. Birth weights were not taken by midwives. The mother's weight was not recorded at prenatal checks, and a vaginal examination was not included. No drugs were administered during delivery, so that home-delivered mothers experienced milk in their breasts. Midwives advised binding the breasts tightly to inhibit milk formation and advised against allowing the baby to suck the breast when the delivery occurred in Houston.

Following the delivery it was the midwife's duty to bathe the baby and pierce her ears if female. The midwife also prepared a cup of tea for the mother. Home-delivered mothers in Houston were generally left with the care of older children and housekeeping duties immediately following delivery. Costs of midwife delivery ranged for $40 on the Mexican side of the border to $400 in Houston. It was considered a mark of poverty not to be able to afford hospital delivery, and midwife-delivered mothers received the sympathy of their countrywomen for their travail.

Hospital delivery was apparently uneventful, partly because little or no communication took place with the Engish-speaking staff. No mother raised any objections to any hospital procedures; the cost, $800 for full-pay patients at the county hospital, prohibited this luxury in a number of cases. All hospital-delivered babies received glucose water and formula in the hospital. If nursing was adopted, it was established later at home.

Support for pregnant and lactating mothers depends entirely on cultural definitions of appropriate roles and attitudes. Thus, while work loads, diet, sex information restrictions, and father absence in traditional Mexican village settings seem harsh by middle-class American norms, they were part of the supportive arrangements that fostered virtually universal breast-feeding.

Strong taboos existed traditionally against the discussion of sexual information or the recognition of pregnancy. The protection of young girls from early entry into sexual unions was the rationale for the perpetuation of the first taboo; the second functioned to protect the pregnant woman and the fetus from malevolent magic if their delicate state should become known to the wrong persons. Respondents were aware of both a need to adopt new ways and a lingering anxiety over taboo violation in the Houston setting.

Traditionally mothers did not prepare their daughters for menstruation, sexual intercourse, pregnancy, or childbirth. Such matters were considered bodily functions, somewhat dirty, shameful, to be hidden from view even of oneself, and thus to be virtually invisible to the well-mannered girl. The taboo was sufficiently strong that violation was termed ''a holy sin.'' No confidences between sisters, or games, or jokes within friendship groups elucidated sexual matters for the young Mexican girl. There was close supervision of the girl in mixed groups outside the household. Girls reached menarche somewhat later under poorer nutritional conditions, and the preferred age of marriage was 15 years. This system functioned effectively to prevent premarital conceptions and to provide two parents and an extended kin group for every newborn. This constituted a distinct advantage for Mexican babies over other lower-class babies in Houston.

Once married, girls were not expected to retain a slender, girlish figure. Only a sweet face and beautiful eyes were desirable attributes for married women. Dark, shapeless dresses and large shawls that could hide any pregnant swelling from view were adopted. The pregnant woman and fetus were protected in their delicate condition by never drawing attention to themselves. Thus, informants reported that as children they never noticed that any of their female kin were pregnant. If a midwife came and went, they were never informed of her profession. No preparations were made by the mother, no special diets, no change in work load, and no preparation of nipples or breasts for nursing. Female kin sometimes prepared baby clothes, but usually this could be afforded only for the first birth.

On the day of a birth in the family, the children were distracted from the event by being sent on an errand, usually to the house of a relative far enough away to cause some delay. On their return they would find the new baby and would be told an airplane had brought it. Respondents laughed a bit incredulously to discover that each had unquestioningly believed that explanation until the moment of birth of their own first child. It was a considerable shock to the primipara to comprehend that her baby grew inside her body, and then that he did not emerge magically from the umbilicus but painfully by the vaginal route.

The father frequently absented himself during the weeks directly preceding the birth, going out to his fields, or looking around for work in other towns. Sometimes he did not return until the 40-day seclusion period had ended. Although the father's role was distant, violations of expectations had severe repercussions in mother's and baby's health. Mother's emotional well-being was heavily dependent on the father's sexual abstinence during late pregnancy and the postpartum period. If the father was known to be going to another woman, his behavior could cause the fetus to develop heart problems or a weak character and could inhibit the milk supply of the mother. Two mothers confided, aside from the group, that this was the underlying cause of their infant's heart murmur and poor health, although both mothers were quite willing to allow the doctor to try to help the child.

Other continuities can be readily traced from these traditions. Prenatal checks were considered a mark of modernity but not essential to the health of the fetus. The public nature of health clinics also made mothers nervous in view of the traditional secrecy concerning pregnancy. Vaginal examination was refused by one woman as she did not see any relevance to the pregnancy. Many of the mothers were acutely aware of styles of dress in the city, which required the slender figure fashion. As their bodies swelled with the pregnancy, they believed that they should go on a diet. Three mothers reported that they had gone to the doctor to request diet pills and that they had received and were following prescriptions to lose weight during pregnancy.

When questioned about decisions to breast-feed, all mothers reported that health personnel had advised them against it for the following reasons: that breast-feeding was considered a hippie behavior and all agreed that they did not wish to be associated with hippie culture; that it would cause cancer; that Mexican mothers had too much work to do; that the milk was bad for the baby; that it was not really milk; that it was indecent to expose the lactating breast to other children in the family or to the husband; and that mothers could not produce enough milk to feed the baby adequately. Planning and decision making concerning the new baby were new and modern activities for migrant women; breast-feeding was never a matter for decision under traditional conditions. Thus, it was always an unexpected question, and the mothers were quite willing to take the advice of health personnel. Routine injection of Deladumone at delivery inhibited the milk supply. Only one mother understood this however. Most of the mothers felt that the medical advice had been accurate and that milk was not possible to produce in Houston conditions. The adoption of medication regimes postpartum was also very common. Hospital-delivered mothers had been placed on birth control pills, hypertension medication, diet medication, tranquilizers, and diabetic medication—all of which were given by health personnel as further reasons for the inadvisability of breast-feeding.

Initiation of lactation. Grandmothers and older mothers referred to breast-feeding as "the natural way," saying for example "she fed them the natural way," suggesting the rarity of not lactating after childbirth under traditional conditions. The presence of milk in the breasts was expected, observed, and experienced by all women who had delivered in rural Mexico. Two exceptions among all remembered deliveries were reported. A grandmother had nursed a neighbor's child when the neighbor died in childbirth. The grandmother called the baby her "niño de crianza," or nursling child, and remembered the incident fondly. Her own baby was born about the same time and she produced enough milk for two babies when the occasion required it. In the second case the informant was a younger woman born in Mexico whose own mother had not had milk for her at her birth. She herself was nursed by an aunt who had a nursing baby about the same age and provided milk for both babies when requested to do so. The incident was not remembered fondly because the mother's lack of milk was attributed to the father's taking another woman during the pregnancy and early postpartum period. Chronic health problems of the informant were traced back to the same prenatal cause. No instance of crossing class boundaries in nursing behavior was remembered by informants, suggesting that wet nursing for upper-class infants was not a factor in the villages of the informants.

The naturalness of lactating when social supports were in order and the mother felt secure was a distant memory, clearly separated from the situation of childbearing in Houston. With newly acquired modern viewpoints the same women in another part of the interview now reported feelings of pity at the memory of women in Mexico who were so poor they had nothing to give the baby but their breast, even when it was not really milk in the breast. Women doubted that the secretions of the lactating breast were really milk, or constituted infant food. Women were told by "someone at the hospital" not to try to nurse their baby, and this modern medical authority completely changed their evaluations of lactation. Real baby food was Similac, and the entire family would sacrifice to provide it for the new baby. Two women reported that after 3 and 4 weeks postpartum they still had milk in their breasts but did not consider giving it to the baby because it would be harmful. Two other mothers admitted in private that they clandestinely nursed their babies at night or when no one could know about it and clearly wished that this behavior would not be brought to the notice of the doctor. Such behavior indicated the strength of the admonitions received not to breast-feed but to give the baby real food, which was Similac.

Deladumone administered at delivery inhibited the formation of milk. But later when home in their own surroundings, several mothers felt frustration at the insufficiency of milk supply. For example, one mother reported that during the first week at home only one breast developed milk. She managed to satisfy the baby for 3 months nevertheless, but finally he began to complain and she worried that he was not getting enough milk. She weaned him to Similac. With the next baby she had even less milk and with the last baby none at all. She remembered nursing the first baby, who was delivered by a midwife in the border area, with plenty of milk in both breasts. She had no memory of being asked to discuss her lactation plans prior to any delivery.

A range of personalities and attitudes was evident in the composition of respondent groups. One mother expressed disgust at the idea of lactation. She said breast-feeding was associated in her mind with slovenly habits of person and housekeeping. She was unusually neat among the group of migrant mothers, held her child at arm's length, and sat somewhat removed from the conversation group.

Under village conditions, the colostrum was thrown out for the first 2 or 3 days until the true milk came into the breasts. In its place the baby was given sweet tea. Some mothers took a different view of the first postpartum day. They admonished the interviewer that one should never throw anything away, that the baby should be given whatever was in the breasts. In 2 or 3 days, the breasts became full to engorgement; the baby was put to breast to suck and relieve the hardness. From that time forward the baby was fed exclusively on breast milk and sweet tea for approximately 6 months. One mother reported 10 months of exclusive breast feedings. At that time the baby was started on a gradual weaning diet to family food and to milks other than breast milk.

Teas of the mountains made of wild leaves gathered in the high dry areas of northern Mexico were considered beneficial to both mother and baby, in fact for all persons of delicate constitution. The most popular teas mentioned were oregano tea for colic, *te de salvia* for the phlegm in the newborn's lungs, cinnamon tea for diarrhea, te de zacate de limón, te de ojo de naranjo, Manzanilla tea for general well-being, and te de agua buena, which was made of water that had been blessed during the "Day of the Dead" ceremonies. These tea leaves can be purchased in Houston at Mexican *farmacias* or can be brought to Houston by the many relatives and friends who come from Mexico frequently. The method of preparation is to fill a medium size pot with water and put it on the fire. When the water boils well, the leaves are thrown into it along with the desired amount of sugar. Some families used more sugar than others, it being a mark of status to be able to sweeten the baby's tea and the father's coffee. Adding the sugar during boiling rather than after cooling requires more sugar to produce a definite sweet taste. Thus both mother and baby ingested 2 to 4 tablespoons of refined sugar to the cup of tea where families could afford the expenditure. A new mother felt very soothed after receiving the tea; it was seen as a facet of the generally supportive and comforting environment that surrounded her at delivery.

The lactation diet. In addition to tea the mother was given *atole* to hasten her recovery and to enhance her milk supply. *Atole* is an ancient Aztec beverage prepared of ground corn, water, and spices such as cinnamon. It is also sweetened, and once again, the higher status the family the sweeter the atole. Atole may be made of ground corn that is dry, or corn in a moist mass such as is used in tortillas; it may be made of toasted ground corn, or even of ground wheat. The corn or wheat is stirred into warm water and then warmed again with sugar and spices. The cup of *atole* often constituted the evening meal for the lactating mother along with a tortilla.

The mother's traditional lactation diet consisted of something warm to drink in the morning, usually coffee with warm milk, and a warm tortilla. If there was a bit of meat or beans to put on the tortilla it was eaten in that manner; if not, it was eaten with salt, or merely toasted. At the main meal of the day ideally the mother would share in a soup made of lamb or chicken with a bit of peas or other vegetables cooked in the broth. The lactating mother must avoid chili or beans, the staples of the family diet. Often lamb or chicken soup was a luxury, so that the mother would have soup made only of water and noodles. Food taboos for the nursing mother were based on the homeopathic theories of traditional Mexican thought (Clark 1959); however, none of the mothers knew the rationale for the avoidances they remembered from village life. All agreed that chili and beans were to be avoided, but there was much variability in advice concerning other foods.

Seclusion. The most important aspect of proper care for the new mother under traditional conditions was her seclusion from possible magical contamination of *"aires,"* which were essentially malevolent spirits present in public places, graveyards, and hostile areas. The *aires* had to be kept out by closing up the house so that no breeze of any sort could enter. The baby in particular was to be kept in a completely closed room. The mother was in danger each time she was exposed to wafts of air; thus she should even refrain from sweeping the floor during the postpartum period in order not to invite contamination from the *aires*. Even a light might cause drifts of air in the room according to some mothers.

To maintain such seclusion, a cadre of female relatives had to be in close attendance, bringing food, taking out laundry, and seeing to the older children. The female relatives should be matrilineal. In-laws were to be excluded, but would be the first persons visited following the seclusion period.

Continuities and adaptations. The supportive rather than restrictive rationale of the seclusion period was demonstrated by the tears of the women who had no female relatives in Houston to make such a period possible. The tears were a sign of the strain experienced in the new setting during the early postpartum days when it was necessary to go out to the grocery store and the clinic, thus violating these strong traditions. In spite of an inability to honor the totality of the rule, recognition of tradition was evidenced in the custom of bringing the babies to the church at 40 days of age to mark the successful passage of this vulnerable period.

Mothers were pleased to report that they were able to purchase Similac for Houston-born babies. Only one grandmother believed her grandbabies were lazy because the liquid flowed so easily from the bottle that their suck became weak. The youngest mothers had no comparison for strength of suck and were unconvinced that this was a legitimate concern.

For those mothers who continued to breast-feed in Houston, there was a suggestion that the quality of breast milk under Houston conditions was not as good as breast milk produced under traditional conditions owing to an inability to honor the seclusion period.

Postpartum diets were somewhat more restricted in Houston where fast foods instead of farm-style soups were used for the children during the day, but the cost was often prohibitive to provide these for the mother. About half the mothers reported that they had coffee with warm milk and a toasted tortilla in the morning and then waited until their husband was served in the evening before eating anything else. Beans and chili were avoided if the mother was lactating, as was traditional.

Postpartum work loads were thought to be heavier in Houston where there were fewer maternal relatives to help with the chores. Mothers were expected to wash the baby clothes separately from those of the rest of the family. Clothes were usually washed by hand in the bathtub or kitchen sink. Hot water was often in short supply. Clothes were hung outside to dry. Cloth diapers were cheaper than disposable diapers and were used almost entirely by the group. In order not to cause a chill to the baby, all clothes had to be ironed till they were warm and quite dry. Older children had to be tended at the same time. Girls of 5 or 6 were often assigned the job of nursemaid while the mother attended to the washing and ironing. Older girls were often kept home from school to help with the household and baby tending chores. Grocery shopping required walking to the store unless there was enough money to hire a neighbor to transport. Less than half the mothers had cars in their immediate family.

Thus, heavy work loads and restricted diets were common in the Houston setting for migrant women. The emotional strain of violation of traditional taboos and efforts to modernize the conduct of childbirth and infant feeding was apparent in their discussions. Of these factors, the violation of seclusion was thought to be the most serious detriment to successful lactation.

Table 5-1. Duration of lactation among Mexican-born and Houston-born babies of migrants

Duration	Born in Mexico		Born in Houston	
	No.	%	No.	%
0			15	60
1 day			1	4
1 month			1	4
2 months				
3 months			2	8
4 months	1	8	3	12
5 months				
6 months			3	12
7 or more months	12	92		
TOTAL	13	100	25	100

Duration of lactation. Table 5-1 shows the distribution of respondents according to the duration of lactation for all babies born alive to the informant group. Since group sessions were open ended, only 38 respondents presented sufficiently complete lactation histories to enter into the calculations. Among babies born in Mexico, 92 percent were breast-fed for 7 or more months. Only one Mexican-born baby was terminated from breast milk as early as 4 months. Among Houston-born babies, 60 percent were given only commercial formula from birth forward. One more child was nursed for only one day in the hospital.

Notwithstanding all of the difficulties of lactation in the Houston setting, 36 percent of the migrant mothers breast-fed their babies for lengths of time varying from 1 to 6 months. No mothers continued to breast-feed in the Houston setting beyond 6 months.

Feeding schedules, whether breast or bottle, were entirely on demand. Bottle-fed babies were observed to have a bottle in their mouths almost continually as a pacifier during group sessions. It was not considered either healthy or virtuous to allow the baby to cry. Nursing babies usually slept in the bed with the mother and father, effectively reducing sexual activity and risk of conception. Nevertheless two mothers curtailed nursing at 3 months and 4 months postpartum because they believed they were pregnant, although in each case conception did not actually take place for several more months.

Bottle babies slept separately from their parents and usually consumed one bottle of milk during the night. Most mothers of bottle babies were taking contraceptive medications, suggesting that "Similac and the pill" were part of the package ordered routinely by the doctor. The need for fertility regulation and fear of conception were the most frequently reported causes of curtailment of lactation in Houston. However, it should be noted that several conceptions occurred among mothers who were not nursing and were taking the pill in the early postpartum period. Other causes of discontinuation of breast-feeding were dislike of leaking breasts, fear that strangers would surmise that the mother was lactating, and the baby's dislike of breast milk. Problems with engorged breasts were known from Mexico, and several effective folk treatments were reported, but no such problems were experienced in Houston. On the contrary, frequent crying by breast-fed babies was apparently a signal of insufficient milk supply, and five mothers reported weaning from breast to bottle for this reason.

Breast-feeding under traditional conditions had been continued through the second year of life. Nearly all mothers could recall an instance from their childhood of the extension of breast-feeding beyond the second year. But weaning from the breast has been considerably accelerated even in Mexico in recent times. Respondents reported the curtailment of breast-feeding shortly after 7 months for their Mexican-born babies. Commercial bottles and nipples were substituted. No babies rejected the easy flow of sweet liquid, so that weaning from breast to bottle was not problematic for the respondent group.

Supplements. All babies whether breast- or bottle-fed were supplemented with sweet herb teas from the first day at home and throughout the first years of life. Teas were administered through a commercial nursing bottle and rubber nipple. Amounts varied depending on the age of the baby, his appetite between feedings, and his state of health. Administration of tea supplements up to three times per day were used in the treatment of colic, phlegm in the lungs, and diarrhea. Breast-fed babies received tea only occasionally, dropped from a teaspooon into the mouth in the traditional manner as a safeguard to their health.

Milks. Sixty percent of the mothers who allowed the hospital to initiate bottle-feeding at the first feed and 4 percent of the mothers who weaned from breast to bottle after 1 day in the hospital all continued to use the same commercial formula issued by the hospital for 4 to 6 weeks. Highly valued gifts of formula for the new baby from relatives and neighbors indicated both the affection that was lavished on him and the strain on the family budgets by the purchase. Any fussing, diarrhea, or other distress that occurred after the first month was interpreted as a sign for a change to a less expensive milk.

Table 5-2 shows the ranking of prestige values of milks and milk substitutes for the group. The rankings did not change between Mexico and Houston; only the opportunity to secure the higher prestige items appeared as a situational advantage in the Houston setting. Every effort was made to give the baby the highest prestige milk or milk substitute that could be afforded.

Under traditional conditions, temporary substitutes for breast milk were used only for treatment of serious illness; milk of the female burro was used for treatment of diarrhea, as was rice water and sweet herb tea. Goat milk was not advised for infants but was used for children over 2 years of age. Evaporated and pasteurized milk were highly valued as occasional cash purchases. Commercial formula, which is an imported item in Mexico, was outside the ability of respondent families to secure.

Substitutes. On payday all babies and young children received milk undiluted, but when the food budget was low at the end of a pay period, water had to be added to stretch the supply of either milk or substitute, and substitutes had to be used more frequently.

Table 5-2. Prestige value of infant milks or substitutes

Rank	Milk or substitute
Highest 1	Commercial formula
2	Fresh homogenized, pasteurized milk
3	Evaporated milk
4	Fruit punch; Kool-Aid
5	Tea
6	Rice water
7	Burro milk
Lowest 8	Breast milk

Canned fruit punches and Kool-Aid were popular for their sweet taste and red color. No babies rejected commercial nipples that allowed an easy flow of liquid into the baby's mouth. Nursing bottles containing substitutes were also used as pacifiers throughout the day, particularly in public.

Rice water is the water strained away from the refined cooked rice. It is white in color, thus seen as a satisfactory substitute for milk in the nursing bottle. Rice baby cereal and tea were frequently ordered by Houston doctors in the treatment of diarrhea, so that prolonged use of rice water was interpreted by mothers as prophylactic as well as traditional.

Additives. One or two tablespoons of sugar were routinely added to the nursing bottle when milk was being administered. Chocolate was frequently added and enjoyed. Sugar was added to Kool-Aid and fruit punch by about half the mothers. Several tablespoons of sugar and a pinch of salt were added to rice water before offering to the baby. Sugar alone was added to tea.

Family foods. Beans, the staple food of the Mexican diet, were the first food for all infants, initiated around 4 to 6 weeks of age, whether born in Houston or Mexico and whether breast- or bottle-fed. The method of introduction was well known to all respondents. A bit of the water in which beans were cooked was offered the baby in a spoon. If he accepted, several of the soft, cooked beans were squeezed from their skins into the baby's mouth. Alternatively, several beans might be mashed on a plate in a bit of the cooking water and the soft bean mash placed in the baby's mouth with a spoon. The same liquid might also be prepared with tiny pieces of corn tortilla soaked in the soup and then placed with a bit of liquid in the baby's mouth. The soup was usually well salted. Most mothers added chili to the beans early in the cooking stage, so the baby's portion had a bit of chili flavor also.

Chicken broth was given to the baby as a higher status food. After 6 months of age, small bits of cooked fruit might also be offered. In Houston all mothers offered the babies canned baby foods after 4 to 6 weeks. This was considered part of the modern mileu and a mark of status. Babies tended to reject all but the sweet foods, and the cost was sufficiently high that canned baby foods were not routinely used.

Bottle-feeding was extended well into the second year of life as breast-feeding had been earlier under village conditions. If behavior problems developed in the transition from bottle to cup, bottles were allowed until the child spontaneously made the change. In one case the change occurred around 4 years of age.

Weaning illnesses. Diarrhea was the most frequently reported illness by mothers during the first year of life, unidentified fevers the second most frequent, and stomach ache with distended abdomen the third. No association was made by mothers between type of milk or milk substitute, family foods, and the occurrence of these illnesses. To the mothers, the causes of illness during infancy included getting chilled, the spontaneous depression of the soft spot on the baby's head, getting into a draft of air, evil intent by malevolent persons, and not removing enough of the bean skins before feeding to the baby. Modern medicine as offered by the clinic played an intermediate role in the health care of the families; germs were readily acknowledged as the culprits in babies' illnesses, but what, the mothers reasoned, had caused the germs. Thus the clinic might be consulted secondarily if the problem did not resolve on treatment of the primary cause. Furthermore, if the problem became chronic, folk curers were again sought in order to remedy the underlying cause. The sacred quality of folk medicine was expressed by the saying, "We cure ourselves in the . . . church."

Contact with clinic medicine did not appear to offer a completely satisfactory alternative because, with the exception of illnesses that responded to antibiotics, other treatments were not instantly effective. The high cost of care was also prohibitive. Only the most superficial problems could be treated for a reasonable price at the Catholic clinic; further tests, x-ray examinations, or hospitalization all required entry into the low-cost county medical system, but there was a fear that citizenship papers would be required for registration, so migrants tended to avoid this step. Private treatment was available only at a much higher cost.

Another reason for the perpetuation of the folk medical system was the difficulty of interacting with doctors, who did not speak Spanish, and the impersonal manner of clerks and nurses, who wished to clearly differentiate themselves from the poor and recent immigrants. The prestige value of medical consultation was not a determinant in times of serious stress, so that the same families who consulted physicians for prenatal checks did not, as a first resort, consult them for the baby's illnesses.

The most frequent cause of diarrhea in the folk system was a sudden chill to the baby's abdomen. This could have been brought on by inadequate ironing of the diapers when they were brought in from drying, leaving the baby's head uncovered and exposed to drafts, or giving him foods that were believed to be cold according to homeopathic theory. The cure thus consisted of warming him up with heavy covers and hot tea. Cinnamon tea was frequently recommended in these instances.

If the diarrhea was caused by the depression of his fontanelle on his soft palate, such that his regular food would cause him distress and his eyes would reveal a heaviness, then the cure would consist of the raising of the fontanelle usually with the help of sticky egg on the baby's head. Prayers and rituals were an essential part of the treatments.

The diarrhea might be a secondary feature of a more serious illness, that of evil eye or malevolent intent. This, unfortunately, could be picked up in the clinic waiting room. Diarrhea could also be caused by a sudden fright, such that the soul was jarred loose or lost entirely from the little body. A sudden fright might occur when the baby was startled by a loud noise, as was frequent among families who lived near the railroad tracks; it could also be caused by a fall. In either case the treatment was quite complex, focusing on the restoration of the soul or the release of the influence of evil eye. When either of these matters was accomplished, the diarrhea would automatically stop.

In cases of abdominal distention and stomach ache, the presumptive cause was the ingestion of too many bean skins. The cure was to symbolically remove the bean skins by cupping the skin on the infant's back with a large popping sound. Massage with warm oil and the administration of hot cinnamon tea or homemade cathartics were also part of the treatment regime.

SUMMARY AND CONCLUSIONS

Differentials in the incidence of breast-feeding by social class were examined in nations with very different degrees of demographic advancement. Three greatly contrasting patterns were described: the concentration of breast-feeding among lower-class women in high birth–high death nations; the concentrations of breast-feeding among upper-class women in low birth–low death nations; and a U-shaped pattern in the United States with both upper and lower class women tending to breast-feed more frequently than middle-class women.

Small group sessions with women migrants from northern Mexico into Houston, Texas revealed an abrupt shift in the practice of lactation. The social conditions that required the shift were traced, and the implications for explaining the social class patterning of breast-feeding were developed.

Psychological explanations appeared not to be relevant, as emotional trauma as well as satisfactions were reported in both traditional village settings and urban Houston. Prestige rankings of milks and milk substitutes appeared to be the same in both circumstances; only the opportunity to acquire the highly valued commercial formula was afforded by city employment as compared to village settings.

The low value accorded to breast milk in the Houston setting led to clandestine breast-feeding in order not to jeopardize the mother's acceptance by clinic personnel. Nevertheless, low income precluded extended use of commercial formulas. Favored substitutes were highly sugared and colored either red as in fruit-flavored drinks or white as in rice milk. Diarrhea was the most frequently present complaint among migrant babies.

Traditionally restricted lactation diets were even more restricted in the city because of adoption of high-cost fast foods over low-cost farm-style soups. Heavy work loads continued in both settings for the postpartum mother. However, the most difficult change from the mother's point of view was the necessity to go out among strangers wearing revealing clothing while lactating.

Contact with hospitals and clinics in Houston resulted in anesthesia use during labor and delivery, milk-inhibiting injections following delivery, and heavy use of prescription drugs both pre- and postpartum. Any advantages of breast milk to either the baby's or the mother's health apparently were unknown or thought not to be relevant to migrant mothers whether they delivered in hospitals or at home and whether they consulted folk curers or clinics at times of illness.

It seems unlikely that a "filter down" theory of emulation of upper-class behavior can predict the future direction of change in the practice of lactation in the United States. Very low-income women, such as mothers who have recently migrated from rural settings into urban settings, suffer the disabilities of breast-feeding only until they can release themselves from this burden. Their lack of nutrition education, their own poor lactation diets, the pushing of prescription drugs and commercial formulas, and the lack of support for an at-home period for the establishment of lactation all function to inhibit successful breast-feeding in Houston. Variations in the social supports for women in childbearing and childrearing are probably the best explanation of the contrasting social class patterns observed between nations of different demographic advancement.

REFERENCE

Jelliffe, D. B.
    1968 "Breast milk and the world protein gap." Clin-
        ical Pediatrics 7:96-99.

Part II

GENDER ROLES

Those who control the distribution of food or wealth, irrespective of sex, are the wielders of power (Martin and Voorhies 1975:11). As has already been noted in the introduction to this volume, women's status seems to have generally declined with the passing of her extradomestic economic importance during the transition from foraging and horticulture to agricultural economies. Mexico's culture, as well as its economy, is still basically agricultural, and Mexican Americans possess a large degree of this same legacy.

It is not enough, however, to speak of a decline in status or of the inequities of resource distribution and power in order to paint an accurate picture of the content of female gender roles and the degree of control Mexican American females have over their lives. It is essential to consider the parameters of gender roles if one wants to analyze and appreciate the differential power accorded to an individual merely by being a member of one sex or the other.

Gender roles are one of the principal means of social specialization; class, age, and other biological traits, such as skin pigmentation, are others. Because of their femaleness, the occupational roles, both economic and noneconomic, open to Mexican American women are severely restricted. The restrictions need not be objectively enforced. In fact, they seldom are. Socialization is the critical factor in developing attitudes and behavior considered characteristic of a specific gender role. If a female has been socialized to believe that she has little control over her occupational options, she is not likely to aspire to the education, experience, and attitudes necessary to expand those options.

Limón analyzes the socializing function of a girls' folkgame. The culturally expected role and perception of a mother in Mexican American culture are evidenced in this game. Female children depend on their mother for their basic identity, even though, in adulthood, independence may be their goal. The game's highlights illustrate some of the basic tenets of Mexican American culture. For example, home is safe; there is danger outside; and some of that danger comes from competition with other females. Eventually, all girls must grow and leave their mother's protective presence, someday to become mothers themselves.

Mason looks at the change in women's status as perceived by politically active Chicanas and reflected through the medium of theater. One of the skits she analyzes

represents female relatives as primary socialization forces. It emphasizes the value placed on a woman's nurturing skills both at home and in the community at large. It also represents the ideal of a woman involved politically—not individually, but with her family as the unit. A second skit features the idea that unity among women is secondary to ethnic unity. Loyalty to family and kin is thus portrayed as a major value without rejecting the need for a woman to assert her independence and freedom. The differences in strategies and values that are characteristic of the Chicano and Anglo feminist movements are contrasted. Cotera picks up on this comparison, reviewing the history of the women's movement in Part III. Mason shows that Chicanas are interested in creating new gender role patterns that remain, nevertheless, within the context of the traditional family institution.

Culture is in constant flux. The chapter by Whiteford illustrates the strategies and choices that, in response to external causes, generate innovation. Mexican American women are the innovators in Frontera where they introduce changes in family relationships and life-styles. Whiteford's chapter is also valuable in that it describes the so-called traditional lifeways of Mexican Americans in a semirural setting. This traditional lifestyle is often referred to in the literature, but a current description has been lacking. Her chapter thus provides a suitable baseline for comparison and for the analysis of changes.

When a Mexican American woman becomes a healer, her status within her circle of devotees surpasses that of any man. It is as if her role of mother is expanded to include all those who are in need of her nurturing ministrations. Macklin's analysis of the role of *curandera,* and its place within Mexican American culture, reveals aspects of the female role that are often ignored by researchers. She also explores the supernatural models for gender distinctions that still characterize Mexican American culture. Although a vast

majority of Mexican Americans are urban dwellers (85 percent according to the 1978 census report), the folk traditions of rural days persist among many, even though they have been somewhat modified.

REFERENCE

Martin, M. Kay and Barbara Voorhies
  1975 Female of the Species. New York: Columbia
      University Press.

Chapter 6

"La vieja Inés," a Mexican folkgame

A research note

José E. Limón

The respective folklores of Mexican women and children on either side of the Rio Grande remain relatively unexplored in analytical terms, although we can note several significant recent studies in both of these areas (Cardozo-Freeman 1975; Hawes 1968; Jordan 1975; McDowell 1975). This chapter is intended as a contribution to this corpus of work. Specifically, I will present a combined ethnography of a girls' folkgame performance in two Texas settings and offer an interpretive analysis based largely on the works of Georges (1969) and Sutton-Smith (1972) in the area of folkgames. The folkgame performance is called *la vieja Inés* (the old woman Ines) or sometimes *la virgen Inés* (the virgin Ines). After describing the settings, the performers, and the performance, I will suggest an enculturating function for this folkgame—a function affecting language, kinship, and sex roles in Mexican working-class culture.

Such a function for a children's game is, of course, not new and is perfectly consistent with what we already know conceptually of folkgames in particular and childlore in general. My contribution then is largely descriptive and intended to further verify this general function cross-culturally. On the other hand, I will be making at least one new conceptual observation in regard to intrawoman's social relationships suggested by this game. Let me begin by describing the general and particular social settings for these game performances, since they appear to have a direct bearing on their cultural significance.

LORETO AND SAN ANSELMO, TEXAS*

The two communities of Loreto and San Anselmo share at least three general sociocultural characteristics and are significantly different in others. They were both colonization sites for the Spanish in the northern borderlands; largely as a result of this early colonization and of their close proximity to modern Mexico, the two areas are heavily populated by individuals of Mexican descent. Finally, because of its history in Mexico coupled with its continuing repressed position in the United States, the Mexican population in both communities is in a general state of socioeconomic deprivation. The dif-

---

*Fictive names for these communities.

ferences, however, may be more pertinent to this study. Loreto is a small city of approximately 80,000 citizens, predominantly of Mexican descent, on the United States–Mexico border; while the Mexican sections of San Anselmo are, of course, part of a major national urban complex with a slight majority of Anglo Americans in the city, the city in turn is located in the largely Anglo American south-central Texas area. As a result, native Texas-Mexican cultural values and behaviors in such areas as kinship and language appear to be under less stress and change in small, largely Mexican border towns like Loreto.

In both cases, however, I studied game performances in lower socioeconomic federal housing project units. The apartments in these projects house a predominantly Mexican working-class population, while some in the units are chronically unemployed. The men in these households are engaged in a variety of unskilled and semiskilled occupations, while the women are predominantly homemakers. This latter role is crucial to my thesis. While some of these women have outside jobs, most of them are engaged in the daily tasks of housecleaning, meal preparation, childrearing, and articulating relationships with the outside world necessary for the maintenance of the home. Indeed, even those with outside work appear to have these responsibilities anyway. In all of these tasks and responsibilities, these women are probably not at all unlike the great majority of American working-class wives and mothers. Nevertheless, it is possible that as members of a linguistically distinct and socially subordinated class and cultural group, these women may develop a somewhat greater attachment and focus on their home and familial life. Perhaps these same factors also account for certain features of the children's culture in these projects.

The children in these projects appear to share the sociocultural characteristics of the Mexican barrio children studied by Goodman and Beman in Houston, Texas (1968). Both the Loreto and San Anselmo children I interviewed give their first loyalties to their parents and family and view the external world with some degree of awe and apprehension. Doing something "bad" for these youngsters usually means doing something against the wishes of or inimical to the kin group. While male children have much greater freedom to wander beyond the confines of the project, the females are much more restricted and confined save for the necessary excursions to school or to the store. In addition to understandable fears concerning the dangers posed by the outside world for little girls, there is also a more practical consideration for this culturally expected confinement to the home area. Like Goodman's children these youngsters, especially the little girls, are persistently trained in the care of little brothers and sisters and in the care of the home. Commands and inquiries like "¡Cuida a tu hermano!" "¡Divierte a la bebita!" and "¿En donde está tu hermano?"[1] are constantly aimed at these youngsters. An older girl rarely plays alone and must be watchful of an ever-present brood of toddlers. If there are small babies in the household, a little girl will also quickly be pressed into service for feeding and diapering.

THE GAME AND ITS PARTICIPANTS

When they are not engaged in household tasks or childrearing, these little girls play like children everywhere. Perhaps as working-class children they play more than other children, since some of them do not have the distraction of a television set. Nevertheless, it is also clear that they do not play perhaps as much as their mothers did owing largely to this distraction. They may play jump rope, jacks, tag games, guessing games, and, according to their testimony, they play the game called *"la vieja Inés"* or *"la virgen Inés"* about "one time a week," although others say they play it "every day."

I observed two game performances in Loreto and San Anselmo. The game is played in the afternoon or at night by window and door light. In both regional cases, the game players are almost exclusively little girls ranging from 4 to 9 years of age. The only exception is in Loreto where two little boys, one 4 and the other 5, also played. As such, the predominantly female definition of the participants is consistent with what older women have told me about their participation in this performance when they were little. There is no set number of participants; although in these cases there were eight and nine players. In the Loreto case, the game called *"le vieja Inés"* was stimulated by an older little girl who functioned as a "plant"—a cooperative informant who agreed to suggest the game to a group of children. They readily agreed and the game was on. In the San Anselmo case, I walked into the middle of the first game in progress after learning that these children played every night. They called the game *"la virgen Inés."*

In San Anselmo, the children open the game by selecting the two major role players by a kind of pressure consensus. By nearly unanimous yelling agreement, one older little girl is selected to play the role called *la mamá* and another was chosen (with much voiced opposition) as *la virgen Inés*. The other children constituted a collectivity, but they did not have a name. Each individual child, however, acquires a game name, for *la mamá's* first game task is to assign each child a color name such as *colorado, azul, verde,* and so on, although two of the children were particularly insistent on their own color selections and *mamá* agreed to them. The Loreto players were more democratic and yet authoritarian; that is, *mamá* and *la vieja Inés* are chosen through a traditional counting game, "one potato, two potato," but played only among those children who nominated themselves as candidates. Thus, these candidates vie for the privilege of being *la mamá,* a prized role, yet run the risk of being counted out first and thereby having to play the stigmatized role of *Inés*. The last one to be counted is *la mamá* and once selected she assigns colors to the children in a forthright, uncontested, authoritarian fashion. The color assignment in the Loreto case differs somewhat from the San Anselmo performance in other ways. The assignments are made totally in Spanish and the color selection seems a bit more varied and complex; the children became *aquamarino, guindo, rojo, blanco, morado,* and a little fellow was called *verdecito*.

The two game performances then share a number of features. The color assignments are made in secret between *mamá* and the rest of the children and are *not* shared with *la vieja Inés* who by this time is supposed to take a physical position at some distance from the group. In both cases, the children play in their front yards with the *mamá*-color group standing (in San Anselmo) or sitting (in Loreto) on the front concrete porch of an apartment unit. Each unit is connected by a sidewalk to a main central walkway running between the rows of rectangular buildings. *Inés* takes her position at this intersection of sidewalks. We now have *Inés* at her position and the *mamá*-color group on the porch; the more dynamic portion of the game unfolds. The symbols go into action as *Inés* approaches the porch group, faces *la mamá,* who is in front of the others, and says "¡Tan, tan!" or in English "Knock, knock!" and the following rhyming dialogue ensues with *mamá's* reply:

> **M:** ¿Quien es?
> **V:** ¡La vieja Inés!
> **M:** ¿Que quería?
> **V:** ¡Un color!
> **M:** ¿Que color?
> **V:** ¡Rojo![2]

If *Inés* does not guess a color in the group, she returns to the intersection and then comes right back to try again. In the Loreto variant, any child who is "guessed" must go with *la vieja Inés.* In San Anselmo, however, *la vieja Inés* has an additional obstacle. If she guesses a child's color, the latter is not an automatic victim. She runs around the yard within prescribed boundaries "de el tree, al sidewalk, a las matas" while *Inés* gives vigorous chase. The rest of the color group cheers loudly for their own, while *Inés* attempts to freeze-tag her and prevent her returning to "home," as the porch is called, and safety.

In both regional cases, the game ends when *Inés* has captured all of the color children or, more than likely, when either child fatigues and boredom sets in, or when a real *mamá* calls her brood home. It is rarely the case that *la mamá* and the color children "win" the game. *Inés* will almost always guess at least a few of the color children.

LA VIEJA INÉS AS SYMBOLIC ACTION

I have not been able to determine the origins of this game. To my knowledge it has been reported only once in a recent collection of Mexican folklore in the United States (Robe 1972). Like so many children's games, however, there are similar performances to be found in other parts of the world, although the closest one is a variant of Bar the Door reported by Sutton-Smith in New Zealand in which a "he" figure chases a girl after guessing her color from among a group of girls, each of whom has selected her own color. This variant is clearly not as complex as *la vieja Inés* nor is it as specific in its roles. A colleague and expert in Mexico City tells me he has never heard of this game. However, I have interviewed women from Monterrey who tell me they played the game as little girls but knew it as los *listones* (the ribbon game), a name also reported to me by older Texan-Mexican women and the name given to the variant in the Robe collection. By my informants' recollections, another line appeared in the rhyming dialogue; after "¿que quería?", *Inés* would reply "¡un listón!", then *mamá* would say "¿de que color?" and *Inés* would guess. At least one older informant reports the actual use of small colored ribbons obtained, interestingly enough, from real mothers. The little girls would hold the little ribbon hidden in their fist and would unfold it and use it to wave goodby if they were guessed.

The contemporary versions that I have reported have maintained most of the traditional elements of the game played by my older informants. I have described the formal elements of this game using Sutton-Smith's guide to the formal analysis of game meaning. Sutton-Smith requires that the analyst present an account of the game challenge, the player participants, the players' performance requirements, and the spatial setting and temporal structure of the game (1972). I believe I have done this for *la vieja Inés*. Knowing these things is, however, only a precondition for fully understanding the game's meaning, or so I think Sutton-Smith would agree. By interpreting the activity in each of these sectors, one can perhaps infer the social significance of the game, that is, its social function and our inferential knowledge thereof as postulates in our approach to games. For the children, the game is only contestative fun; for the analyst, the game may have a sociocultural significance and function. Social functions in games, Georges tells us:

> . . . are the correspondences and/or non-correspondences between the whole play activity or any one or more of its aspects and the total social structure or any one or more of its aspects . . . (1969:11-12)

as perceived by the analyst of course.

For this analyst *la vieja Inés* is a reflection of and a reinforcement for certain sociocultural values and behaviors within the Mexican community in the United States. It would seem to enculturate female children into culturally expected roles and perceptions. Some of this enculturation is perhaps obvious by now, but let us analyze the game as a dynamic symbolic structure—as symbolic action in particular social contexts. The role of *mamá* or *la que habla* is highly valued, while that of *Inés* is stigmatized. The mother's first game (and real life) function is to give the children identity by assigning them names, so that the child is dependent on her mother for her most basic identity. As I noted, urban San Anselmo children exhibited some independence in this regard. Further, the children depend on mother to speak for them to the outside world, and indeed their fortunes depend directly on mother's ability to manipulate language and use it effectively against the outside world. She may fail or she may be quite good. The San Anselmo variant, however, has a subsymbolic action that again speaks for greater child independence.

If *mamá* fails, they have the option of individual running action against the world, although home is always safety. It is my contention then that this game is a symbolic learning experience in which predominantly female children "learn" and "practice" something about the need to take responsibility for children by naming them and speaking for them against the world beyond the kin group. They learn and practice the language manipulation that they need to deal effectively with the outside world. In one game performance, one little girl objected strongly to the candidacy of another little girl for the *mamá* role saying "¡ella no sabe hablar bien!"[3] Fundamentally these children are reinforced in the cultural value of the kinship group; they learn loyalty to the group and its individual members, as the wailing and cheering indicate. Both the Loreto and San Anselmo children learn these things, yet clearly there are interesting differences in the two game areas. I can only offer the most tentative of hypotheses for these differences. It is as if Spanish language use and family structure are more conserved in the Loreto area so that in San Anselmo the children have developed the running option. To take the matter to another symbolic level, one might suggest that an urban environment might encourage and be more conducive to less reliance on the family unit as social and linguistic protection and more on individual freedom of action, although even in the urban center, "home" is still quite important.

In both cases, however, the polarized structure of the game is the same. *Mamá* and her family stand against the outside. This "outside force" remains to be explored. This force is not a simple "it" or "he" figure opposed to "home," characteristic of so many children's run and tag games. Nor is it a "bogey man"; indeed it is a bogey woman. For unlike other Mexican folk games, this symbolic world is populated by women. In her study of games played by Mexican girls, Cardozo-Freeman notes the importance of these games as symbolic structures that teach young girls about men and the oppressive dangers they pose for women. Her children do not play *la vieja Inés* or at least they did not play it for Cardozo-Freeman. Had they done so, she might have wanted to revise her thesis to include not only men as oppressors but other women as well. In this game it is *Inés,* a feminine figure, who introduces elements of insecurity, anxiety, and competition for *mamá* and the kin group. Like the legendary *Llorona* who is without children, her threat to the *mamá*-kin group is enhanced by her symbolic identification as a *vieja* (an old, presumably infertile, woman) or a *virgen* (an equally childless woman). In an indirect symbolic way, are these female children also learning something about the threats posed by *vírgenes* and *viejas* in a sexual competition for the male in the kin group? I do not wish to belabor this latter speculative point, but I am struck by the way Mexicans sometimes use the phrase *vieja* as in "¡Andaba con una vieja!" referring to illicit male sexual activity.

Yet this learning experience about cultural perceptions and values concerning language, kinship, and females may ultimately be secondary to another, perhaps more profound, learning conveyed by this game. Let us return to it. *Mamá* manipulates colors for the children as best she can in the face of the *vieja Inés* and persistent guessing efforts. The children may also run to escape, but is there not a significant lesson in inevitability here? If the game lasts long enough, the children must eventually be captured—they must leave home. *Mamá* may use all the linguistic forces at her command and the children may do what they can, but the rules of the game seem to dictate that eventually each child must leave and not return. While indeed these children may be learning about the values of the mother, family, and home, they are also learning about the ultimate limitations of these values.

NOTES

1. "Take care of your little brother." "Entertain the baby." "Where is your brother?"
2. Who is it?
   Old lady Inés
   What did you want?
   A color.
   What color?
   Red!
3. "She does not know how to speak well!"

REFERENCES

Cardozo-Freeman, Inez
   1975 "Games Mexican girls play." Journal of American Folklore 88:12-24.
Georges, Robert
   1969 "The relevance of models for analysis of traditional play activities." Southern Folklore Quarterly 33:1-23.
Goodman, Mary Ellen and Alma Beman
   1968 "Child's eye-views of life in an urban barrio in

Spanish Speaking people in the United States. In June Helm (ed.), Proceedings of the 1968 Annual Meeting of the American Ethnological Society, Seattle: University of Washington Press.

Hawes, Bess Lomax
1968 "La llorona in juvenile hall." Western Folklore 27:255-267.

Jordan, Rosen
1975 "Ethnic identity and the lore of the supernatural." Journal of American Folklore 88:370-382.

McDowell, John H.
1975 "The speech play and verbal art of Chicano children: an ethnographic and socio-linguistic study. Unpublished dissertation. University of Texas at Austin.

Robe, Stanley
1971 Antología del Saber Popular. Los Angeles, California: University of California Press.

Sutton-Smith, Brian
1972 A Formal Analysis of Game Meaning in the Folkgames of Children. Austin, Texas: University of Texas Press.

Chapter 7

Symbolic strategies for change

A discussion of the Chicana women's movement

Terry Mason

The recent interest in studies focusing on women, in anthropology and in other disciplines, has begun to produce rich data on variety in the female experience and in women's position in different cultures (see, for example, Reiter 1975; Rohrlich-Leavitt 1975; Rosaldo and Lamphere 1974). Much of this work has been concerned with analyzing different forms of power and sources of status available to women in male-dominated societies (questioning the meaning of "male domination"). Few have actually examined and compared women's movements aimed at changing and enhancing the power and status of women.[1]

In this chapter, I propose to look at some limited aspects of the ways politically active Chicanas, through the medium of a performance form (a type of political theatre), represent and advocate a change in women's status. The performances are dramatizations of an ideology that defines some of the social and cultural expectations limiting women and indicates how they should be changed.

The values and symbolic strategies for change represented in the skits (called *actos*) to be analyzed are different in certain key respects from those characteristic of the predominantly Anglo women's movement in the United States. They represent the ideology of a distinct movement, for Chicana feminism is structurally and ideologically integrated into the Chicano movement.

The primary purpose of this chapter is to delineate some of the distinct features of the Chicana feminist ideology and to discuss some of the social and political factors influencing it. To clarify the distinctness of this ideology I will compare some of its basic values and symbolic strategies to those of the Anglo women's movement, drawing on my own experience and on the literature for the analysis of the latter.

The analysis must be viewed as tentative and preliminary, as the data on which it is based are limited. Nevertheless, the analysis of women's movements as social movements has been neglected in anthropology, and they are a potentially rich source of information on women's situations in different social groups. The variations in the forms of these movements must therefore be addressed. As social scientists—both Chicano(as) and others—begin to destroy the stereotypes and oversimplifications about Mexicano[2] culture that have pervaded the social scientific literature, it is especially important that attention be paid to the way Chicanas portray their situation and their role, even as they are changing it.

The research from which the data on Chicana feminist ideology are drawn was a field project that explored the philosophies and activities of two Chicano political groups in two Texas cities. It did not focus specifically on feminism. The study involved interviewing the members of the theatre groups and attending public performances held at different Chicano social and political functions in central Texas, including functions focusing on women.

The data that I will use as an example of Chicana feminist ideology consist of two *actos* on the subject of women's changing roles performed by two political groups for a conference on Chicanas held in Texas in 1976. Before describing and analyzing the *actos*, however, it is necessary to provide some brief background information on *Teatro Chicano* (Chicano Theatre) and its role in the Chicano movement.

TEATRO CHICANO

Teatro Chicano is the theatrical branch of the Chicano movement. It is a national theatre movement that began in California with the formation of the *Teatro Campesino* (Farm Worker's Theatre) in 1965, the original members of which were involved with the unionizing activities of César Chavez. As *Teatro Campesino* evolved into a professional theatre publicizing the situation of the farm workers, and later of Mexicanos in general, they encouraged the formation of other *teatros*. By 1973 there were at least 64 active groups in all parts of the United States (Kanellos 1975; Ramirez n.d.). *Teatro* is a recognized vehicle for the communication of political ideas by all groups in the Chicano movement, and *actos* are performed by groups that are not primarily theatre groups.

As part of the Chicano movement, *teatros* present interpretations of characters, situations, and events from the perspective of *Chicanismo,* the movement's dominant ideology. One of the basic tenets of *Chicanismo* is that Mexicanos living in the United States have the right to—and must for the survival of their group identity—preserve their cultural distinctness. One of the major goals of the movement is to promote knowledge about and respect for Mexicano/Chicano culture among all Mexicanos and to fight the pressures by the majority culture to assimilate. In addition, Chicanos argue that just as the United States' power structure has pressured them to assimilate culturally, the Anglo-dominated political and economic system has systematically discriminated against Mexicanos by depriving them of access to economic opportunity and political power. Thus, a second major goal is to organize to enhance the political power and economic conditions of Mexicanos. There is a high value placed on intragroup solidarity in opposition to the Anglo majority group in order to realize these goals.

Partly in order to promote social unity in the face of the actual cultural and social diversity within the Mexicano population, the movement promotes certain values as symbols of a shared culture and deemphasizes others. The Spanish language, particularly

Chicano speech varieties, is an important symbol, as is loyalty to family and friends. There is a deemphasis on individual achievement for the purposes of individual gain, but achievement is encouraged as it contributes to the good of the community.

The performers in *teatros* translate these goals of the movement into aesthetics by stressing the social and political message of their *actos* and emphasizing the personal exchange between performers and audience. Their ideas are communicated through characters, settings, events, and other symbols that they feel most Mexicanos can recognize or identify with (at least those who will be likely to be the audience at a particular performance).

Groups generally create their *actos* communally by thinking of a situation and a political interpretation of it that they wish to convey; then they select the characters, settings, and events that the members feel are most appropriate to communicate their ideas.

Two *actos* will be analyzed in this chapter. The first is a short play entitled *Reflexiones de Una Mujer (A Woman's Thoughts),* created and performed by a *Teatro Chicano* of male and female university students in Texas. The second is a series of skits (that I will call an *acto*) dealing with dilemmas of identity that a Chicana must confront and resolve in the process of becoming politicized and participating in the Chicano movement. This latter *acto* was created and performed by the members of a Chicana women's organization of primarily university students in another Texas city. I have seen the *teatro's acto* performed twice and the *acto* of the women's group once. Both were performed at the same Chicana conference in 1976. Since the performers (almost all female) and most of the audience were active participants in the Chicana women's movement, I assume that the views and realities the *actos* present are representative of a common Chicana perspective.

THE ACTOS

In this section, I will describe the scenes as they occur in the *actos* in order to demonstrate the way that the female role is depicted and the strategies used by the performers for advocating a change in that role. The manner in which different characters are portrayed—that is, the interpretation of the characters and the tone of the scenes—is of interest because it is here that the attitudes of the actors toward the social types that are represented are conveyed.

Reflexiones de Una Mujer

The *acto* entitled *Reflexiones de Una Mujer* is set in the home of a working-class Mexicano family, and the central character is a housewife and mother. The *acto's* form is repetitive, not progressive (to use Kenneth Burke's terms, quoted in Peacock 1975:138), meaning it develops a theme, not a plot, by embellishing on the same ideas throughout the piece. The overriding tone as it is performed is a friendly humor as opposed to derisive humor or satire. The performers attempt to create the feeling of common, everyday events in a typical household, and there is much code-switching between English and Spanish.

The central concepts and values are introduced in the opening scene through an exchange between the woman, Carolina, and her young daughter. Carolina is sweeping the house, worrying about her housework, when her daughter comes home looking for food to eat quickly before going out again to a political meeting. The mother responds by helping her, commenting with a sigh that young women today do not know how to stay at home. Her daughter reminds her that Mexicanas have historically been involved in work for the community and mentions a number of her mother's friends who work in community services and politics. The daughter also stresses how Carolina contributes to the well-being of the community by making tamales for fund-raisers and caring for the sick. When the mother responds with pride to the complement to her cooking skills, the daughter encourages her to think of additional ways she could help out.

The scenes that follow are presented as flashbacks in Carolina's mind to earlier critical stages of her life cycle as she keeps interrupting her housework to daydream; they are framed by the contrast offered in the first scene between herself and her daughter. Carolina is depicted as a new mother turning down a part-time job offer because of her baby and her husband's desire for her to stay at home. This flashback is interrupted by her husband's return home from work. He hands her his hard hat and lunch bag, tells her how easy she has it staying home all day, and goes out to drink with his *compadre.* In the next flashback, Carolina is shown as a young girl with her own mother, who is combing Carolina's hair and giving her motherly advice about how she will soon want to leave her mother's home, marry a good man, and take care of her own husband's home. (While most of the scenes received laughter, this one was greeted with the strongest bursts of laughter.)

In another scene, Carolina is pregnant and worried about losing her job because her boss does not think she should work, and her *tía* (aunt), while fussing solicitously over her pregnant state, agrees definitely that she should not work. The final flashback is to a typical hectic day in Carolina's life when her children were small; her husband and his *compadre* are drinking beer and watching television while she handles the housework and rowdy children. Carolina's reaction to all these memories is not regret but a recognition of how much responsibility and work she has taken on for her family over the years.

The final scene begins when Carolina's daydreaming is interrupted by a call from the local health clinic asking her if she would be willing to come and work as an interpreter for women who cannot speak English; after a brief hesitation, she accepts the position. Her daughter and husband return, and both parents agree to help their daughter circulate a petition in the neighborhood. All leave the house together.

In the first scene, as I interpret it, the mother symbolizes a woman who has devoted her life to her role as nurturer and housekeeper and accepts this as her proper role. The daughter represents a new kind of Chicana and a new conception of the role of women— one that includes her freedom to work outside the home and contribute to a larger social unit than the family, the community. However, these two roles are not presented as conflicting or mutually exclusive but rather as having parallels: they both involve working to help others. In addition, both mother and daughter place a positive value on the traditional domain of women's work. The tone of their conversation is warm and mutually supportive, although the daughter implies that additional opportunities should be available to women. And finally, the goal that the daughter offers as a motivation for extending the traditional role to include work outside the home is not individual achievement or gain but rather a contribution to the good of the community.

In each of the flashback scenes, which because of the sequencing appear to have been sparked by the exchange with her daughter, there is someone who represents the cultural forces that determined Carolina's view of her role. Most of them are symbolized by members of her family—her mother, her aunt, her husband, her children, and also her male employer. In particular, the primary socialization forces are represented by her female relatives, and it is also a female relative (her daughter) who presents her with the concept of an alternative role. In the final scene, the same values and goals expressed in the first scene are repeated: Carolina's nurturing skills are valued (she accepts work as an aide in a community health center), and she becomes involved outside the home in political work to help the community, not separate from but *with* her family.

As I have mentioned, the scenes are all performed with humor. Each of the characters encouraging the traditional role for Carolina are mildly caricatured, characterized by appropriate speech styles and verbal clichés to suggest social types (this is a common technique in *teatro* productions). None are condemned outright, rather the scenes and characters all drew warm laughter of recognition from Chicano(a) audiences.

The second acto

The series of skits performed by the women's group (which have no title) are not structurally integrated into a play, but in notes where members of the group recorded some of their ideas for skits a guiding theme mentioned was to demonstrate kinds of encounters that led them to organize as a group.

In the first scene, a woman counsels a friend who is hysterical because she is pregnant and unmarried. The father of the child has rejected her and she does not want to marry him. She expresses great concern about what her family and the priest will think but rejects the idea of abortion. Her friend supports her decision to have the baby.

In another scene, there is an exchange between a mother and her young daughter similar to the first scene of the *acto* discussed previously. The mother lectures her daughter for coming home late from a women's meeting and at the same time complains about how in her work at community functions the women stay in the kitchen working while the men work out front. Her daughter encourages her to take a stand against this kind of limitation.

In the scene that follows, a young Chicana from the barrio (stage directions indicate she should walk *pachuca* style) encounters an Anglo feminist who attempts to persuade her of the necessity and value of unifying as women in the feminist movement in opposition to males. The Chicana rejects the offer because the issues are irrelevant to her situation and because it is apparent the Anglo does not understand the importance of the Chicana's identification with her own culture and ethnic background. For example, the

Anglo suggests a day-care center for the Chicana, which is both too expensive for her and is not run as a bilingual center. The Chicana expresses stronger identification with her husband than with the Anglo feminist.

The next scene shows a Chicana attempting to discuss political organizing with a Chicano, who keeps grabbing her knee and suggesting she make tortillas for political functions; when she objects, he asserts that it was the men who let the women into the movement. She responds with a kind of wry sarcasm and continues to lecture him that they are in the movement together and must be friends and equals.

Although both the Anglo and the Chicano in these last two scenes are attempting to define the Chicana in ways that are unacceptable to her, the characterization of these two and the tone of her response are quite different. The Anglo is portrayed in an exaggerated manner as arrogant and as ignorant of the Chicana's culture and experience, much in the manner of the "stupid american," described for a type of anecdote with that name in the folklore of greater Mexico (Paredes 1966). The Chicana's response to her is hostile and rejecting. The message is that unity among women is secondary to ethnic unity. The Chicano male is portrayed more as foolish, a buffoon, and the Chicana's reaction to him is a persistent and firm rejection of his expectations of her but not a rejection of him as a character.

In the scene that follows, all of the Chicanas come on stage and depict part of a meeting of their group making plans for various activities and lead the audience in three songs that were composed for the performance. The songs praise the strength of Chicanas/Mexicanas and call for unity between them and between all Chicanos. One song entitled *"La Tonta de Antes"* (*"The Fool I Was Before"*) has a wife warning her straying husband that she will no longer wait at home for him but will go seek her pleasures elsewhere, too. Another, written by one of the members of the group in the form of a *corrido* (a type of popular ballad) is called *"La Mujer de la Raza"* (*"Woman of the People"*) and extols the virtues of woman for her hard work and the strength she has given to the home and demands she be given respect. The final scene shows the group protesting to university authorities about a newspaper ad soliciting travelers to New Mexico where they will find "margaritas and mamacitas," and the Chicanas demand that the sexist/racist ad be removed.

In these scenes, Chicanas are portrayed in situations where they face expectations about their "proper" behavior, which limits their autonomy and independence or imposes a stereotyped image. Again, the characters or institutions selected to represent the social and cultural forces limiting her are varied; in the first scene it is her boyfriend, her family, and the priest (representing social mores) that contribute to her predicament; in another, it is her mother; and in another, a Chicano colleague in the movement. Two scenes depict representatives of the larger society—the Anglo feminist and the university officials that have ignorant and stereotyped views of her. In all these scenes, the Chicana asserts her independence of these expectations, although it is only in the scenes with the Anglo and the university officials that she rejects the characters that symbolize these forces.

It is also notable that in only two of these seven scenes is there a clear opposition set up between males and females—the scenes with the Chicano activist and with the university official—and in the latter scene officials also represent the university as an institution not simply the category male. The women in this scene speak not just for women but for all Mexicanos and are thus transformed into a symbol of their ethnic group. In the scene with the Chicana and the Anglo feminist, the Chicana explicitly rejects the Anglo's suggestion that they must unite as females in opposition to males.

In this *acto,* taken as a whole statement about factors leading a group of women to unite (which is depicted in the final scene), it is indicated that they must do this in order to provide support for each other in the pursuit of options for women. The options presented as desirable include the freedom to have a child out of wedlock without censure or being forced to marry and the freedom to do a variety of types of work on an equal basis with males, not just behind-the-scenes work traditionally associated with the female role. The strategy for advocating change in the female role does not indicate a total rejection of activities and values associated with the culturally defined female role. The woman in the first scene wants to have her child—motherhood is thus supported. The young woman in another scene does not condemn her mother for her kitchen work; she encourages her to seek options, to broaden the range of her activities. In the *corrido* sung by a member of the group in the last scene *("La Mujer de la Raza"),* respect for women is demanded in the name of their contributions to the strength of the home. This is the same value and strategy represented in the *acto "Reflexiones de Una Mujer."*

SYMBOLIC STRATEGY IN CHICANA FEMINISM

I have tried to indicate in my analysis of these *actos* the significance of the characters and events selected to represent concepts and the importance of the attitudes conveyed toward these symbols. As I have suggested, *actos* are dramatizations of an ideology using (from the performer's perspective) culturally appropriate symbols, primarily for rhetorical purposes; that is, to enable Chicano/Mexicano audiences to identify with the social reality in the play.

In utilizing these *actos* as representative of the ideology of Chicana feminism, I, of course, do not suggest that all Chicana feminists would present their views in just such a fashion, nor do I suggest that there is no variation in ideology within the movement. Like most social and political movements it includes people of varying political and social affiliations. Nonetheless, I believe there are certain symbolic strategies utilized in depicting the traditional role and how it should be changed and basic values expressed in the changes advocated in the women's positions that appear consistently as themes in Chicana's discussions of the issue (see, for example, Baca Zinn 1975; Cotera 1977; Longauex y Vasquez 1970; Nieto 1974; Rincón 1971).

The chief values or principles associated in these *actos* with the desired change in the women's position are:

1. Commitment to family, community, ethnic group
2. Equal respect for the contributions and abilities of males and females, including work traditionally done by women

3. Freedom of opportunity for women to define the terms of their relationships with men, always based on equality of status and power
4. Freedom of opportunity for women to select work outside the home and work not traditionally associated with the female role

Thus, the key principles appear to be social commitment, egalitarianism between the sexes in access to prestige and power, and the option to pursue these goals in new areas and fields.

The features of the symbolic strategy that appear to be significant are:

1. The positive depiction of at least certain aspects of the traditional female role
2. The absence of an overriding symbolic opposition between females and males
3. The consistent depiction of females—particularly kin—as important in the socialization into female sex roles

As has been pointed out, in these two *actos* there is no condemnation of the nurturing function that marks the traditional female role, represented by the older women with whom their daughters appear to identify. Rather, the performers advocate respect for the women's contribution within this role, while offering women choices for the future. The strategy appears to be, in part, enhancement of the status of women by enhancement of the status of the traditional role they have played.

The absence of an overriding symbolic opposition between females and males is also striking in both *actos*. While men are depicted as stereotyping or limiting women (both groups portray this in at least two scenes), there is no heroine/villain opposition. Men are not depicted as the enemy or the out-group in opposition to which solidarity among women is advocated. The fact that men do not appear to carry the burden of responsibility for the women's limited role is related to the variety in the characters and institutions that are depicted as responsible. In the first *acto,* this is primarily female kin of the older generation; in the second *acto,* the family of origin, the mother, the priest, and the university appear or are mentioned as playing a part in this process. Women's identity appears defined not just by men but in important ways by women of the older generation. It is solely females who are depicted as encouraging the exercise of new options for women, and in both *actos* young women reverse the traditional order by resocializing their own mothers into new roles.

SYMBOLIC STRATEGY IN ANGLO FEMINISM

In the analysis of feminist strategy in the predominantly Anglo feminist movement, I draw on my own experience as a concerned participant/observer over the years, as well as on the literature. Again, there has been tremendous variety in approaches and analyses by women involved in this movement, particularly as the impact of the ideology has filtered into a broad range of institutions and organizations around the country. Nonetheless, there appears to have been a consistency across types of organizations and types of feminism in a few basic values and strategies, despite the variation in the degree to which they are adhered to.

Both Cassell (1977), in her field research on the women's movement in the New York City area, and Freeman (1975), in her analysis of the movement as a whole, have distinguished between two types of feminist groups: the more unstructured types of groups, with a younger membership, that focus on reeducation and ideology (Cassell calls these "women's liberation groups") and the bureaucratically structured, reformist organizations with an older membership, such as the National Organization of Women (Cassell's term for these is "women's rights groups"). Both authors argue that despite major differences in style and structure these types of groups have shared a general ideology, which Cassell argues has been primarily generated by the women's liberation groups.

The basic concept and value associated with the new order advocated by this feminist ideology is egalitarianism. Freeman has analyzed this value into two components that she calls the "egalitarian ethic" and the "liberation ethic" (1975:385-387). Cassell, focusing on its formulation in women's liberation groups, calls it "radical egalitarianism" (1977:160-170). In both their analyses, however, this concept and value is seen as not just advocating equality of access to prestige and power for the sexes but in addition involves the notion that this equality cannot be achieved without the total dissolution of sex roles. As Freeman stresses, this not only means the removal of the limits placed by the stereotyped female sex role but also the abolishment of the content—all features associated with social differences between the sexes (1975:385).

Cassell demonstrates how this concept has been radically interpreted in women's liberation groups to the extent that all differences in individual abilities were considered suspect, and leadership was ideologically discouraged (1977:160-170). Both authors point out that while there is, of course, great variation in the degree of acceptance of this egalitarian ethic by feminists, the dissolution of sex roles is a basic principle of this movement's ideology.

The types of symbolic strategies used in depicting the existing situation of women and in demonstrating how it can be changed also vary, but drawing on my own experience, the analyses of Freeman and Cassell, and some of the classic feminist literature (see, for example, readings in Koedt, Levine, and Rapone 1973; Martin 1972; and Morgan 1970), I suggest the following as basic:

1. A negative depiction of all features and activities associated with the traditional female role, including a condemnation of the key institutions of marriage and the traditional family as responsible for women's oppression

2. The depiction of an overriding symbolic opposition between males and females, such that males most often appear as the "enemy" responsible for the limitations placed on women, and female solidarity is defined in opposition to them

3. A related tendency to depict males as the prime sources of identity formation for females

I stress that these are *symbolic* strategies, not political analyses, for clearly many feminists espousing this ideology do not, for example, believe men per se are responsible for women's limited opportunities but rather the social order, society, and so forth. It is significant that males as a category or the concept "maleness" has consistently been selected as the symbolic representation of the source of the problem.

Cassell argues that in women's liberation groups the consistent symbolic opposition asserted was between "the way men are" versus "the way women are," with the devaluation of characteristics associated with the former and a positive value placed on the latter (1977:150-160). She points out that many of the desired features of radical egalitarianism, such as cooperation, a concern for personal experience, and a rejection of power and hierarchy, are associated in these groups with "the way women are" and are somewhat consistent with characteristics traditionally associated with females. She notes the inconsistency here between this concept and the feminist belief that there are no natural differences between males and females but suggests this can be understood if one realizes that this female/male opposition is a symbolic strategy for creating a sense of female unity or "sisterhood." That is, these same characteristics are those commonly associated with marginal groups in low positions in the social structure and are frequently stressed as characteristics of these groups in social movements. Victor Turner (1969) has called these values and characteristics "communitas," and they are associated with groups and individuals in a stage of social transition.

This stress on positive characteristics associated with females that Cassell describes for women's liberation groups does not include a positive depiction of values and activities associated with the female sex role. Nurturing activities and all work inside or outside the home that is associated with this supportive role—at least as it relates to males in the home or occurs in the public domain outside the home—is devalued and associated with low status and powerlessness. Thus, a tremendous ambivalence is expressed toward the institutions of marriage and the family, ranging from outright condemnation and rejection to a search for alternative social forms. Cassell gives accounts of the unspoken rules in women's consciousness-raising groups where it was permissible to speak of problems with and disillusionment with men but suspect to speak of good relationships with them; it was socially approved to speak of the problems and inconveniences with children but not to speak of the pleasures and rewards of motherhood (1977:59). Thus, the powerlessness and low status associated with the traditional female roles of wife and mother have meant that to raise the status of women, these roles must be symbolically rejected.

The third strategy that I suggest is characteristic of the Anglo women's movement is the depiction of women's traditional identity as defined primarily in relation to men. This would appear to be related to the consistent symbolic opposition to males and the resulting implication that they are the cause of women's traditional limitations. Again, this does not mean that analytically feminists have ignored women's role—for example, their mothers—in their own socialization. But the solution appears consistently to be defined as a breaking away from a primary identification with men in order to shift to a primary identification of self with women—the solidarity of "sisterhood."

This achievement of a feeling of sisterhood has very often been attributed to the change in consciousness as a result of the movement, suggesting the absence of a female-defined identity previously. Again, Cassell notes that in the consciousness-raising groups she observed, members often began with an initial negative view of their mothers as less interesting than their fathers and with more positive depictions of their fathers, with whom they often appeared to identify. But the effect of the consciousness change was to increase respect for the mother and shift in the direction of identifying with her (1977:58-59).

The depiction of the traditional female identity as formed in relation to the male is consistent with and maintained in the movement's symbolic strategy of forming the new identity in opposition to males, thus providing evidence for the pervasiveness of this concept in the movement.

DISCUSSION

The contrast between key features of the ideologies of what I have called Anglo feminism and Chicana feminism has revealed that certain aspects of the goals of the two movements are similar—namely egalitarian relations between the sexes and higher status, increased independence, and power for women. However, they differ in significant ways. I have termed this as differences in symbolic strategies in the formulation of the situation of women and in strategies and values to communicate the changes desired.

These differences are related to the way the traditional female role is used in the enhancement of women's status and the ultimate group with which unity is advocated. In the Anglo feminist ideology, the traditional female role is devalued and rejected (as is the male sex role); in the Chicana feminist ideology, it is valued but "opened up." Its limitations are rejected, and its status is enhanced. In the Anglo ideology, the ultimate group with whom unity is indicated is women; in the Chicana ideology, it is ultimately all Chicanos/Mexicanos.

This, of course, is related to the most obvious factor distinguishing the movements. The Anglo movement is a distinct movement for women, whereas Chicana feminism is integrated into a larger movement for the enhancement of power and status of an ethnic group.

As I have just noted in my brief discussion of key goals and symbols of the Chicano movement, there is a high value placed on intragroup solidarity in symbolic opposition to the Anglo majority group. The Chicano/Mexicano family is a central symbol of this unity. Baca Zinn (1975) has called this emphasis on the family in the Chicano movement "political familism." She notes that it is represented in the key movement concepts of "*La Familia de la Raza*" (The Family of the People) and "*carnalismo*" (the spirit of brotherhood), where it has become a metaphor for the entire ethnic group. She argues that this stress on the family unit is not simply ideological but also organizational, citing evidence that suggests a tradition in Chicano/Mexicano political struggles of the active participation of entire families (Baca Zinn 1975:15-19). She also suggests that it is both part of the cultural revitalization aspect of the movement and an effort to preserve an institution that serves vital psychological protective functions for colonized groups.

The Chicana feminist strategies analyzed here are consistent with this value and goal; the changes in women's roles are presented as compatible with family solidarity. The absence of an overriding opposition between females and males is also consistent with the goals of the larger Chicano movement.

As I have indicated previously, the significance of the family in the Chicano movement is also as a symbol of traditional cultural forms that are being "revitalized." Baca Zinn (1975: 20-21) cites several Chicanas as they explain their view of the compatibility of the apparently conflicting goals of the preservation of traditional culture and the eradication of traditional patterns of female subordination. The discussions share an emphasis on a new female ideal, a woman who respects men, the family, and the home but combines this with better opportunities for work outside the home and active social and political commitment to the larger Mexicano community. Of course, a selection of features of the traditional female role for preservation, while others are rejected, is paralleled by a similar selectiveness in the preservation of features of the traditional male role, often outlined by women in discussions of the positive and negative features of machismo (see, for example, Rincón 1971).

The dual strategies of cultural revitalization and ethnic group solidarity are part of the features of an anticolonial movement and of the political movements of ethnic minorities in the United States in general. They stem from the priorities in these movements of material improvement and the achievement of dignity for the entire group, males and females, in the face of the destructive effects of colonialism on the status of males as well as females. Thus, the goals of nationalistic and anticolonial movements such as the Chicano movement are incompatible with ideologies that advocate the enhancement of female status separate from that of males or that in any significant way denigrate other central institutions of the culture,[3] a point Chicanas often stress.

The concern with cultural tradition in the Chicano movement is not, however, simply a reflection of a past-oriented group identity, as some social scientists have described as characteristic of ethnic groups (DeVos 1975). It is fundamentally dedicated to social and cultural change but not at the expense of identity loss. The movement ideology has therefore attempted to create a framework for change within traditional cultural forms, and this is reflected in the ideology of the Chicana women's movement. Baca Zinn (1975) has pointed out that in the past social scientific literature has attributed any changes in the Chicano/Mexicano family structures in the direction of egalitarianism to acculturation and assimilation to the dominant society. She argues that this assumption has led social scientists to overlook other factors affecting changes in the female role and in the family structure, one of the most important being the periodic resistance movements of Chicanos/Mexicanos against their subordination within United States society. Chicanas often distinguish their women's movement from that of Anglos and make it clear that they are not advocating an Anglo model of sex role equality. In the *actos* analyzed previously, the major influence on the changing role of females that is depicted is indeed their participation in the Chicano political movement.

Therefore, despite the fact that the predominantly Anglo women's movement and the Chicano political movement, as minority movements, may share certain political strategies and goals, their symbolic strategies and goals are quite distinct and in several respects incompatible. The women's movement focuses on the dissolution of sex roles and a total rejection of social and cultural tradition in this regard, while the Chicano movement is concerned to preserve some aspects of tradition in their attempt to create new social forms—including sex roles—within the context of traditional institutions.

CONCLUSION

As a concluding note, I suggest that as social scientists and others examine the female experience in different cultures from the perspective of women themselves, this should include analyses of women's expressions of dissatisfaction with their roles and their conscious attempts to change them. Dwyer (1978) has argued that cultural variation in "ideologies of sexual inequality" (beliefs about maleness and femaleness) will lead to different political strategies by women in attempting to alter their position. One suggestion for future research would be to examine in more depth than I have here the relation of these women's movement ideologies to the cultural ideologies to which they are a response. Certainly the analysis in this chapter of the contrasting attitudes reflected in the two women's movements suggests possible differences in the evaluation of the traditional female role in the two groups. It is more highly valued within Chicano/Mexicano culture, at least in the eyes of the women in the movement. However, to examine the validity of such speculations would require more extensive research and a different kind of data than I have used here. Whatever the approach taken, however, it is clear that women's movements for sexual equality will vary in revealing ways, and the ideologies of these movements will reflect the different circumstances of women in different groups.

NOTES

1. There have been analyses of the Anglo women's movement in the United States by sociologists and anthropologists (for example, see Carden 1974 and Cassell 1977). For examples of discussions of women's movements in other societies, see Davin 1975; Jahan 1975; and Rowbotham 1972.
2. I combine the term Mexicano/Chicano when referring to Chicanos who are committed to the Chicano movement and all people of Mexican descent living in the United States. The term "Chicano (a)" is used when referring only to those active in the movement. In some places (when the hyphenated term was too awkward) I have used only the term "Mexicano" in referring to the entire ethnic group.
3. See Rowbotham (1972) for an interesting review of the dilemmas faced by women participating in a range of revolutionary and national liberation movements in different countries.

REFERENCES

Baca Zinn, Maxine
  1975 "Political familism: toward sex role equality in Chicano families." Aztlan 6(1):13-26.
Carden, Maren Lockwood
  1974 The New Feminism. New York: Russell Sage Foundation.

Cassell, Joan
  1977 A Group Called Women. New York: David McKay Co., Inc.
Cotera, Martha
  1977 The Chicana Feminist. Austin, Texas: Information Systems Development.
Davin, Delia
  1975 "The women's movement in the People's Republic of China: a survey." Pp. 457-470 in Ruby Rohrlich-Leavitt (ed.), Women Cross-Culturally: Change and Challenge. The Hague: Mouton Publishers.
DeVos, George
  1975 "Ethnic pluralism: conflict and accommodation." In George DeVos and Lola Romanucci-Ross (eds.), Ethnic Identity: Cultural Continuities and Change. Palo Alto, California: Mayfield Publishing Co.
Dwyer, Daisy Hilse
  1978 "Ideologies of sexual inequality and strategies for change in male-female relations." American Ethnologist 5(2): 227-240.
Freeman, Jo
  1975 "The women's liberation movement in the United States." Pp. 375-388 in Ruby Rohrlich-Leavitt (ed.) Women Cross-Culturally: Change and Challenge. The Hague: Mouton Publishers.

Jahan, Rounaq
    1975 Women in Bangladesh. Pp. 5-30 in Ruby
        Rohrlich-Leavitt (ed.), Women Cross-Culturally:
        Change and Challenge. The Hague: Mouton
        Publishers.
Kanellos, Nicolás
    1975 "Chicano theatre to date." Tejidos 11(8):40-45.
Koedt, Anne, Ellen Levine and Anita Rapone (eds.)
    1973 Radical Feminism. New York: Quadrangle
        Books.
Longauex y Vasquez, Enriqueta
    1970 "The Mexican-American woman." Pp. 379-384
        in Robin Morgan (ed.), Sisterhood is Powerful.
        New York: Random House.
Martin, Wendy (ed.)
    1972 The American Sisterhood. New York: Harper &
        Row, Publishers.
Morgan, Robin (ed.)
    1970 Sisterhood is Powerful. New York: Random
        House.
Nieto, Consuelo
    1974 "Chicanas and the women's rights movement."
        Civil Rights Digest 6(3):36-42.
Paredes, Américo
    1966 "The Anglo-American in Mexican folklore."
        Pp. 113-128 in Ray B. Brown, Donald M. Win-
        kleman and Allan Hayman (eds.), New Voices in
        American Studies. West Lafayette, Indiana: Pur-
        due University Studies.

Peacock, James
    1975 Consciousness and Change: Symbolic Anthro-
        pology in Evolutionary Perspective. Duxbury,
        Massachusetts: Halsted Press.
Ramirez, Elizabeth Cantu
    n.d. "The annals of Chicano theatre: 1965-1973."
        Unpublished master's thesis. University of Cali-
        fornia at Los Angeles.
Reiter, Rayna R. (ed.)
    1975 Toward an Anthropology of Women. New York:
        Monthly Review Press.
Rincón, Bernice
    1971 "La Chicana, her role in the past and her search
        for a new role in the future." Regeneración
        I(10):15-18.
Rohrlich-Leavitt, Ruby (ed.)
    1975 Women Cross-Culturally: Change and Chal-
        lenge. The Hague: Mouton Publishers.
Rosaldo, Michelle Zimbalist and Louise Lamphere (eds).
    1974 Women, Culture, and Society. Stanford, Cali-
        fornia: Stanford Press.
Rowbotham, Sheila
    1972 Women, Resistance and Revolution. London:
        Allen Lane: The Penguin Press.
Turner, Victor
    1969 The Ritual Process. Chicago, Illinois: Aldine
        Publishing Co.

Chapter 8

Mexican American women as innovators

Linda Whiteford

The subject of this chapter is women who are innovators of social change in a small region in Texas located on the United States–Mexican border. The region, which I call Frontera,[1] is undergoing rapid and sometimes dramatic socioeconomic change. I will describe the setting and population of Frontera, those factors originating outside of Frontera that have changed local conditions, and, in particular, those women who responded to the changed conditions by becoming innovators.

The women in this study are Mexican Americans who are, or were, agricultural workers. All of them migrate seasonally or used to. Some of them have stopped migrating and working in the fields. Many of them have made major changes in their own lives and in the lives of their families. Women who used to cut asparagus in Michigan, pick strawberries in Tennessee, and pick cantaloupes in Texas are now getting their master's degrees in bilingual education and hope to teach in the local schools. Others, who with their families picked tomatoes in Indiana, de-tasseled corn in Illinois, and picked cotton in New Mexico are working as aids in local school programs while getting their bachelor degrees at a nearby university. They are also taking advantage of new local jobs created by a variety of state, county, and federal government programs. While many of the women in the region still work in the fields, other women are taking jobs as store clerks and restaurant employees, jobs that have become available as a result of a minor local economic boom created in part by capital from narcotics smuggling. These and other women are learning to use programs that provide special education supplements for their children and food, clothing, and medical care for themselves and their families. This chapter is about those women who, with their husbands and children, are changing patterns of behavior, expectations, and goals. They are the innovators, the actors in the drama of personal, familial, and social change.

SETTING AND POPULATION

Frontera is a town of 6,000 people, although I use the name to denote not only the town but also an area of about 10 miles radius surrounding the town. It lies within a county in Texas to which I have given the name Seco. Frontera constitutes a miniregion within Seco County, and the county, in turn, is part of a larger, nonindustrial, sparsely

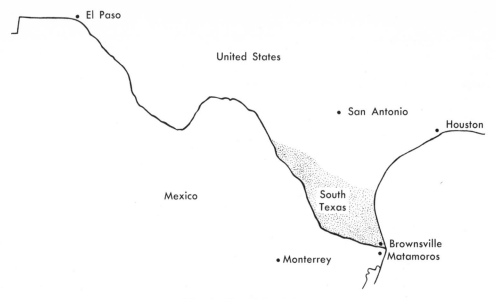

Fig. 4. Map of South Texas.

populated portion of South Texas (Fig. 4). Frontera is located on the Rio Grande River, and 98 percent of its residents are of Mexican descent (Texas Industrial Commission 1977). Geographically, politically, and culturally, Frontera is isolated from the rest of the United States. It is over 300 miles from Houston and San Antonio and more than 700 miles from El Paso; there are no major United States cities in between. However, it is only 100 miles from Monterrey, Mexico.

The ambience of Frontera is one of quiet enjoyment and open spaces. The air smells of desert dust, tortillas, and a dry, clean freshness. The trees covering the gentle hills that roll down to the Rio Grande River are bent and twisted. The Rio Grande, the largest natural body of water in the county, is the southern boundary of Seco, the state of Texas, and the United States. Then Mexico begins.

The county's climate is dry and hot. Its sparse, semidesert foliage makes skimpy forage for domestic animals. Farming is impossible without irrigation, and there is little noncommerical irrigation. Nor is there any large-scale industry. In fact, there are few steady jobs of any kind, so that most residents must seek seasonal employment elsewhere in Texas or beyond. In official per capita income, Seco is the poorest county in the state, the third poorest in the nation. While some neighboring counties have experienced enormous population growth in this century (over 1,000 percent in some cases), Seco's population has grown slowly (U.S. Bureau of the Census 1900, 1970). The 20,000 residents there now represent less than a 60 percent population increase since 1900. What wealth and power there is in Seco is concentrated in a few families, a situation that has changed little in 100 years, although it is changing now.

The population of Seco County shares in the general Mexican American subculture but with many distinctive characteristics of their own. While mass media are available to virtually everyone, the information they provide must pass through a local cultural screen that selects and redefines the information that is received. Whereas migrant farm workers from Seco travel, live, and work in many parts of the United States, their personal interactions are limited to those with employers and fellow migrants; migration only slightly reduces their isolation.

Frontera shows a lack of capital investment. Most streets and roads are in poor repair, and many are unpaved. Perhaps half the housing would be considered inadequate by federal standards. Many commercial buildings in the town are in states of decay (and many of them are 100 years old). With virtually no public transportation, travel within the county is difficult and costly. In many ways, Frontera and the county appear to be a dormant social, cultural, and economic backwater, an anachronism.

Contrary to its appearance, Seco County is neither quiet nor sleepy. Changes from outside the local social system have catalyzed old predispositions in the culture of Seco. Large-scale agricultural producers are converting from labor-intensive to capital-intensive operations. Smugglers bring illegal drugs across the border and through the county by the tons weekly; their profits help the county to prosper. The federal and state governments send money into Seco County through grants and programs to help the indigent and the migrant. Mexican nationals cross into Seco County in search of better jobs, housing, medical care, and education for their children. Within this setting are women who are creating new roles and relationships for themselves and their families; they are the innovators.

Innovation has been defined as ". . . any thought, behavior, or thing that is new because it is qualitatively different from the existing forms . . . every innovation is an idea or constellation of ideas" (Barnett 1953:7).

To conceptualize the qualitative changes that are part of the innovative behavior of women in Frontera, I will describe Frontera at two time periods. The first time period (referred to as "Time One") is until the middle 1960s; the second time period (referred to as "Time Two") is from that time until the present. The time periods are distinguished by two factors: (1) during the middle and late 1960s, economic conditions changed within Seco County in response to forces originating outside of the county, and (2) women, in conjunction with other members of their families, created innovative social and economic strategies to take advantage of new resources. Now, let us begin with a description of Frontera before 1965.

Time One

The local system at Time One (mid-1960s) was characterized by fairly rigid social divisions, with most power, wealth, and information concentrated in a few Mexican American families. Among the handful of Anglo families were the owners and operators of some of the largest commercial farms in the county.[2] Another powerful group were those Mexican American families who had been in Frontera for the last 100 years, had accumulated wealth, had access to political power at both county and city levels, and had access to information concerning jobs, real estate, and potential business enterprises. These "old families" at Time One still occupied most of the positions of respect and authority within the community. They were the doctors, lawyers, and judges. After the Anglos, the old families had the largest farms and ranches. The old families also participated in local business enterprises—the bank and some of the retail stores. Yet another group of families—merchants and their higher level employees, school teachers, and other county employees—had a modest amount of wealth and shared information with old families and the Anglos but had little power.

The rest of the population, by far the largest segment of it, had very little access to wealth, power, or economically important information (Whiteford and Uzzell 1978). These were the agricultural laborers. Except for a few low-level jobs in Frontera's stores and construction projects, most of them worked on farms and ranches in the county. Most of these jobs were seasonal and temporary. Wages were kept low by the constant presence of a reserve labor force across the border ready to work for low wages. These families eked out a living by taking seasonal employment elsewhere, by building their own homes and cultivating gardens, as well as by shopping and maintaining social ties in Mexico (Whiteford 1979a).

While the options of people who were agricultural laborers were powerfully constrained by the local extrafamilial systems, the familial subsystems such as allocation of roles and responsibilities themselves constrained choices of their members. Although I make the distinctions between familial and extrafamilial constraints, it is an artificial distinction to the extent that, although the constraints at the familial level have their origins in the family, they are constantly reinforced by events outside of the family. Familial-level constraints on the system incorporate social norms, beliefs, and roles.

Frontera, during Time One, was a conservative community; domestic roles were repeated in each successive generation. In this community, women (particularly those who were farm workers) were taught to play the role of the "little mother," first in their father's home and then in their husband's. They were prepared to raise and care for their families. They were prepared for lives in which the husband was the head of the household and made all of the public decisions, with little input from the women. The women learned role stereotypes that dictated that they, particularly young married women, must content themselves with interactions limited to their immediate families and their affinal and consanguineous female relatives. Organized religion, be it the Roman Catholic Church or one of the Fundamentalist sects, reinforced local and familial constraints. The lack of communication between mothers and daughters concerning sex and reproduction was encouraged by church norms. Lack of mutual trust and communication between marriage partners stemming from local sociocultural beliefs was also reinforced by religious instruction concerning role segregation, therefore increasing women's isolation even from their family members.

At Time One, women in the agricultural families had almost no access to certain kinds of public information, power, or wealth. They did not even have control over their own fertility. They were separated from society; their social contacts were limited to family members. When they worked, they did so in the fields alongside their husbands or other family members. Their goals for themselves were centered on their families; often their aspirations for their children seemed unrealistic. Many women believed that if their sons could finish high school the young men would be prepared for managerial, or better, jobs. The women had not learned about sex and reproduction from their mothers, nor would they teach their daughters that information. Their families were large (averaging more than seven children), even at the risk of the mother's health. Regardless of the cost, religion and cultural beliefs prescribed large families. Familial and extrafamilial constraints converged to isolate women from the world around them and simultaneously to limit the number of possible options available to them.

External inputs

During the late 1960s, a number of events produced modifications in some of the extrafamilial constraints. Agitation by agricultural workers, both in Seco County and in other parts of the United States, resulted in slight wage increases. In response, the large farms began accelerating the shift from labor-intensive to capital-intensive production. This resulted in a reduction of agricultural employment by one-third between 1960 and 1970 (Texas Industrial Commission 1977). At the same time, the federal and state governments began to release money to communities such as Frontera in the form of anti-poverty programs.

The development of the local Council for the Improvement of Seco (CIS)[3] facilitated the dispersion of the federal money through jobs in local education, health, nutrition, and care-for-the-elderly programs. These programs created new low-level white collar employment. Money flowing into the community from the government, as well as money from an increase of smuggling, stimulated local retail and service activities. The result was an increase of 50 percent in clerical and sales jobs between 1960 and 1970 (Texas Industrial Commission). The 450 agricultural jobs that disappeared were held by both men and women. The 250 new clerical and sales jobs were available mostly to women.[4]

Time Two

During the 1960s and early 1970s, the demand for marijuana grew, the smuggling operations became better organized, and revenues increased. Smuggling has had several important effects on Frontera. It is a possible job for men sometimes in conjunction with another legal job such as trucking, and there is a general increase of wealth in the local system.

During the last 10 years, over 1,000 jobs have been created through special programs (Migrant, Manpower, Headstart). In most of these programs, there is a stipulation that (1) to be eligible for employment your household income must be below national poverty guidelines, and (2) that those employed can and must undergo ''career development'' training at the program's expense.

During this time, there has also been a dramatic increase in television sets in private homes, even those of the poorest families. While it is impossible to evaluate precisely the effect of this development, it is clear that television provides information about roles that are normative elsewhere in the United States, although negatively sanctioned or even unheard of in Frontera.

In this situation, women have taken the jobs that have been made available to them. They are the innovators, not so much because they have taken the jobs as because of the changes in their behavior occurring as a result of taking the jobs. The women take the jobs as stopgap employment for short-term income. Many of them find they enjoy their jobs and do not want to give them up. However, jobs conflict with the normative female role of bearing and raising children. They place the women in the position of earning as much money as, or more than, their husbands do. Some jobs require women to be on the job when, previously, the family would have migrated to take seasonal agricultural jobs. The job gives the woman an alternative to the closed, virtually cloistered, world of her kinswomen. She may even join in extrafamilial activities such as playing on softball teams during the summer months. Her new social contacts and the education she receives give her new sources and kinds of information. She may now have discussions with her husband about many subjects—birth control, jobs, family finances, and role stereotypes—that previously were taboo. Consequently, she limits her fertility and she takes a more active part in family decisions. She may even take an interest in local and county politics (Whiteford 1979b).

Thus, the innovators are transforming their families by bringing additional income and sources of information into those subsystems and changing their own power relative to that of their husbands. They are also changing the local extrafamilial system, mainly as a result of their own increased information, including information about their own efficacy. The likelihood of their children being able to gain a larger share of the resources in the system is considerably greater than it was 10 years ago because the women have learned the value—and the possibility—of higher education. At the same time, these women, together with the male smugglers, are in a much better position to get a greater share of power in the present system than at Time One.

They have gained information that they may transform into political power if they so choose. They, although not their husbands in most cases, have escaped the stigma of working with one's hands. Although they will never join the old families, their children, however, may. Through their innovations, these women have gathered for themselves and their families increased economic wealth, power within their familial subsystem, potential power beyond that subsystem, and sources and types of information that previously had been unavailable to them. They are transforming their lives, the lives of their family members, and, potentially, the social system of Seco and Frontera.

PATTERNS OF INNOVATION

Let us now turn to the specific strategies, choices, and changes that constitute the innovative behavior of women in Frontera. Because the unit of subsistence among the people I am discussing is the family and not the individual, I treat the women's innovations within the context of the overall strategies of their families. There is more than one kind of innovation at work in the present social change in Frontera, and accordingly I present not one but three patterns of adaptation and innovation.

I see innovation as any recombination or redefinition of options, invention of new options, or taking advantage of new options. In this broad sense, nearly everyone's life includes innovations. The migrant farm worker who remains a migrant farm worker innovatively works out the details of his or her seasonal employment and his or her off-season subsistence, while not changing the overall pattern of migrant farm work.

Pattern I: continuing to migrate

The Pattern I life-style represents how migrant farm workers have lived in the past and how many contemporary farm laborers in Frontera still live. Families in this pattern continue to live much as their parents did. I treat this pattern as a baseline with which to compare the changes represented by Patterns II and III. Families in Pattern I migrate during most of the year, often spending as many as 9 or 10 months away from Frontera. The families work and travel in extended kin units, with the eldest male occupying the position of authority and dominance. Procreative families are large; eight or nine children is not unusual. Children are economic contributors in this strategy of migrant farm labor.

Pattern II: modifying migration

Families in Pattern II incorporate innovative behaviors while maintaining some aspects of Pattern I. That is, they continue to migrate but on a reduced scale. They share many values with families in Pattern I, but families in Pattern II have begun to change some of their goals. Families in this second pattern are modifying their schedules of migration to allow their children to finish their school year. Instead of migrating for 9 or 10 months, they migrate during the summer 2 or 3 months. Women in this pattern find local jobs as checkers or clerks in stores to offset the income lost by their limited schedule of migrant labor. The women and children use programs of federal assistance in the areas of health and nutrition; couples have fewer children than their natal families.

Pattern III: getting out

The greatest amount of innovation is found in Pattern III. These families stop migrating. The women and their families of Pattern III demonstrate the most striking changes in life-style and their lives of 10 years ago. Both members of the couple work full-time. The wife continues her schooling, and the couple has, on the average, three children. The women in Pattern III, in particular, appear to be creating themselves out of whole cloth. That is, they are creating new roles for themselves for which no local role models exist. They stop migrating altogether, become full-time economic contributors to the family, and assume a greater responsibility in family decisions. It is such women, and their families, who have the most at risk. They also have the greatest potential for future economic and social rewards.

The innovative women of Pattern III are a minority among the residents of Frontera. Yet they act as role models for others. While actual cultural change "does not occur until the new response is learned and accepted by sufficient numbers of people so that it becomes characteristic of the group'' (Woods 1975:11), change begins when ''individual members of a given society respond in novel ways to environmental modifications'' (Woods 1975:11). The women innovators in Frontera, particularly those in Pattern III, are those individuals whose new responses are causing ripples of change to spread to other members of their community.

CASE STUDIES
Pattern I: continuing to migrate

Patterns of migrant farm work change constantly in response to crop changes, crop failures, and changes in agricultural technology. However, there are more or less consistent parameters within which the behavior of migrants fluctuates. Particularly consistent are the family's periods of absence from Frontera and the domestic organization of the family.

The life-styles of families who continue to migrate have changed little in recent generations. The domestic organization of such families is typified by a close, authoritarian, patriarchal family structure. The father of the family maintains his control of his family well into his old age and his children's adulthood. He still decides where they will migrate, when they will leave Frontera, and when they will return. In most instances, it is he who interacts with the employer on behalf of his entire family: his wife, their children, and the children's spouses and children. Behavioral changes within these families are superficial, amounting to shifts of style rather than changes of family relationships. The following examples are from families whose life-styles fit this pattern.

Pita, who with her husband and grown children still migrates with her extended family, told me of a change she saw between her and her husband's natal family and her family of procreation. ''All my children smoke in front of me. They even smoke in front of their father. I never told them not to, but not even my brothers, nor my husband's brothers smoke in front of our fathers. Both fathers know we smoke, but it would be disrespectful to smoke in front of them. We are different now than we were then.''

Another family who still migrates is composed of the parents, three married sons, their wives and children, two unmarried daughters, and an unmarried son. Three other sons either never came across to the United States (when the adult members of the family did) or have married Mexican women and gone back there to live. The two unmarried daughters are 18 and 23 years old, and while they work the fields in Michigan every year, they are not allowed to go out alone in Frontera, except to the store. Their father is very strict with them and will not allow them to date or attend parties. When they go out socially, they do so with their parents and siblings.

Lea and Juana married brothers. Each April Lea, Juana, their husbands, and their children migrate with their father-in-law's family. The extended family includes the husband of Lea, Lea and their children, Juana and her husband and their children, and a third brother, his wife and children. Lea's father-in-law is the patriarch of the extended family; his wife, their two married daughters, and an unmarried son also accompany the group. While the extended family is away from Frontera, every member works in the fields. Every person contributes to the family's economic support.

Yet, when they return to Frontera in October, the father-in-law will not allow any of the women in his extended kin group to work outside of the home. "Women should stay at home and take care of the house and children," he says. He does, however, allow his wife, daughters, and daughters-in-law to work in the fields away from Frontera because the men of the family are there in the same fields to watch them and protect them. During the 6 months of the year that the family is in Frontera, the men try to find temporary work in construction or on road crews instead of working in the local fields. Agricultural labor is not well paid in Frontera and for that reason the men look for other kinds of work. The result is that for 6 months of the year the women are not allowed to engage in economically productive labor.

The women in these families, particularly the unmarried women, are kept virtually cloistered. They visit no one except other family members, not even neighbors. They rarely go out alone, even to shop. Education for them is not considered important, while education is considered important for their brothers, at least a high school diploma. The attainment of the high school diploma, because it is difficult and rare in these families, holds unreal expectations as to what it will "automatically" make available to the young men who hold it. Most of the women in this group did not express a desire to get their high school diploma or regret that they had not finished high school. Several women in this group did say they wanted their sons to finish high school "so they would always be able to get a good-paying job." The same women also wanted their daughters to have a chance to go to high school. However, their husbands will have the final say.

These women have little or no say in deciding when they will migrate, where they will go, or what they will do in the off-season. Even their own fertility is not under their control. The women in this category show apprehension about the subject of birth control and a lack of knowledge about their own reproductive functionings and birth control methods. Nevertheless, the size of their families is smaller than that of their natal families (six to nine children versus eleven to fourteen children).

For many of these families, the cost of raising children consumes a significant portion of their income, particularly before the children are old enough to work in the fields. Some families are controlling their fertility until they have enough financial security to allow them the luxury of beginning a family large enough to help them in the fields later on.

All families say they want at least one son, but the spacing of the births of the children, particularly among the young women, does vary. One woman told me that, because her family lives far away and her sisters have married and are not able to visit her, she would be terribly lonely without her children. "My children are all my friends." Another woman, more gregarious and outgoing than her sister-in-law quoted above, visits her sisters-in-law daily, and she and her husband visit her parents in Mexico every weekend. She has three small children, 5, 4, and 2 years old. She wants to wait a little while before she has more children. She wants to be able to work, to be less tied down. She would like those three children to be her entire family, but she knows she will have more children because her husband wants a large family. She is presently using the "pill." Her husband wants her to wait before having any more children until they can get running water and an inside toilet. So with his permission she is controlling her fertility; however, she knows that he wants more children and she will have them when he decides she should.

It should not be assumed that people in this population set do not innovate, but only that their innovations are such that as a result of their behavior they maintain their present life-style. The very conditions of their lives require constant creative methods of coping. They cope by establishing and maintaining social contacts that will provide access to information about jobs, by transforming relations of power to help them secure the jobs, by securing transportation and housing, by finding informal sources of credit, and by stretching their meager incomes to allow minimum subsistence. The women in this set, their options severely restricted by both extrafamilial and familial constraints, must devote great amounts of energy to manipulating their few alternatives in order to cope with their environment. Their innovations *sustain,* rather than *change,* the social system.

Pattern II: modifying migration

Some of the families in Frontera, while they continue to follow the crops, are breaking out of the old patterns in subtle ways. In these families, the wives have taken the newly available jobs at the local stores and restaurants. These are not temporary jobs and pay relatively well. If the women leave their jobs to migrate with their families, they may be replaced by schoolgirls during their summer vacation and may be able to return to work in the fall. Taking these jobs is a radical departure for many of the women because it means working for extended periods out from under the observation of their husbands or kin.

Families in this category reduce their migration schedule; that is, they limit the amount of time they spend away from Frontera to fit the wife's work schedule and their children's school calendar. They do not take their children out of school before the regular school term is over. These families migrate only after school is out and return to Frontera just before the school term starts again. They do this even though, by curtailing their work schedule to fit the school term, they reduce the amount of money they can make. Not only do they reduce the total number of working days available to them, but because of the reduced amount of time, they work somewhere in Texas instead of Michigan, Indiana, Tennessee, or California where wages are higher than in Texas.

Women in this group regularly use the federal program services; they take their children in for free shots, health checkups, dental care, and eye tests. They sign up their school-age children for free lunches and snacks; they collect nutrition supplements if they are eligible. They make sure their children are at the right place when free clothing orders are being taken.[5]

The families who continue to migrate but also use the federal programs to help them get ahead—or who allow their young women to take jobs as clerks—differ from other families in several ways. They tend to be more politically aware, to feel that they have "rights" to aid, and in general, to perceive themselves as a part of a larger scheme over which they have some *control.* They encourage not only their sons but also their daughters to finish high school. Children of both sexes work in the fields and in local shops. In contrast to households where the father has absolute control, both the mother and children have a voice, albeit unequal to the father's, in family decisions. Children are encouraged to seek scholarships and aid based on their status as migrants.

Beatriz and "Tucho" have been married 14 years and have six children. Beatriz does not plan to have any more children. The family used to migrate every year; they would go to Michigan usually, but they sometimes went to California. Now they migrate only during the summer months, and they stay in Texas. Beatriz would rather go to California instead of staying in Texas, but she says that the summer just does not give them enough time to make it worthwhile to get to California. They used to take their children out of school to migrate, but the children began to do poorly in school and Beatriz and Tucho decided to change their work schedules so that the children could stay in school.

Beatriz has also learned to use some of the federally-funded programs that are designed to assist migrants. Her children qualify for tutorial help, educational programs with a bilingual component, and free eye and dental examinations. The nutritional supplements for infants and free school lunches greatly help Beatriz and Tucho care for their family even when they reduce their already meager income so that their children can stay in school.

To compensate for that portion of their income lost when they are not migrating, Beatriz took a job in Frontera. Tucho did not want his wife to work, but even with the various forms of assistance, they still needed more income. During the last several years, Beatriz has worked a variety of jobs, as a school aid, a checker in the grocery store, and a clerk in the courthouse. Something always comes up and she has to quit or she loses her job. Beatriz's health and her children's health frequently force her to stop working, but as soon as she can, she begins to look for another job.

Tucho also works at a variety of jobs. Like most men in Pattern II, Tucho is constantly looking for work, for a better job, or a second job. Sometimes he gets work on construction crews. Recently he has rented specialized machinery (earth mover) from a man in Brownsville, which Tucho then rents out in Frontera. But the machine has broken down and Beatriz and Tucho cannot afford to fix it. So, it sits in their yard, costing them money but making no money for them. Sometimes Tucho will hire on to someone else's crew and work for them for several months.

Beatriz believes that she is doing the best for her children by leaving them in school:

> We leave the first week in June and return by August 19th. That's when school starts. We always have the kids in school, and so have to be back by then. There are some people who don't care about their kids' schooling, and switch them around to different schools in different parts of the country. My sister-in-law goes to California and they leave here in February and return here in December and it's hard on her kids. I heard a teacher say that they can never catch-up with the other children if they are moved around like that. That's why we decided that we may not have any money but at least we could give our kids an education.

Decreased family size seems to correspond to the family's degree of innovation. Families in this group have fewer children than families in the previous group. Instead of having six or more children, these women have six or fewer children. A woman's increased control over her fertility, I believe, can be seen as a manifestation of her perception of her increased control over her own life. Women in this second group of laborers see themselves as efficacious in shaping their own lives and the lives of their families. Their involvement in the many federal programs increases their feelings of efficaciousness.

Family relations in the second pattern are markedly more egalitarian than those of families in the first pattern. In the second group are families who do allow the women in the family to work in town. They encourage education for both sexes (although if the girl wants to drop out of school, it is not discouraged). They make use of the federal programs for health services, clothing, education, and so on. They limit their families to a size that is large enough to make it worthwhile to work the fields and still small enough so that the mother can work. They are families who want to continue migrating but are trying to prepare for a time when they either cannot migrate or will not have to.

The futures of the parents, like the futures of parents in the first category, are bound up with their children. The difference is that while a family in Pattern I seeks to replicate itself through its children, a family in Pattern II seeks to enhance the opportunities for the children, to prepare the children to be able to leave the migrant labor force. In many cases, this family strategy is made possible not only by the federal programs but also by the ability of the wife to find employment in previously unapproved and unavailable jobs.

Both the government programs and, indirectly, smuggling (that is, increased service businesses) have offered new opportunities to these people and they have taken advantage of the opportunities.

Pattern III: getting out

In the third and most innovative pattern, the women take jobs in federal programs and the family drops out of the migrant stream. The husband may continue to be involved in migrant farm labor, but as a *troquero* (crew boss or trucker) not as a common laborer. These families best demonstrate the degree of change occurring in Seco's social system. They are people who, finding themselves in a liminal situation, bring their creative forces to bear on redefining the social reality and changing the constraints on their options.

Until the federal programs arrived in Frontera and created a variety of jobs, when a family stopped migrating they were forced to depend on either the husband's wage or the combined salaries of the entire family. There were very few jobs available in Frontera, and those that were available rarely were open to women with the educational levels typical of migrants. The federal programs, with their jobs and subsequent career training combined with the need for acceptable outlets for women's creative energies, have been partly responsible for producing the liminal situation.

The new opportunities have continued to be channeled by the preexisting values and identities. When the new federal jobs became available, they were not equally available to men and women. Most of the jobs were for aids or clerks—in most cases, working under the direction of female professionals such as teachers, nurses, and so on. These positions were far more acceptable to women than to men in Frontera because men in Frontera are not accustomed to being subservient to women. As a result, suddenly many jobs became available to women, and women took them. They took jobs at first because their contribution to the family income was desperately needed. But some of the women decided to stay at their jobs long after the initial financial urgency was over. These women enjoyed their work, its responsibility, and the companionship they derived from the other women with whom they worked. The steady, relatively high income[6] allowed their families the opportunity to stop migrating.

Another way for a family to get out of the pattern of labor migration, and one that in many cases is combined with the wife's taking a job in a federal program, is for the husband to buy a truck and become a *"troquero."*[7] In this case the husband may still follow the crops, hauling work crews and produce. If he takes crews to the field, he usually serves as crew boss. In any event, he no longer performs stoop labor and his income is considerably higher. Thus, it is no longer necessary for his wife and children to migrate. If they can, the *troqueros* try to get enough work locally to keep them occupied. Often they act as entrepreneurs, buying a load of "cull" cantaloupes, for example, and hauling them to Dallas, San Antonio, Houston, or some other city for sale to supermarkets. On such trips, the families need not accompany them.

These strategies often work in tandem. During the time the husband is establishing himself as a *troquero* (2 or more years), the family still needs the wife's income. It is during this period that many of the women first take jobs in federal programs. For many of them it is their first employment other than agricultural labor. Of the women in my sample of agricultural workers who had government jobs, two thirds were the wives of *troqueros* (one deceased). The other third were married to men who had permanent, nonagricultural jobs.

Women who keep their jobs (based on federal grants) receive "career counseling" as a condition of their employment. For most of them, this means resuming their long-interrupted education. The career counseling component is designed to prepare workers to hold skilled jobs after the government grant expires. To do this, most of the workers choose to finish their education, usually to get their high school diplomas (instead of a skill-training program). Career counseling must be shown to have been implemented each year that the individual has worked for the program. Therefore, people who complete high school must find another way to demonstrate that they are actively receiving career counseling. Most people continue going to school. The program director is paid not only to provide the counseling but also to make educational opportunities feasible for employees. This means the program (the federal grant) pays for books and tuition for the employees to attend college if they choose to do so.

As a result, women who start working to try to bring in desperately needed income can both work and get a low-cost college education. This is no easy task. Although their employers pay for books and tuition, the women must still work, take care of their families, and commute to school (the only university is in the next county 40 miles away) several nights a week. This must continue for several years. Obviously, this way of getting a college education is not for those who are not committed to that end. Although it requires a considerable amount of work from the women (and often for female members of their extended families who may help care for the children), those who continue find new access to many forms of information, power, and potential wealth.

Suddenly, the women are college students; some will even get their master's degrees, usually in bilingual education, and become teachers in Frontera. In their families, a high school diploma is considered quite an achievement; often these women are the first to receive a college degree in their families. The women who continue to work and go to school are creating new identities for themselves. They personify a new social identity: someone who both was a migrant and is a formally educated person. They are taking control of their lives by using their jobs to propel themselves into new life-styles and expectations. They see the world around them not as out of their control but very much shaped by their own hands. Their situation stands in real contrast to that of their sisters in the first two populations sets I have discussed.

One manifestation of their perception of increased control over their lives is family size. People in this group have small families, often only three children. In a community of large families (often nine to fourteen children), this is a radical departure from the previous pattern.

Lara is representative of the innovative women in Pattern III. She is 28 years old, married to a man from Frontera, and has two sons. She lives with her husband and two sons in the house her grandparents used to live in and works full-time in the bilingual program in Frontera.

Her grandparents built a new house on the same lot and live next door to Lara. Lara and her husband used to work in the fields; they met there when Lara was 16 years old. Lara is acutely aware of the changes between her life-style and those of her grandparents and mother. Neither her grandmother nor her mother has worked in an office or a store. Her grandmother never worked in the fields; she believed that her role was to care for her children, while her husband's was to support the family. After Lara's father left, her mother worked in the fields, but always near other members of her family.

Lara now works in an office, has finished high school, and is taking courses at a nearby university. Joel, Lara's husband, works as a *troquero,* usually for a local farm. He works locally so that he can stay near his family. Lara does all of the cooking and cleaning (both for her nuclear family and for her grandparents), but Joel helps Lara and watches the children so that Lara can study. They have decided to limit their family to the two children they have because they are already supporting other members of their extended families and because they want their children to go to college.

> My grandmother's and mother's lives were hard. They did not have time or money to make life better for us. Joel and I will be able to make life better for our sons.

Lara and Joel are changing their lives. They are conscious and aware of some of the changes they are making; other changes are more subtle. As Lara said: "Es una vida nueva." (It is a new life.) And so it is.

Another family that has been able to use the new economic resources to facilitate a change in their life-style is that of Rafael and Apolonia. Both of them were brought up on small ranches outside of Frontera. Each of them had seven siblings, and both were eldest children. They met at church and dated for 10 years before they married.'' . . . after I graduated [from high school] I still stayed at home and helped my family because there were eight children and there were seven girls to get at least through high school, so I didn't get married right away.''

For 6 of the years that Apolonia spent helping her family, she worked as a nurse's aid at a local hospital. She wanted to go to nursing school but could never afford to. She now works full-time in the federally-funded E.S.E.A. program, while Rafael is a heavy equipment operator on a local farm. She comes from a family she describes as being very close; yet she did not continue to migrate after she married. Instead, she maintained a position of responsibility and shared economic productivity with her husband, a position she had played in her natal family also.

> Well, we did cotton for years; I guess since I was a little girl. We did the cotton and then I stopped after I had been out of high school for two years. Because I was working in a hospital in Santa Rosa, and every summer I would come and I would go with my family. And I finally started learning that I was losing all my seniority and all benefits, pension and vacation because I was leaving. So my father said to me, ''Apolonia, you will have to stay this year,'' and that was very hard for him. Because we are a very, very close family. We stay together and so from then on I didn't migrate. When I lived at home and commuted to Santa Rosa and then they migrated and I took an apartment in Santa Rosa. So I could just go to work, but it was very hard on father. He didn't want his daughter not with him, and he didn't approve of me living there. But he knew that if I was going to work there so that I could help the family, I had to be able to have those benefits, so that was the last time I ever did migrate. My family continued migrating until my sisters married. Then they moved away, and there were left in the family not enough to migrate.

Apolonia and Rafael have three children and will not have any more. She said that the two of them discussed how many children they wanted and decided to have a small family.

> I came from a very large family, and very poor. Although we were very happy in our close family I don't want my children to have to suffer that much. I want a smaller family. My husband agrees with me so we decided that we would just keep a family of three. It's all we want.

Although Apolonia recalls her early life with happiness, she and her husband have chosen to create a different life-style for themselves.

Preconditions for Pattern III. The question arises: Why don't all the families follow the innovative pattern? Or, given that there are not enough federally-funded jobs for all laborers, why do some women and not others take that option?

Among the innovators in my sample, three characteristics stand out.

1. In every case, their families have been in the United States for more than one generation.

2. In every case, both husband and the wife have worked as migrants during their childhoods.

3. In every case, the women, though of childbearing age, are over 25 years of age. In the following discussion, I consider the significance of these characteristics in terms of the women's access to information, the relative power that they have in their relationships with their husbands, and the relative wealth available to their families.

Obtaining the information that the jobs are available and finding someone who is in a position to influence program directors to hire them, require that the women have social networks that connect, however indirectly, with people already involved in the programs. Having this kind of network is more likely for women who are not first-generation residents. Time is not the only variable in establishing effective networks, but where it is important that the networks include people outside the category of laborers, the family's length of time in the county is probably the most important variable. The women's networks are important for other reasons, too. They must include kinswomen or friends who are willing to care for the women's children, and they must also include members who tolerate or approve of the women's behavior and so give them emotional support. It is not surprising, then, that the innovators I found are clustered within three social networks.

Once a woman establishes herself in a federally-funded job, she becomes a source of information and influence for other women in her network. Also, most of the women in Pattern II are in the networks of women in Pattern III. The reasons for this are twofold. First, the information that it is acceptable for a woman to take a job outside the control of her family and information about the availability of benefits from federal programs flows through the networks. If my sister works in the supermarket, it is more likely that it will be acceptable for me to work full-time, and conversely. If I work in a federal program, I tell my friends and kinswomen about the programs. Second, the overlap of networks is, in some cases, the effect rather than the cause of the innovation. A woman who, following her partial emancipation from the household, joins a softball team becomes friends with other women on the team. And of course, she makes friends on the job.

The job requirements themselves favor women whose families have lived in Seco County for several generations. Although most of the jobs do not require high school diplomas, they do require that the woman speak English. More subtly, the work situation demands that they either have some knowledge of nonlaboring group behavioral norms or have the flexibility and self-confidence to learn those norms. The longer one's family has resided in the United States, the more likely she is to have these abilities. Also, the more mature the woman is, the more likely she is to have encountered women with other subcultural norms. This may be one of the reasons that very young women are not included among the innovators.

The other conditions that affect the likelihood of women taking the federal jobs involve the relationships within their families. If a woman's husband does not approve of her taking the job or if her relationship with her husband is not such that she can override his disapproval, then she cannot take the job. Although this pivots on the distribution of power in the relationship between the husband and wife, it also may be affected by the force of opinion of other family members. If the husband is against the wife's taking the job, for example, but the husband's mother favors it and lends the wife her support, the wife may gain enough power to overcome her husband's objection. Also, the family must be able to bring in enough money so that they can afford to delay migration until the wife's summer vacation or stop migrating altogether. In other words, they must have sufficient access to wealth to take the new step without seriously jeopardizing the family's subsistence. This applies to families in Pattern II as well as to those in Pattern III. Finally, the woman's age and her power in the family determine how old her children are. None of the female innovators have children below school age. This requires that the women have been married for at least 6 or 7 years, and it also requires that they have stopped—temporarily or permanently—bearing children. The latter implies that, except for women who have become physically unable to bear children, the women have taken steps to control their reproductivity.

The fact that all the innovators have been migrant workers as children and that their husbands have also can be explained in one or all of three ways. First, it may be that those who have *only recently* begun to migrate generally have failed at some other mode of adaptation, and the very disabilities (social, psychological, or circumstantial) that caused them to fail previously prevent them from being able to take advantage of the new opportunities. Second, in over half of the cases in my sample, the husbands of innovative women were themselves becoming *troqueros,* a circumstance that was partially made possible because the women utilized the new options. Without long experience at migrant farm work, though, it is unlikely that one could develop the expertise and social contacts required for a *troquero* to become successful. And third, but not to be counted lightly, is the fact that, as many of my informants told me, spending a childhood as a migrant farm laborer is strong motivation to get out of the migrant stream.

Thus, just as shifts in the distribution of basic resources (wealth, power, and information) in the larger social system have created new options, so a very complex array of factors in the women's social networks and their families creates a configuration of personal access to wealth, power, and information that allows certain women, but not others, to take the new options and thus become innovators.

CONCLUSION

As the innovations show themselves to be successful adaptations to the environment, they are directly responsible for changing the social system in Frontera. The innovators and their families are changing their expectations, their jobs, their education, their communication patterns, and the size of their families. In doing so they are also affecting those people with whom they work, their extended families, and their neighbors. As the innovative women and their families become increasingly aware of their own efficaciousness, they are more willing to take risks they would not have taken before. They are increasingly taking an active part in local political and educational activities.

Innovations require and generate information both about the possibility of innovating and about how to do it. Thus, innovation breeds innovation, both in those who act and in those who observe. The process may begin because of extrafamilial factors, but once begun it continues in a positive feedback loop until another event or another element of the system stops it. At the moment, women taking full-time economically productive employment are the key, self-amplifying innovation in Frontera.

This does not mean that the change now in motion in Frontera will cause large numbers of people to stop migrant farm work. For every family that stops, there are several others to take their place. Nor does it mean that the innovative women, once set on their course, will live happily and effortlessly ever after. The new behavior has produced severe strains in some of the families. For many innovative women in Frontera the future is as uncertain as it is promising.

NOTES

1. Frontera, Seco County, and all personal names of people mentioned in this article are fictitious.
2. People who are not of Mexican descent constitute only 2 per cent of the population of the entire county of Seco. Those who are not of Mexican descent are, for the most part, considered by both Mexican Americans and themselves to be "Anglos" or whites. Although some of them own or operate the large agri-businesses, they do not actively participate in political elections nor hold positions in the County Commissioners Court. Without a doubt, they influence what happens in the county, but they are usually "behind the scenes." The Anglo owners of the large agri-businesses are not perceived by the women innovators as being directly involved in those factors that shape the women's options and so will be presented only in structural terms in this work.
3. Psuedonym.
4. Local cultural dictates indigenous to the region disqualified many of these jobs for men. In Seco County, men rarely worked for women and almost never took jobs as aids or semiskilled health or social workers. These were the types of jobs that had become available and thus were filled primarily by women.
5. All of these services are provided at little or no cost to the user through federal programs for the indigent and migrant farm workers.
6. The wage, about $3,500 per annum, is significant locally.
7. There is more involved in becoming a *troquero* than simply buying a truck. The *troquero* contracts with farmers to deliver crews to the field as well as to haul produce. Thus, he must be able to recruit reliable work crews, he must speak English, and he must have con-

tacts with farm owners and managers. In some cases, women perform all of the activities of *troqueros*, although, because they are women, they are not regarded as *troqueros*.

REFERENCES

Barnett, H. G.
  1953   Innovation: The Basis of Cultural Change. New York: McGraw-Hill Book Co.
Texas Industrial Commission
  1977   "General community profile on Rio Grande city. Austin, Texas.
U.S. Bureau of Census
  1900   U.S. Census of Population.
  1970   U.S. Census of Population. "General social and economic characteristics." P.C.(1)-C45, Texas.
Whiteford, L.
  1979a "The borderland as an extended community." In F. Camera and R. V. Kemper (eds.), Migration Across Frontiers: Mexico and the United States. Albany, New York: State University of New York Press.
Whiteford, L.
  1979b "Family relations in Seco County: a case study of social change." Unpublished Ph.D. dissertation. University of Wisconsin-Milwaukee.
Whiteford, L. and J. D. Uzzell
  1978   "Innovation and cultural change in two economically marginal populations." Unpublished paper.
Woods, Clyde
  1975   Culture Change. Dubuque, Iowa: Wm. C. Brown Co., Publishers.

Chapter 9

"All the good and bad in this world"[1]

Women, traditional medicine, and Mexican American culture

June Macklin

> To cure—it is a very hard thing, and demands much sacrifice and suffering. I did not desire the ability, but the Virgin of Guadalupe and El Niño Fidencio told me spiritually that I had to serve—and no one can refuse that: the sainted Niño is lawyer for us all. Now I have surrendered. I do not believe that there is another road that is better, even though many people believe that I am a witch *(bruja)*.

So commented Angelita de E. (fictitious name), a second-generation, 40-year-old Mexican American curer *(curandera)* living in a small town in Indiana. Her mother, mother's sister, and maternal grandmother are *curanderas;* two of her daughters also have the gift *(el don)* to heal.

It is the purpose of this chapter to examine the relations between the role of women and traditional, or folk, medicine in Mexican American culture, many of which are suggested in the preceding quote. As a healer, a woman epitomizes all of the *good* associated with femininity: she is knowledgeable, self-sacrificing, nurturant, caring, submissive yet protecting, loyal, chaste, and close to divine power; but the same arcane knowledge and ability to traffic with spirits suggests all that is dark, mysterious, and *bad* in the power of being a female.

Mexican American folk medicine refers to that amalgam of beliefs and practices comprising pre-Columbian and sixteenth to seventeenth century Spanish medicoreligious ideas. There are certain illnesses to which only Mexicans are vulnerable, and these can be diagnosed and treated only by folk healers. The more commonly known of these include *mal de ojo* (evil eye); *mal aire* (literally, bad air); *bilis* (bile), resulting from strong emotions, especially anger or fear; *mollera caida* (fallen fontanelle), from which babies suffer; *empacho* (gastrointestinal blockage); and *susto,* or *espanto* (soul loss, or severe fright), which apparently is pre-Columbian in origin rather than European. Nonetheless, they constitute a comparatively well-integrated system in that much of its theory and therapy conform to an ''equilibrium'' model of health that is expressed

> . . . in the attenuated humoral pathology belief that the healthy body maintains a balance between 'hot' and 'cold' *calidades*—qualities or elements—and that illness results when an excess of 'heat' or 'cold' strikes or enters the body and destroys this equilibrium. The

127

equilibrium model is also expressed in the belief that parts of the body . . . can be displaced; recovery then depends on manipulation and other treatment to restore these parts to their normal position (Foster and Anderson 1978:74).

Foster and Anderson add that because Spain's "obvious" contribution is so recent, there has been no time for local variants to develop (except in New Mexico and Colorado). Therefore, we are discussing a comparatively homogeneous folk medical system "which makes little sense unless the reader understands its humoral antecedents, and Catholic ritual and belief having to do with supernatural patrons, petitions for help, and the fulfillment of vows" (Foster and Anderson 1978:75). Accordingly, even the details of the system are familiar to many Mexican Americans from Texas to the Middle West and California to Florida—wherever people of Mexican descent have gone. Therefore, I shall use data collected on both sides of the border and shall refer to traditional curers, who see themselves as good Catholics and are guided by the spirit of the North Mexican folk saint, El Niño Fidencio; (Garza Q. 1972; Gonzalez V. 1970; and Macklin 1967) spiritualist mediums *(espiritualistas),* who oppose spiritist mediums whom they believe are using "spiritualist power for evil ends" (Kearney 1977:312; Lagarriga A. 1975:75); and spiritist mediums *(espiritistas),* who vigorously oppose spiritualists as well as the "cajolement of *curanderismo,* fortune telling, divination, and all the perverse arts which denigrate spiritism" *(Armonia* 1957:13). Although there is much inter- and intragroup competition and constant attempts among these practitioners to distinguish themselves one from another—in vocabulary, dress, organizationally, and in perceived histories—the variations are ethnographically superficial[2] (Velimirovic 1978).

Although the knowledge and behavior found among Mexican American folk healers can be learned by either males or females, the role is more compatible with that of traditional Mexican American female role than that of the male. I shall argue (1) that those women who are divinely "elected" to cure enjoy more personal and economic independence than others, and (2) that they acquire real and permanent power and authority over men and other women alike, in both domestic and public spheres. Finally, (3) in order to persist, Mexican American curers need a public, an ethnic group that shares their world view and the symbols that give expression to it. As Mexican Americans become more powerful—socially, economically, and politically—fewer and fewer will rely on miraculous intervention for solutions to their health and other problems. The symbols of their ethnic identity will be modified accordingly.

To define the traditional Mexican American female role is a task fraught with more hazards than defining traditional medicine. Until recently, data on women's roles in any society have been collected very inadequately, as we are being reminded sternly on all sides (Ardner 1975; Flora 1973; Knaster 1976; Lavrin 1978; Quinn 1977; Rosaldo and Lamphere 1974). First, our models of society have been too simple, leading us to assume too much homogeneity of behavior among the members of a given society and, of course, also within gender roles. For example, there is likely to be considerable variation in women's roles within a given nation, as is emphasized by the apt title of a recent paper, *Mexico: the Many Worlds of Women* (Elmendorf 1977). Elsewhere, Elmendorf (1975) has shown that even within a comparatively homogeneous group, such as the Mayan Indians in one village in the Yucatán, variations appear in the roles of individual women.

Second, social scientists—males and females alike—predominantly have studied men's models of society, while ignoring elements that would contradict these models (Ardner 1975:15). Quinn convincingly argues that we must treat the different aspects of women's status as independent: women may have a very " 'low' status in some domains of behavior, approach equality in others, achieve equality with men's status in others, and even in some domains, surpass the status of men" (1977:183). This point is directly relevant to understanding the status of women who heal. The "myth of male dominance"—the idea that sexual asymmetry exists everywhere (Rosaldo and Lamphere 1974)—also has caused us to overlook the kinds of power women may exercise in the domestic sphere.

Third, women's roles, as well as those of men, have a "developmental style, so that a particular woman's relationship to the allocation of power and authority changes as she grows older and her children mature" (Lamphere 1975:118). This dynamic view of role is of particular importance in understanding the relation of Mexican American women to traditional medicine.

Fourth, the supernatural models for gender distinctions must also be regarded as dynamic. While they constitute symbols that embody "deep myths of culture" (Turner 1974:123) and give form and content to male and female roles, the symbols themselves are responsive to the processes that have altered the relations between men and women in the Mexican American social and cultural arenas.

While the many roles of Mexican American women may be as complex as the "many Mexicos" (Sánches Morales and Domínguez 1975) from which they have been derived, there nonetheless seems to be consensus in the literature (Elmendorf 1977; Paz 1961; Pi-Sunyer 1973; Wolf 1958; Wolf and Hansen 1972), ably summarized by Stevens, that Latin American mestizo cultures:

> exhibit a well-defined pattern of beliefs and behavior centered on popular acceptance of a stereotype of the ideal woman. This stereotype, like its *macho* counterpart, is ubiquitous in every social class. There is a near universal agreement on what a 'real woman' is like and how she should act. Among the characteristics of this ideal are semidivinity, moral superiority, and spiritual strength. This spiritual strength engenders abnegation, that is, an infinite capacity for humility and sacrifice. No self-denial is too great for the Latin-American woman, no limit can be divined to her vast store of patience with the men of her world. . . . She is also submissive to the demands of the men: husbands, sons, fathers, brothers (Stevens 1973:94-95).

Termed *"marianismo"*—the model for the ideal woman having been derived from the religious cult of the Virgin Mary—the female pattern of behavior has its corollary in reciprocal male traits, termed *"machismo,"* a cult of virility, the chief characteristics of which are "exaggerated aggressiveness and intransigence in male-to-male interpersonal relationships and arrogance and sexual aggression in male-to-female relationships" (Stevens 1965; 1973:90). While the Virgin and women preside over the domestic sphere, a trusted warm circle of kin within which "morality is strong and certain" (Wolf and Hansen 1972:115), men represent their households in the public sphere, "the sphere of distrust, questionable loyalties, conflict and violence," a male-dominated world represented by either a helpless little Jesus, or as "the suffering Christ who has taken the suffering of the world upon his shoulders but is not yet certain of resurrection" (Wolf and Hansen 1972:114-115). Successful female healers modify and manipulate these supernaturals and introduce others to validate their new identities in the public sphere.

The specific Mexican American communities from which my own data come (Ohio, Indiana, and Texas) as well as other ethnographic studies on Mexican American life support these descriptions of family roles (Moore 1976:106). Male and female role rights and obligations, informed and validated by ideas about supernaturals, are directly related to the generic definition of the healer role. Men and women alike have become internationally known healers (cf. Macklin 1967; Macklin and Crumrine 1973; Romano 1965; Spicer 1962), while those of lesser repute exist and flourish by the hundreds on both sides of the border (Aguirre 1978; Cheney and Adams 1978; Kearney 1978; Macklin 1978; Trotter and Chavira 1978). But the role of highly successful, full-time healer demands that all of one's time and energy be devoted to "humanity": conflictive obligations of *any* other role cannot be met. Further, the role demands an androgynous combination of nurturing compassion and openness along with a willingness to exercise the power, authority, and decisiveness necessary to confront and conquer spiritual and existential dangers. In these senses then, full-time healing constitutes a role that transcends gender. However, the role orientations of females as described in the preceding are more consistent with being a healer than are those of males, and the orientations of the powerful supernaturals that guide and assist in curing also are more traditionally feminine than masculine.

THE MAKING OF A *CURANDERA*

To illustrate the relationships just suggested, I will describe briefly the career of Lila G. (fictitious name), an internationally known *curandera* who has been living and practicing in Indiana since 1946. Mrs. G.'s development as a healer may be taken as prototypical and is of particular interest because she is the second of four generations of women who heal; she also is the mother of Angelita, whose statement opened this chapter.

Lila G. was born in 1909 on a small border farm between Brownsville and Harlingen, Texas. When she was very young, Lila's mother, also a *curandera*, returned to her small home town in San Luis Potosí, Mexico; there Lila grew up. Her mother continued to cure until her death in 1968, using only her vast knowledge of herbs for healing. She never received supernatural assistance, although she knew of and believed in El Niño Fidencio, according to Lila. Lila's sister, 4 years her junior, is also a well-known healer in this town where she cures with the assistance of Fidencio. Later, Lila returned to Harlingen where she married. Shortly after Angelita's birth, Lila's husband was killed violently, for reasons that seem unclear to Lila. She and her daughter then spent the next

18 years or so traveling between her mother's home in San Luis Potosí and the valley of Texas, during which time she herself was developing a reputation for skill in curing. She then suffered from a series of severe hemorrhages that "doctors with titles" could not cure; she received help through the intercession of Fidencio, working through one of his "elected" *curanderos*. As Lila tells it, it becomes clear that the *curandero* enjoyed the gift of "seeing" as well as curing:

> He [the *curandero*] *knew* that I was ill for he told others that they should go to Mercedes (where Angelita and I were then living) and they would find a woman who cured there who was very ill, and that they should bring me to him. He then told me that my neighbor, whom I thought to be a close friend, was causing my illness because she was jealous of me; she thought I was bewitching and attracting her husband. The *curandero* told us to leave that area if I wanted to get well, and we did. That was about 1945 or 1946; we began to work the crops, first in Michigan, and then we came to Indiana. It was at that time that I remarried, just after Angelita had married.

She had devoted much of her early mature life to supporting herself and her daughter and curing part-time. Her daughter, no longer dependent on her, she had no close kin obligations to demand her time, energy, and concentration; her second marriage produced no more children. Her second husband, given to drinking, was somewhat improvident and it became necessary for her to find employment in one of the local factories, work she loathed; she also returned occasionally to the fields to engage in the back-breaking stoop labor she had wanted to leave. It was about this time that she finally realized that the spirit of El Niño Fidencio had been assisting her with her curing. For 8 years she had "denied his presence, his aid, and his attempts to be recognized." Clearly El Niño had been influencing her life in significant ways; it was he who had known that she was desperately ill in Texas and had apprised one of his "chosen vessels" of her condition so that she could be healed; it was he who had directed her to the Midwest, where she contracted her barren second marriage; and it was he who had provided the successes she had enjoyed as a curer. But her actual knowledge that he had elected her to be one of his "favorite" chosen vessels *(vasos preferidos* and *vasos escojidos)* came convincingly while she was visiting her brother who lived in a tiny village in the northern Mexican state of Coahuila. Her brother's wife had been cured by Fidencio when the great and sainted *curandero* was alive; Fidencio himself had visited this village. The *centro* or *templo* erected here after his visit is considered to be the mother church *(matriz principal)* for many healers and "missionaries" (devotees who do not heal, but who do have some mission in the service of the Niño) on both sides of the border. These followers of Fidencio are all nominal Catholics, rural or lower-class urban—*fidencistas*— dwellers who have had little or no formal education. If they are healers, they say that they "lend" their bodies *("le presto mi cuerpo")* to Fidencio, which carries further the imagery of their being chosen, favorite vessels, offering a passive, submissive, body, open to receive and be filled by Fidencio. A female healer is referred to, and refers to herself, as a *caja,* and a male is a *cajón.* They are, literally, "boxes" that receive the spirit of Fidencio.

SPIRITUAL MESSAGES: DIVINE OR DEMONIC?

Three of the curers in the Coahuila village where Mrs. G. learned of her "election"—a *cajón,* his wife, and another *caja*—had known Fidencio personally, which gave them great authority in the healing hierarchy. I will describe briefly the function of the old *cajón* who announced Mrs. G's mission because he represents a typical solution to the problem inherent in every attempt to organize charismatic healers and validate revealed knowledge. How does a person know that he or she has been divinely elected? How is he or she to know that the spiritually revealed messages are divinely rather than demonically inspired? And how is a client to know who is a true curer and who is a charlatan?

Each of the groups—*fidencistas, espiritualistas,* and *espiritistas*—that has organized its members has to try to control and interpret the messages from the spirits, whether these come through trance possession, dreams, visions, or visits "in the flesh." Victor Z., the old *cajón* in Coahuila, is known as the *Revisador*, the official interpreter or reviewer of Fidencio's mission. "He is the foremost, the chief one *(el principal)* in the things of the Niño," asserts Angelita. When people aspire to become *cajas* or *cajones* for Fidencio's spirit, they must come to the *Revisador* and "see" a vision (a *revista* in their terminology) that he, too, must see exactly as the petitioner sees it. These *revistas* are formulaic in vocabulary and in the sequence of events that occur in them. After beginning "In the name of the Father, and the Son, and the Holy Spirit," the petitioner describes everything he or she sees, while proceeding down a road, usually described as "very straight and illuminated": flowers and palm trees may appear, and all is beautifully colored. The petitioners always encounter the Virgin of Guadalupe, who tells them, "Continue following your road." El Niño Fidencio appears and also urges the petitioner to continue on the road *(camino)*. Often God himself appears and says: "Continue on your way, *for it is your salvation*" (my emphasis). Symbolically, the "road" is a life dedicated to curing and serving Fidencio and humanity. The symbolism is recognized explicitly by the curers, who frequently observe that the "way" of El Niño is very hard *("el camino del Niño es muy duro")*. These accounts *(penitencias*[3]*)* must be written down, dated, and signed by the *Revisador*. A heavenly trip and encounters with supernaturals is a typical route to healing power in many societies throughout the world.

During Lila's visit to the mother church, both the highly respected *Revisador* and one of the *cajas* received spiritual communications from Fidencio telling them that Lila was going to serve him. "He said that 'when you have plucked out the sin from your own eye, you will serve me.'" She knew that she had not had that ecstatic trip to the supernatural world and said that she did not have a *penitencia* that the *Revisador* could verify, but he responded, "Oh, yes, you do; that you are a favorite vessel shows in your hand; it is marked."

The recruitment of Mrs. G. illustrates a complex of traditional features common to shamanistic-like curing and ritual specialists in Mexican American society, whether traditional *curanderos,* spiritualist, or spiritist mediums.[4] The data I have on twenty-two healers—eight in the United States and fourteen from northern Mexico—vary only in details from those descriptions offered by Aguirre (1978), Cheney and Adams (1978),

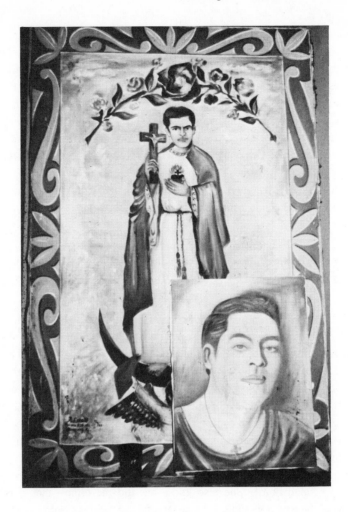

Clark (1959), Kearney (1978), Lagarriga A. (1975), Romano V. (1965), Rubel (1966) and almost could be interchanged with those cases of Guatemalan midwives presented by Paul (1978), Paul and Paul (1975), and Macklin's (1977) analysis of non-Hispanic spiritualist mediums from Connecticut. Mrs. G.'s claim to power is unassailable: apparently some of it is perceived as having been inherited from her maternal ancestors. All of the eight Mexican American healers on whom I have data claimed that at least one relative— usually on the maternal side of the family—had been a gifted healer.

Mrs. G., like Fidencio, had considerable empirical knowledge of healing techniques, having been reared in a home where she was exposed to the folk diagnostic system and appropriate remedies; she also had been socialized in several healing centers when she needed treatments for her own lingering illness, caused by another woman's jealousy and envy. She, like most such healers, uses both traditional and scientific western medicine but knows that no "doctor with title" can be expected to understand or treat the range of "unnatural" Mexican illnesses that includes suffering evoked by other humans. In some ways, she and other healers like her share a medieval world view in which the doctrine of signs is still meaningful; that is, visible outward marks signify inner spiritual states and qualities. Mrs. G. carried in her hand the *mark* of her divine election; El Niño Fidencio reportedly carried a crucifix in his hard palate, the mark of a gifted healer *(saludador)* from early Spanish times on (Foster 1953). Parents watch for other signs. For example, being the seventh son of a seventh son; having cried out in the mother's womb before birth; and being born with a caul are among the signs announcing one's divine grace and the gift to heal.

A further typical element in the recruitment of Mrs. G. is that she was recognized by proven healers, and, typically, she resisted the call:

> I could not believe them—that I was marked to serve Fidencio, and went back to my brother's house. But the next morning, I returned to the *matriz principal,* and fell into trance for the first time. There, at 9:00 A.M., I received the first communication I ever had from El Niño; he identified himself through me, and then I knew it was true.

Now the possessing spirit had spoken, and Mrs. G. set about reorganizing her perception of her own past, another feature that is common in the ecstatic experience. She now understood that her apparently secular ability to heal had been divinely inspired after all. Often at this point the healer "realizes" in retrospect that she had been a prescient, gifted child. She also had had to purify herself—get the sin out of her eye—before entering service to her possessing spirit; as the mother of only one now grown child, she was at the point in the female life cycle where very few of the demands usually made of women were being made on her. She could devote herself to helping "humanity"—most of whom are, of course, nonkin. Her second husband not only did not believe in Fidencio, he attempted to stop her from serving the Niño. She knew that she could reject the Niño's call only at her own peril; she defied her husband and built a curing room to the Niño that was as large as their small home. She also knew—as did the Niño—that if one charged for one's service, the power would go. Material gifts she receives from grateful clients are supposed to go back into the service of the Niño, either to help other needy clients or to glorify El Niño himself. In 1975, she had constructed a second larger curing temple. She also told me that she has invested "more than $15,000" (U.S. dollars) in the repair and renovation of the tomb room of El Niño in Espinazo, Nuevo León.

She, like others who have been recruited successfully, continues to receive regular help from supernatural sources in diagnosing and treating clients, as well as other assistance. She reports that Fidencio came to her once in the flesh *(la carne);* she carefully distinguished this appearance from a vision or dream.

> It was 2:30 A.M. and Mrs. G. was in her bedroom. Her husband was out with their car, and she knew that he had been drinking. Furthermore, he had two of their grandchildren with him. Mrs. G., worried about her husband, had been sleeping very fitfully, when suddenly she became aware of a presence, and there was El Niño. She pretended to be sleeping and did not want to open her eyes; then came a light blow on the knee, and then another, and another. El Niño was determined to attract her attention. When she did open her eyes, she

saw him exactly as she knew him to be from his photographs but felt no fear. She knew he was there assisting them—and later learned that her husband, although drunk, had driven unnoticed right by two local policemen and had returned safely with the grandchildren.

Her case also illustrates the roots of contention and competition among the divinely elected themselves. The source of their revealed knowledge poses a threat, the same threat with which charismatics always have challenged established religion. The dilemma is this: If knowledge is something one inherits or if it comes supernaturally revealed through dreams, visions, or spirit possession, then it always is possible that others, outsiders, can claim equal or superior knowledge. Some of the followers of Fidencio have accepted the authority of the *Revisador* to audit and validate their own communications; others do not and match their revealed message against the revealed messages of others, each claiming to know best what El Niño wants. Of course, those receiving revealed knowledge are caught in a double bind. If one denounces a competitor's revelations as false or misguided, then one's own revealed truths are suspect. *Fidencistas, espiritualistas,* and *espiritistas* of all stripes struggle constantly for the authority to control which messages are to be accepted as valid and which individuals are to be admitted to their groups as qualified healers.

Mrs. G. is very much aware of spiritualists and spiritists healers but dismisses them as having only *some* "light," being in "other lines" *(otras líneas)* than she; she says that the "Niño is so different from others that he is in a separate category." To illustrate the Niño's superiority, Lila told of a *caja* who had come to her Indiana temple from California and wanted to "develop" spiritually with her, having heard of Lila's reputation as a great healer:

> She was a pure spiritualist. I asked her, "Develop what? Study what? What is there to develop? What is there to study?" She said that she had been communicating with Don Pedrito Jaramillo, San Martín de Porres, Santa Teresita de Jesús, and a General who can get in touch with at least five other spirits.

Then, warming to her subject, Lila went on:

> I told her that here we are very simple people, and had no more than one spirit, that of the Sainted Niño. I told her that if they had so much intelligence out there *(mucho cerebro),* she would be better off to return to California, that here we had not so much to offer. What did she have to learn from me?

The pointed sarcasm and mock humility with which Lila related the above case emphasizes another difference between intuitive, inspired knowledge, and rational knowledge that one comes by through studying and reasoning. Lila believes that either you have it or you don't; you are among the chosen and *know,* or you are not, and all the studying in the world cannot change that. The status is ascribed, not achieved, and emphasizes the God-given specialness of her ability. Daughter Angelita, who lives with her nine children across an alley from Lila's house and curing room, assists and administers the temple while her mother is in Mexico during the winter months. Lila says that she never wanted the two granddaughters with the gift to heal, because you "know how people talk. They might think that we were just trying to exploit them, to make money from them.'' She also says that the other Mexicans in her town, most of whom settled out of the migrant stream in the early 1950s, do not believe in the Niño nor do they come to be treated; but then, ''Jesus was not respected in his own town, either, was he?'' she asks rhetorically. She says that she has no friends among her neighbors but really has no time to sit and have coffee with them, in any case. Serving her supernatural patron is far too demanding.

KNOWLEDGE, HEALTH, AND SOCIAL STRUCTURE

Medical beliefs and practices comprise a major part of every sociocultural system. Among Mexican Americans, home remedies are a part of a woman's knowledge and experience. Applying her knowledge in the domestic sphere is an extension of her obligation to nurture and care for her husband and children. She knows, for example, that she must bring in the baby's drying diapers before sunset or *los aires* (malevolent air) will enter them and cause the child to be inconsolably irritable. She knows that following an afternoon among strangers, young children almost invariably will suffer from *mal [de] ojo* (evil eye); she also knows that some foods are ''hot'' and some ''cold,'' and too much of one or the other can cause her children to become ill. She knows that she herself is particularly vulnerable during pregnancy and that for the 40 days *(cuarenta dias)* following the birth of a child she must be particularly careful not to eat too much of either the hot or cold foods. She and her family must be careful not to attract envy—as was illustrated in the case of Mrs. G.—or someone might inflict illness through bewitchment. She must be particularly concerned that other women not make a slave of her husband with *toloache* (jimson weed) or other magical potion and therefore cause him to act ''crazy'' and forget his responsibility to her and their children. Although all of the examples just cited came from a sample of second-generation women now living in Toldeo, Ohio, folk medical knowledge that is common among first-generation women in the Southwest appears to be considerably attenuated in the Midwest. It is in the breach that second- and third-generation women surmise that they must have broken a taboo and become vaguely anxious and uncertain about the rules of healthful behavior. For example:

> One young matron reported that although her own mother followed very strict rules for *los cuarenta dias* (such as wearing only long-sleeved garments, never washing or even combing her hair during this period), she herself did not follow these rules very carefully. She added, however, that there was no question in her mind that the problems of her sister (who had had a hysterectomy before she was thirty-four) was because she ''didn't take care of herself.'' Doctors tell you not to bind yourself after the child is born, and that it's all right to take showers, but I don't know. You hear so much more about cancer and I think it's because women don't take care of themselves [during the *cuarenta dias*] like they should (Macklin 1976:224-225).

Another woman, although she knew nothing about the general underlying theory of displaced parts causing illness, constantly attempted to discipline her children by telling them that rambunctious play, or anything else she didn't want them to do, would injure their ''nerves.'' She attributed her own failure to recover rapidly from an operation to the fact that "they had not left things in the right place in there." Mrs. G. herself, as a curer, frequently attributes slowness in postoperative healing to the doctors' "not having left things right in there." Therapy is invariably massage, usually with her feet. She walks up and down the patient, her weight being supported on either side by an assistant.

Often the need to treat oneself or one's family occasions social interaction between a woman and her mother, thereby reinforcing and extending traditional belief patterns. Many second-generation Midwestern Mexican American women have knowledge of the appropriate folk medicine remedy but do not have access to the broad range of *materia médica* necessary to apply their knowledge. Therefore, they enjoin their mothers or other female relatives in Texas to send them herbs, oils, and appropriate printed prayers that they are unable to locate in the *botanicas* in the Midwest. A pregnant woman often elects to return to the home of her mother to give birth; she may also return to solicit her mother's care if a serious or protracted illness strikes her family. On the other hand, a mother may travel from Texas for a several weeks' sojourn to help with her daughter's health or other family problems. Such a protracted visit is likely to affect several other members of the feminine social network her daughter has built in the new community.

> A Texas mother, in Toledo attempting to resolve her daughter's marital problems, learned that a Mexican American neighbor's baby daughter was running a fever, had suffered apparent convulsions, and had been taken to the local hospital. She was ready to help at once: "Ha—obviously *mal [de] ojo!* They will kill her in that hospital!" The anxious young mother of the child acquiesced to the older woman's insistence that they treat the child properly. The two women went to the child's hospital room in which there also were five other small patients. Armed with a used handkerchief of the afflicted child's father the *tejana* [Texas woman] treated her, surreptitiously rubbing the child with the handkerchief and repeating seven *Padrenuestros* [Lord's Prayer]. She subsequently burned the handkerchief—just to teach the offender 'a thing or two.' That will produce a terrible pain in the eyes and he will learn not to give *ojo* to another child (Macklin 1976:186-187).

Romano discerns ten "positions" in the healing hierarchy he proposes (1965:1154-1158): daughter[5]; mother; grandmother; experienced neighbor; full-time healer; town or city healer; regional healer; international healer; international, religious folk saint; and international, religious, formal saint. However, the major criteria that discriminate one category from another appear to be (1) whether or not there has been divine intervention on behalf of the healer; and (2) the extensiveness of the geographical area from which the healer's clientele is drawn. Only two of Romano's positions—mother and grandmother—are limited exclusively to women. Further, these are the only two categories in which the healer relies entirely on experience and empirical knowledge and where those served are confined primarily to the bilateral extended family. Once there is a suggestion that the individual is divinely gifted (has *el don*), the role becomes that of exceptional *person* and is not necessarily linked to gender. It remains to be explained, then, why the overwhelming majority of divinely elected *curanderas* and mediums *are* women.

First, the role has been an acceptable one for women, historically, in Latin America. Jacinto de la Serna's discussion of pre-Columbian healers in the valley of Mexico *(medicos nahuas)* has a remarkably contemporary ring. He reports that some curers "inherited" their medical knowledge directly from their parents who passed on their experience. Such knowledge also could be communicated to a curer during the course of an illness or trance that was considered to be a transitory "death." Serna gave the example of an Indian *woman* (my emphasis), a child of *curanderos* who acquired her "gift" *(gracia)* as well as the "instruments" to cure from all of her relatives during a 3-day "death" she experienced when she was a child. De la Serna might well have been describing the validating trip taken by contemporary curers when he reported having discovered some twenty people who had the art of curing, all of whom had "died" and in the other life had been given the gift of healing as well as the instruments of the cures: to some went cupping glasses, to others the lancet, and to yet others herbs and medicines that they were to apply (cited by Anzures y Bolaños 1976:43 [my translation]). During the colonial era some women continued in this role. For example, the eighteenth century Jesuit Johann Nentuig commented that women curers in nothern Mexico were "respected for their knowledge of 'herbs which have been discovered, either by the Indians of this land, or by the old Spanish women who have either set themselves up or have become in the natural course of events the College of Physicians of Sonora' " (cited by Kay 1978:88).

The preponderance of women serving as intermediaries between the supernatural and natural worlds is characteristic of many societies in which trance possession is found. Therefore, a sociological analysis must complement such a historical explanation. Kearney reports that "about 80 percent of those attracted to spiritualism are women, and of the seventeen mediums of whom" he had data, all but one were women (1977:322). Upwards of 300 folk Catholic *curanderos(as)*, spiritualist, and spiritist healing mediums from Texas, California, New Mexico, Arizona, and Indiana as well as from Mexico attend the March and October fiestas honoring Fidencio; women outnumber men almost 5 to 1, insofar as one can estimate.[6] From my own data on mediums (non-Hispanic) who have been licensed by the National Spiritualist Association of Churches in the United States, women outnumber men 2.5 to 1 (Macklin 1977; cf. Zaretsky 1974:175). Lewis, discussing trance possession cults in southern and eastern Africa as well as northern India, found that spirits regularly expressed a "marked predilection . . . for women in general, and . . . for certain depressed and despised categories of men'"[7] (1971:86).

There is no question that the role of healer has provided Mexican American women an alternative to the circumscribed, traditional role definition outlined in the introduction to this chapter. Most possessing spirits are powerful, knowledgeable males, and while possessed by one of them, the trancer is no longer the submissive, long-suffering, patient woman *marianismo* has prescribed that she should be. For example, in trance Mrs. G. is addressed by others as "he" or "El Niño Fidencio." Her social identity has changed, and she is transformed for the time into "quasi-woman, quasi-divine man" (Kearney 1977:324). In some ways, the healer has transcended her feminine role: she can be aggressive; she can dictate, chide, berate, and correct others, males and females alike. Lewis concludes that a "structural analysis demonstrates that treatment accorded those who fall in such 'peripheral' social categories [that is, as women and homosexual males] enhances, even if only temporarily, position and status'' (1971:295).

In common with female ritual specialists in many other societies, then, the Mexican American healer "puts domestic, child care, and wifely tasks aside during communication with divinity in her role as a sacred professional'' (Hoch-Smith and Spring 1978:15). However, the healers discussed here accrue unto themselves power in the secular world as well as during those times in which they are in trance and acting as sacred professionals. Although it was a supernatural "call" that enabled Mrs. G. to leave the domestic sphere legitimately, she was not in a trance and it was not the revered folk saint speaking through her when she said firmly, "The only people I have to respect are my mother and El Niño; I obey my husband but only up to a certain point. Beyond that, I actually don't care how he feels about it." She could have sent him packing without suffering economically had he continued to object to her obedience to the supernatural world. Her specialty, like those of the more independent women in late Mayan societies, who were weavers, potters, tradeswomen, healers, and midwives, permits her to be beholden to no man (Leacock 1975:614). Her husband did not pay for the two curing temples, nor decorate the altars, nor build the parking lot; nor does he pay for the food she provides and the matériel that she redistributes to clients during the curing rituals. She pays the bills with El Niño's help and the donations of the grateful. In this redistribution of goods, she clearly exercises power based on the continuing demand for her product: healing and counseling beyond the domestic unit. From late May until the first frost, she works indefatigably every weekend during 12- and 14-hour sessions to serve between 150 and 200 clients, the overwhelming majority of whom are migrant farm laborers and a few first- and second-generation Mexican Americans who have settled in the Midwest in the last two decades.

The healer functions to reinforce the values and social structure of both the traditional extended family and folk Catholicism. For example, Mrs. G.'s reputation is such that some families bring their ailing relatives from Texas to stay for several weeks' consultation. The presence of such a relative in Midwestern homes shores up the belief system surrounding traditional medicine and raises doubts about scientific medicine in the minds of skeptical young Chicanos. Mrs. G's reputation was recently (1978) enhanced when a a well-known, economically successful and very religious first-generation Mexican American father from Toledo traveled to Texas in search of a good *curandera* to help him solve a family problem. He was told in San Antonio, "There is none here better than Mrs. G. of Indiana—and she is in your own backyard."

When she orders people to travel or not to, chides a mother for working outside the home and for not having been home when her child was subjected to a severe fright, and merits donations sufficient to support her operation, she is exercising power over others, their time, energy, and resources.

She has other powers. While apparently asleep, she says she can travel out of her body—as could Fidencio—in order to treat patients in distant places.[8] Often in the *templos* she assures patients that she (or Fidencito) will come in the night and perform an invisible operation on them and that they should not be afraid although it will hurt somewhat. But her mobility is not confined to spiritual travel. She can and does also travel annually in the mundane world from Indiana to Nuevo León and San Luis Potosi. On these journeys, she is healing and talking of the Niño's power constantly; she is dealing frequently with other healers, observing, discussing, and competing.

The healer has the power to alter the social networks of the client when she initiates the latter into two new dyadic contracts, one with the supernatural patron who assisted in the cure and the other with the healer herself. Both he must now repay in one way or another. The client also may enter into a brotherhood of missionaries, joined by their faith and service to El Niño and God. The *cajas* and *cajones* themselves are *madrinas* (god-mothers) and *padrinos* (godfathers) to the mission of El Niño and use these ritual kinship terms reciprocally when addressing each other, usually employing the affectionate, sup-plicating form, *madrinita* and *padrinito*. Since most of the chosen vessels *are* women and they do aid and assist each other during the fiestas of Fidencio, there is something of a "sisterhood of charisma" here (Middleton-Keirn 1978); however, it is such a highly competitive lot of sisters that it can hardly be considered an example of female solidarity and power.

Spiritualists and spiritist mediums and their followers become "brother" and "sister" to each other. Both of these groups appear to be more prevalent in urban areas than the traditional, folk Catholic *curandero,* perhaps because they offer the client a more complex network of spirits, with differing abilities and knowledge, to support and assist him in understanding the multiple roles he has to play in the fragmented, complex world in which he must act. Having powerful, knowledgeable spirits such as Fidencio, Benjamin Franklin, Pancho Villa, Napoleon the First, or Santa Teresita in your corner is just the kind of *palanca* (influence, pull) the rural Mexican migrant and *barrio* Mexican American need in this world and the next. But it is also precisely this kind of power, this ability to at-tract the cooperation of supernatural beings, that creates the ambivalence with which the miracle working healer has met since time immemorial. All claim to work only for the good of their clients, but each accuses others of using their knowledge and power for evil ends.

Certain common features concerning the role of women in traditional medicine emerge from the cases presented here and in the literature:

1. All of the practitioners under consideration are applying syncretic and constantly evolving belief systems. They borrow from each other, are socialized in various curing *centros* or *templos,* and as practitioners come into contact with each other's clients; they often read the same texts and sometimes attend fiestas where they can observe others at work. They share underlying assumptions about the world-taken-for-granted and about the nature of human nature and that of super-natural nature.

2. The empirical knowledge needed for healing is passed through the oral tradition from mother to daughter. Some modernizing occurs—penicillin in the pomade,

for example—but the main corpus of beliefs and practices as well as the *materia médica* remain a synthesis of pre-Columbian and Spanish concepts.

3. It is assumed that women are by nature different from men and that a part of that difference is an inherent ability to heal. The ambivalence toward the assumed dual nature of woman is reflected in the constant anxiety about the source of supernatural intervention: is it divine or demonic?

4. Purity is an important, powerful criterion for being able to attract pure spirits; therefore, children, regardless of sex, are eligible because of a Rousseauistic assumption that they are naturally good and as yet uncorrupted. So are virginal women and men and postmenopausal women. Although the absence of sexually mature, childbearing women from the ranks of healers is explained in practical terms ("She wouldn't have the time to devote to it."), the implicit assumption seems clear.

5. The curer or medium is the instrument of God, who is the ultimate source of power. (*"Es el Altísimo quien cura."*) The imagery describing the instrument is feminine: "vessel," "vase," "box," and bespeaks a passive, submissive, open, receptive role for the curer, who must turn over the body to the possessing spirit, which penetrates and fills it.

6. An important ingredient in the healing process is faith on the part of the patient. Often, the practitioner initiates the curing encounter with "Do you believe . . . ?"

7. All agree that there is a close connection between illness and offenses against others as well as against the gods.

8. All groups are mildly messianic and millenarian. Fidencio reputedly announced just before his death that there would be many *niños* after him, some true and some false; Roque Rojas (to whom most spiritualists trace their historical origin) spoke of the "new era," and the spiritists are working toward the judgment day, also.

9. Once there is supernatural intervention on behalf of the curer, the role may be occupied by either a male or female. The possessing spirits usually are those of powerful males and are usually peripheral to the established, central "cult" of the society—in this case, Catholicism. The spirit messages are egalitarian and declare explicitly that distinctions are to be made between neither the sexes nor among those of different social classes.

10. Women and men (especially those men who are not able to fulfill effectively the expectations of the dominant male role) are able to obtain higher social status and economic power both in and out of the trance states than would otherwise be possible for them.

11. All of these curers help the client to construct a personal community comprising social networks in both the natural and supernatural worlds, which give him leverage and assistance in coping with his problems.

12. Although all appear to agree that the "wisdom of the spirit is superior to the science of the mind," traditional curers without formal education claim their "gift" to be sufficient, while others (spiritualists and spiritists) see the development of one's God-given power to be both possible and desirable. As Anzures y Bolaños says: "In both prehispanic and colonial times, transgression of natural laws and religious precepts caused illness" (1976:143), and a healer needs talents in both of these worlds.

13. The role of healer has been one of the few specialities open to women from traditional, rural, peasant-oriented groups of Mexican Americans. As more roles become available to educated young Chicanas, one may hypothesize that fewer and fewer will find that of *curandera* or medium attractive.

SUPERNATURAL SYMBOLS AND GENDER

Although the intercession of the saints (and by extension other spirits) in human affairs has little authority in the Scriptures (Warner 1976:293), such activity has long been an important part of the reality experienced by the folk. As has been pointed out, the Mexican Guadalupe always has been concerned with the well-being of her children, and her relationship to them prefigures the contracts they strike with other saints and curers. Typically, an altar in a curing temple is lavishly and lovingly adorned by several different virgins particularly well known for their curing miracles, including not only Guadalupe but also the Virgin of San Juan de Los Lagos and La Purisima. In the case of the many healers assisted by El Niño Fidencio, there are photographs of him, appearing in various poses and costumes (Fig. 5). Although the healing virgins dominate, which serves to emphasize the appropriateness of this model for women healers, there are also symbolic models for a dimension of masculinity not included in that secular model summarized in the concept of *machismo*. San Martín De Porres and San Francisco de Asis are popular. However, I would like to suggest that one major supernatural figure, significant to many of the patients and healers discussed in this chapter, demonstrates a "multivocality" (Turner 1974) that permits both men and women legitimately to become outstanding healers. This is symbolized by a composite photograph of the figure and face of El Niño Fidencio dressed in a long white gown. The figure is ensconced splendidly in the blue cape and dazzling, illuminating rays that unmistakably merge Fidencio's identity with that of the powerful Guadalupe, the Dark Virgin, Patroness of Mexico and Queen of the Americas. She represents the "female *eros,* the emotional, passionate, metaphysical principle in the nature of things" (Northrup 1966:28). But the third personage embedded in this particular icon, which has become the center of many home altars and adorns every healing altar Fidencio visits, adds another "voice" to the many already expressed through Guadalupe and Fidencio. This element is the Sacred Heart of Jesus, emblazoned on Fidencio's robe, and his (Jesus' or Fidencio's) right hand is raised in benediction. As was mentioned earlier, the uncertain, violent, secular world in which the Mexican *macho* lives and acts is usually represented by a baby or crucified Jesus. In El Niño Guadalupano—for that is what this icon is called—the Sacred Heart represents the

Fig. 5. A Mexican American *curandera* practicing in Indiana. Her left hand rests on the throne *(trono)* into which the spirit of El Niño Fidencio sometimes descends. The initials FSC stand for *F*idencio *S*intora *C*onstantino.

redemptive love of Jesus, expressing the "dignity and importance of the family" (Moell 1967: 812). Stressing the love of a father for his children and wife as well as "pre-figuring the Messiah's sacrificial love in the new Covenant" (Moell 1967:815), the Sacred Heart became the focus of devotion of groups, families, and communities after the middle of the nineteenth century. By choosing to emphasize this aspect of Jesus, rather than the Christ of the "male *logos,* the rational doctrinal principle of orthodox Catholicism," the symbol embraces a facet that permits some men also to become divinely elected healers and yet keep a masculine identification. This, and role models provided by compassionate male saints, suggests that the social scientists' models of male as well as female behavior have been oversimplified. Fidencio, a chaste, androgynous figure, mediates between male theological *dogma* and evolving female *charismatic* knowledge. He is both Jesus and Guadalupe.

But a compassionate Christ[9] is not yet very popular in a world of socially, economically, and politically marginal people, such as Mexican American migrant farm workers or those living in *barrios* in many southwestern cities. So finally, the Virgin, the female principle, dominates, and in providing "unfailing assistance to her devotees, she undeniably usurps the unique privileges of Christ" (Warner 1976:323). Salvation is available to all, even those who do not merit it, if they have sufficient faith. An amoral, loyal Virgin prevails, and "Through her the whole gay crew of wanton, loving, weak humanity finds its way to paradise. No wonder the devils are puzzled . . ." (Warner 1976:325).

Perhaps even more significant, she is the Dark Virgin, for: "In Catholic countries where blackness is the climate of devils, not the angels, and is associated almost exclusively with magic and the occult, Black Madonnas are considered especially wonder-working, as possessors of hermetic knowledge and power" (Warner 1976:275). The symbolism of El Niño Guadalupano, Fidencio merged with the Virgin, is particularly appropriate for powerful, independent women healers who must contend with the continuing ambivalence of their clientele.[10] Since the sixth century, she has been "The one creature in whom all opposites are reconciled" (Warner 1976:336), all of the good and all of the bad in the world.

EPILOGUE

One may predict that women will retain a dominant role among folk healers for some time to come, even though many Mexicans and most Mexican Americans are now living in urban areas; many are still first- and second-generation rural people and have brought their traditional beliefs with them (Balán, Browning, and Jellin 1973). Although the traditional kinship system over which women and Guadalupe preside continues to be a powerful socializing social unit (Keefe 1979; Macklin 1976), her importance seems to be fading among those acculturating and assimilating Mexican Americans who have moved away from the southwestern states.

The parish priest (ethnically Polish, but Spanish-speaking and a Latinophile) of the Toledo, Ohio, Mexican American congregation thinks that a partial explanation for this may be found in the recent popularity of the *cursillo* and charismatic movements within the Church itself, both of which are much more Christ-centered than traditional Latin American religion. But why has an optimistic, powerful, wise, Americanized Jesus become acceptable to a group brought up to venerate a supplicating Guadalupe and a problematic, suffering, and helpless Christ? On the basis of their Toledo data, Macklin and de Costilla conclude that success in the Anglo world (in which Guadalupe has no part), along with the identification of themselves as Americans, has opened that personal, trusted, intimate world of family and kin over which she presided. Many Mexican Americans *do* feel competent in the public sphere and *do* feel themselves to be masters of their own fates. Relations between them and their society have changed; accordingly, so has the arrangement of ideas about the supernatural and their relations to it (Macklin and de Costilla, 1979).

NOTES

1. "All the good and bad in this world, one may unerringly state, are caused by women." Juan Luis Vives, *Instruccion de la mujer cristiana*, 1524. Cited by Lavrin (1978:26).

2. Various attempts have been made to classify the syncretic, evolving ideas and organizations of these practitioners and groups. In 1974, I suggested that they might be best arranged along a continuum from: (1) the more or less traditional *curanderos,* who consider themselves to be Catholics and who practice according to a set of assumptions and rituals usually classified by investigators as "folk" Catholicism; to (2) spiritualists (ably described by Lagarriga [1975] and Kearney [1977; 1978]), who regard former Mexican seminarian, Roque Rojas, as having founded their groups in the 1860s in Mexico; to (3) spiritists, whose philosophical and "scientific" tenets are based on the books of Allan Kardec (d. 1869), the nineteenth century French author (whose ideas were in Latin America by 1853 and Mexico by at least 1857) and those of Joaquin Trincado (d. 1935), a Spaniard-become-Argentinian, who published twelve volumes on spiritism. Formally affiliated spiritualists and spiritists cannot be members of other religious groups, while those healers who regard themselves as Catholics consider their participation to be a part of their religion and hold the Church's criticism of their devotion to folk saints and healing rituals to be misguided. There are also individual healers who do not consider themselves to be part of any organized group. Each group appears to borrow, eclectically, from the others.

3. This group of Catholic healers use the word *penitencia* in at least two ways, both of which help one to determine whether or not he must serve as a healer. First, one may have to do penance, for example, go on the knees or back from one sacred place to another at Fidencio's shrine or suffer through other self-sacrificing, painful acts. Second, one may fall into a trance and "see" encounters (*revistas*) with the supernaturals who validate one's healing power. These *revistas* are strikingly similar in vocabulary and in content to the *videncias* seen by spiritualists. These Catholics also sometimes "see" messages in special glasses of water, as do the spiritualists, although they vehemently deny any connection with the latter.

4. The vocabularies are similar, for example, the gift of seeing (*revista, videncia*) and what one sees, the marked person (*marcada*), use of the word temple (*templo*), the chair or throne (*trono*), the use of water to assist divination, the resisting of the "call" but finally the necessity of acquiesing, and then one has the light (*luz*). The details of the life history of the medium of the *templo* in Jalapa is almost identical to that of many of the folk Catholic *curanderos* on whom I have data. Of course, many have been treated in a number of spiritualists or spiritist centers (*centros*) or temples (*templos*) during the period in which their supernatural illness could not be diagnosed, so such paralellism should not be surprising.

5. Romano regards this category as being filled only by an adolescent girl, which my data support if one is discussing children who heal with empirical knowledge alone. However, several cases of gifted or divinely elected young boys (as well as girls) have been documented in the state of Nuevo León, Mexico alone (Garza Quiros 1972, Macklin 1967).

6. It is extremely hard to estimate the number of practitioners in Espinazo, Nuevo León during these fiestas. Between 10,000 and 15,000 persons attend; among them are grateful clients, mediums in various stages of spiritual "development," mediums with small groups of followers, and mediums with large groups of followers. During the four different fiestas I have attended (October 1965, March 1966, October 1967, and March 1973), I counted those who were self-declared and those whose behavior—being in trance and healing—seemed to warrant their inclusion.

7. The degree of Fidencio's feminine identification is striking. He never married and was called "mama" by several of the children for whom he was caretaker, some of whom he adopted. There is evidence that he was a transvestite; he often preferred a long, loose gown (*bata*) for clothing and frequently disguised himself as a woman in order to escape briefly the crowds of demanding, suffering people (up to an estimated 50,000 during his heyday). He surrounded himself with a group of young male assistants, or "apostles," and many of the contemporary male healers who receive his spirit are considered to be "effeminate" by Mexicans and Mexican American observers. I have been told repeatedly by spiritualists in both Connecticut and Indiana that the males who

have become mediums, or are developing, are "effeminate," or "Well, not really homosexuals, maybe, but not very masculine, either" (cf. Zaretsky 1974:175). Although this seems to be a widely shared insiders' view, I have no independent, quantifiable evidence.

8. Many formal saints, for example, San Martín de Porres, reputedly have had this ability and provide the model for this expected ability.

9. Although she is discussing Mexican villagers rather than Mexican Americans, Nelson goes so far as to say that the Holy Family offers males no appropriate role models: "Christ—for all his compassion—or because of it—is effeminate" (1971:74).

10. This discussion is based, in part, on the provocative analyses offered by LaFaye and Wolf as well as that of Warner. Wolf refers to the Virgin of Guadalupe as a "master symbol," "one which seems to enshrine the major hopes and aspirations of an entire society"; he goes on to say that this symbol provides the "cultural idiom of behavior and ideal representations through which different groups of the same society can pursue and manipulate their different fates within a coordinated framework" (1958:34). LaFaye's insights are particularly useful in understanding Mexican American women healers and their followers. He points out that "each historical moment is capable of giving a sacred 'recharge' to a pious image, by endowing it with a new power adapted to new aspirations." He concludes that someday "Guadalupe will become an extinct star, like the moon, with which she is associated; it would be fascinating to study the emergence of the mythical image that will replace her" (1976:310).

REFERENCES

Aguirre, Lydia
1978 "Alternative health practices along the western Texas border." Pp, 60-66 in Boris Velimirovic (ed.), Modern Medicine and Medical Anthropology in the United States–Mexico Border Population. Washington, D.C.: Pan American Health Organization, Scientific Publication No. 359.

Anzures y Bolaños, Carmen
1976 *La medicina tradicional en México: processo historico, syncretismos y conflictos.* Tesis que presenta para optar al grado de Maestria in Cincias Antropologicas en la especialidad de Ethnologia, México: SEP—Escuela Nacional de Antropología e Historía.

Ardner, Edwin
1975 "Belief and the problem of women." Pp. 1-17 in Shirley Ardner (ed.), Perceiving Women. London: Malaby Press.

Armonia
1957 Monterrey, N. L., México, No. 81, p. 13.

Balán, Jorge, Harley L. Browning and Elizabeth Jellin
1973 Men in a Developing Society. Austin, Texas: University of Texas Press (for the Institute of Latin American Studies).

Cheney, Charles C. and George L. Adams
1978 "Lay healing and mental health in the Mexican-American *barrio.*" Pp. 81-86 in Boris Velimirovic (ed.), Modern Medicine and Medical Anthropology in the United States–Mexico Border Population. Washington, D.C.: Pan American Health Organization, Scientific Publicatiton No. 359.

Clark, Margaret
1959 Health in the Mexican-American Culture. Berkeley, California: University of California Press.

Elmendorf, Mary Lindsay
1975 "The Mayan woman and change." Pp. 111-127 in Ruby Rohrlich-Leavitt (ed.), Women Cross-Culturally: Change and Challenge. The Hague: Mouton Publishers.
1977 "Mexico: the many worlds of women." Pp. 129-172 in Janed Zollinger Giele and Audrey Chapman Smock (eds.), Women: Roles and Status in Eight Countries. New York: John Wiley & Sons, Inc.

Flora, Cornelia Butler
1973 "The passive female and social change: a cross-cultural comparison of women's magazine fiction." Pp. 59-85 in Ann Pescatello (ed.), Female and Male in Latin America: Essays. Pittsburgh, Pennsylvania: University of Pittsburgh Press.

Foster, George M.
1953 "Relationships between Spanish and Spanish-American folk medicine." Journal of American Folklore 66:201-247.

Foster, George M. and Barbara Gallatin Anderson
1978 Medical Anthropology. New York: John Wiley & Sons, Inc.

Garza Quiros, Fernando
1972 El Niño Fidencio y el fidencismo, 2° edicion. Monterrey, N. L., México: Privately published.

Gonzalez Valdes, Pedro Angel
1970 Vida y Milagros del Niño Fidencio. Saltillo, Coah., México: Privately published.

Hoch-Smith, Judith and Anita Spring
1978 "Introduction." Pp. 1-23 in Judith Hoch-Smith and Anita Spring (eds.), Women in Ritual and Symbolic Roles. New York: Plenum Press.

Kay, Margarita
1978 "Parallel, alternative, or collaborative: *curanderismo* in Tucson, Arizona." Pp. 87-95 in Boris Velimirovic (ed.), Modern Medicine and Medical Anthropology in the United States–Mexican

Border Population. Washington, D.C.: Pan American Health Organization, Scientific Publication No. 359.

Kearney, Michael
1977 "Oral performance by Mexican spiritualists in possession trance." Journal of Latin American Lore 3:309-328.
1978 *"Espiritualismo* as an alternative medical tradition in the border area." Pp. 67-72 in Boris Velimirovic (ed.), Modern Medicine and Medical Anthropology in the United States–Mexico Border Population. Washington, D.C.: Pan American Health Organization, Scientific Publication No. 359.

Keefe, Susan Emley
1979 "Urbanization, acculturation, and extended family ties: Mexican-Americans in cities." American Ethnologist 2:349-365.

Knaster, Meri
1976 "Women in Latin America: the state of research, 1975." Latin American Research Review XI: 3-74.

LaFaye, Jacques
1976 Quetzalcóatl and Guadalupe: the Formation of Mexican National Consciousness, 1531-1813. (Translated by Benjamin Kenn.) Chicago, Illinois: The University of Chicago Press.

Lagarriga Attias, Isabel
1975 Medicina Tradicional y Espiritismo: los Espiritualistas Trinitarios Marianos de Jalapa, Veracruz. México: Sep/Setentas.

Lamphere, Louise
1975 "Women and domestic power: political and economic strategies in domestic groups." Pp. 117-130 in Dana Raphael (ed.), Being Female: Reproduction, Power, and Change. The Hague: Mouton Publishers.

Lavrin, Asunción
1978 "In search of the colonial women in Mexico: the seventeenth and eighteenth centuries." Pp. 23-59 in Asunción Lavrin (ed.), *Latin American Women: Historical Perspectives.* Westport, Connecticut: Greenwood Press.

Leacock, Eleanor
1975 "Class, commodity, and the status of women." Pp. 601-616 in Ruby Rohrlich-Leavitt (ed.), Women Cross-Culturally: Change and Challenge. The Hague: Mouton Publishers.

Lewis, I. M.
1971 Ecstatic Religion, An Anthropological Study of Spirit Possession and Shamanism. Middlesex, England: Penguin Books, Ltd.

Macklin, June
1967 "El Niño Fidencio: un estudio del curanderismo en Nuevo León." *Anuario Humanitas,* Centro de

Estudios Humanísticos, Universidad de Nuevo León, pp. 529-563.
1974 "Folk saints, healers, and spiritist cults in northern Mexico." Revista/Review Interamericana 3:351-376. Also appeared in Spanish as Santos folk, curanderismo y cultos espiritistas en México: elección divina y selección social." Anuario Indigenista XXXIV:195-214, deciembre.
1976 Cultural Change and Structural Stability in a Mexican-American Community. New York: Arno Press.
1977 "A Connecticut Yankee in summer land." Pp. 41-85 in Vincent Crapanzano and Vivian Garrison (eds.), Case Studies in Spirit Possession. New York: Wiley Interscience.
1978 *"Curanderismo* and *espiritismo:* Complementary approaches to traditional mental health services." Pp. 155-163 in Boris Velimirovic (ed.), Modern Medicine and Medical Anthropology in the United States–Mexico Border Population. Washington, D.C.: Pan American Health Organization, Scientific Publication No. 359.

Macklin, June and Alvina Teniente de Costilla
1979 "La Virgen de Guadalupe and the American Dream: the melting pot bubbles on in Toledo, Ohio." Pp. 111-143 in Stanley West and June Macklin (eds.), The Chicano Experience. Boulder, Colorado: Westview Press.

Macklin, June and N. Ross Crumrine
1973 "Structural development and conservation in three North Mexican folk saint movements." Comparative Studies in Society and History 5:89-105.

Middleton-Keirn, Susan
1978 "Convival sisterhood: spirit mediumship and client-care network among black South African Women." Pp. 191-205 in Judith Hoch-Smith and Anita Spring (eds.), Women in Ritual and Symbolic Roles. New York: Plenum Press.

Moell, C. J.
1967 "Sacred Heart, devotion to." Pp. 812-820 in New Catholic Encyclopedia, Vol. 12. New York: McGraw Hill Co.

Moore, Joan W.
1976 Mexican Americans, ed. 2. Englewood Cliffs, New Jersey: Prentice-Hall, Inc.

Nelson, Cynthia
1971 The Waiting Village: Social Change in Rural Mexico. Boston: Little, Brown & Co.

Northrop, F. S. C.
1966 The Meeting of East and West. New York: The Macmillan Co., Collier Books Edition.

Paul, Lois
1978 "Careers of midwives in a Mayan community." Pp. 129-149 in Judith Hoch-Smith and Anita

Spring (eds.), Women in Ritual and Symbolic Roles. New York: Plenum Press.

Paul, Lois and Benjamin D. Paul
1975 "The Maya midwife as sacred specialist: a Guatemalan case." American Ethnologist 2:707-726.

Paz, Octavio
1961 The Labyrinth of Solitude: Life and Thought in Mexico. (Translated by Lysander Kemp.) New York: Grove Press.

Pi-Sunyer, Oriol
1973 Zamora: Change and Continuity in a Mexican Town. New York: Holt, Rinehart & Winston.

Quinn, Naomi
1977 "Anthropolgical studies on women's status." Pp. 131-225 in Bernard J. Siegel (ed.), Annual Review of Anthropology, Vol. 6. Palo Alto, California: Annual Reviews, Inc.

Romano, V. Octavio Ignacio
1965 "Charismatic medicine, folk-healing, and folk-sainthood." American Anthropologist 67:1151-1173.

Rosaldo, M. Z. and L. Lamphere (eds.)
1974 Women, Culture, and Society. Stanford, California: Stanford University Press.

Rubel, Arthur J.
1966 Across the Tracks: Mexican-Americans in a Texas City. Austin, Texas: University of Texas Press.

Sánchez Morales, Aurelia Guadalupe and Ana E. Domínguez
1975 "Women in Mexico." Pp. 95-110 in Ruby Rohrlich-Leavitt (ed.), Women Cross-Culturally: Change and Challenge. The Hague: Mouton Publishers.

Spicer, Edward H.
1962 Cycles of Conquest: the Impact of Spain, Mexico, and the United States on the Indians of the Southwest, 1533-1960. Tucson, Arizona: The University of Arizona Press.

Stevens, Evelyn P.
1973 "*Marianismo:* the other face of *machismo* in Latin America." Pp. 89-101 in Ann Pescatello (ed.), Female and Male in Latin America: Essays. Pittsburgh, Pennsylvania: University of Pittsburgh Press.

Trotter, Robert T. and Jan Antonio Chavira
1978 "Discovering new models for alcohol counseling in minority groups." Pp. 164-171 in Boris Velimirovic (ed.), Modern Medicine and Medical Anthropology in the United States–Mexico Border Population. Washington, D.C.: Pan American Health Organization, Scientific Publication No. 359.

Turner, Victor
1974 Dramas, Fields, and Metaphors: Symbolic Action in Human Society. Ithaca, New York: Cornell University Press.

Velimirovic, Boris (ed.)
1978 Modern Medicine and Medical Anthropology in the United States–Mexico Border Population. Washington, D.C.: Pan American Health Organization, Scientific Publication No. 359.

Warner, Marina
1976 Alone of All Her Sex: the Myth and the Cult of the Virgin Mary. New York: Alfred A. Knopf.

Wolf, Eric R.
1958 "The Virgin of Guadalupe: a Mexican national symbol." Journal of American Folklore 71: 34-39.

Wolf, Eric R. and Edward C. Hansen
1972 The Human Condition in Latin America. New York: Oxford Unviersity Press.

Zaretsky, Irving I.
1974 "In the beginning was the word: the relationship of language to social organization in spiritualist churches." Pp. 166-219 in Irving I. Zaretsky and Mark P. Leone (eds.), Religious Movements in Contemporary America. Princeton, New Jersey: Princeton University Press.

Part III

CULTURAL CONFLICT

Ethnic groups interact along boundaries that are often fraught with conflict. It is precisely the we/they dichotomy that reinforces identity and contributes to mutual misunderstanding. Part III deals with characteristics that distinguish Mexican American females from Anglo American women, as well as from other minority women. It also points out some of the areas that are particularly prone to creating conflictive situations, such as employment, institutional dealings, and acculturation itself.

"Acculturation" has remained a classical concept in anthropology over the years, and generally it has represented a process whereby bearers of a minority or dependent culture traveled across a continuum of increasing familiarity with an internalization of a dominant culture's values and behavior patterns. Thus, for social scientists in the 1950s and 1960s, the solution for the "problems" of Mexican Americans lay in Americanization or Angloization (Madsen 1973). Currently, most anthropologists recognize that what actually occurs between two cultures in close contact is selective acculturation (Clark, Kaufman, and Pierce 1976) based on patterns of interaction and conflict. I have described this process as experienced by women newly arrived from Mexico in my own chapter in this section. I conclude that aspirations to social class mobility are determinants of the degree and type of acculturation that takes place.

Long and Vigil demonstrated that acculturating Mexican American female adolescents can be stereotyped neither as faithful to traditional values nor as committed to radical feminism. Rather, the picture that emerges is young people who recognize pragmatic values but are respectful of some of the traditions of their heritage. Theirs is also a case of selective acculturation.

Wagner and Schaffer found that there are proportionately fewer female household heads among Mexican Americans than among Anglos or blacks. However, single parenthood is increasing among Mexican American women. They argue that one of the differences between single Mexican American women and Anglos or blacks is that the former rely more frequently on siblings, parents, and *comadres* for help and advice than do the latter. An important concomitant is that Mexican American women more often choose to live close to their relatives. Nevertheless, the constrictions of the United States

149

urban life, such as lack of transportation especially for people with low income, are evidently contributing to culture change.

Women of Mexican heritage in the United States acculturate to varying degrees according to the study by Manzanedo, Lorig, and Walters. Newly arrived Mexican women from rural areas are more likely to espouse traditional Mexican values and health beliefs, while United States-born ''Chicanas'' have assimilated many American practices. In either case, there are two important factors that should be considered for improving health services to the population of Mexican heritage. One is the increased involvement of Mexican American women in the health professions. This can be both as neighborhood aids and as professionals. A second factor is the treatment of an individual's illness within

the family context. To be more effective, medical information and counseling sessions should involve both wife and husband. Despite Manzanedo's recommendation, the proportional participation of Mexican women in the nursing professions is diminishing. Alvarado cites two official reasons given for withdrawals from nursing schools: "poor educational preparation" and "unsuitability for nursing." However, the fact that most nursing school dropouts are minority women requires further investigation, especially when there is evidence that the enlistment of minority faculty, recruiters, and counselors has stemmed the tide of dropouts in at least one instance.

Cotera documents the struggle of Mexican American women for civil rights and labor

organization, as well as their attempts to be incorporated into the women's movements. At the turn of the century, women achieved suffrage but minorities did not. Currently, in their attempts to get the equal rights amendment passed, the leadership of the women's movement often bypasses and discriminates against Mexican Americans. Cotera's chapter analyzes the barriers faced by Chicanas in their attempts to gain equality in the United States society and to promote the rights of the Chicano community. Cotera's chapter echoes some of the concerns of Mexican women recorded by Elmendorf. The latter says that in Mexico today even the more radical women believe that women's problems should take second place "to the Indian problem, the development problem, the population problem" (1977: 161). At the same time, women express their need to be more involved themselves in resolving these basic problems.

The interface between an Anglo institution and Mexican women can become a cultural battleground as illustrated by Velez's empirical study of a nonconsenting sterilization suit. He states that for Mexican women born in a rural context, motherhood is an essential componenet of their social role. The physical sterilizations suffered by a group of

Mexican women resident in California resulted in their "cultural sterilization," as well as severe depression. Yet, the judge's decision excused and legitimized the medical institutions violation of these women's basic human rights. The decision, in fact, negates the validity of cultural pluralism.

The empirical data collected by Stephens, Oser, and Blau demonstrate that older Mexican American females suffer from the circumstances of being old, female, and members of a minority group. Even though relatively more elderly Mexican American women own their own home than do ederly Anglo women, those homes are in a sorry state of disrepair and constitute a reason for worry. Mexican American women are more alienated from society in general than are Anglo women, yet they are less depressed. These contrasts have important implications for policy recommendations as well as intercultural understanding.

REFERENCES

Clark, Margaret, S. Kaufman and R. Pierce
    1976 "Explorations of acculturation: toward a model
        of ethnic identity." Human Organization 35(3):
        231-238.
Elmendorf, Mary
    1977 "Mexico: the many worlds of women." In J. Z.

Giele and A. C. Smock (eds.), Women: Roles
and Status in Eight Countries. New York: John
Wiley & Sons, Inc.
Madsen, William
    1973 Mexican Americans in South Texas, ed. 2. New
        York: Holt, Rinehart & Winston.

Chapter 10

Selective acculturation of female Mexican migrants

Margarita B. Melville

Through extensive interviews and observation, I found that Mexican women migrating into a large Southwestern city adapted in different degrees and with varying stress to urban life in a United States setting. This chapter examines the covariation of adjustment (or acculturation) to the aspiration of social class mobility, as well as the factors that facilitated acculturation. In the fall of 1977, 47 recent migrants to Houston were interviewed.* All had been in the city for 2 years or less. Sixteen had come from rural Mexican American communities in the United States, and the remainder came directly from Mexico.

I used the sixteen women who had been long-time United States residents as a control group to compare them to the women who migrated directly from Mexico. Thus, I compared two groups of women who had similarly experienced relocation during the previous 2 years but had come from distinct cultural backgrounds. I will analyze the factors affecting the rate and degree of adaptation. Elsewhere (Melville 1978) I have detailed the types of adjustment problems these women encountered. I found that some women adapted to the new environment without apparent stress, while others remained in near isolation. At first, I attributed this to English language ability, but then I noticed that some of the informants from Mexico, who had little previous exposure to English, were becoming more active in their new environment than those from rural communities in the United States who had been in an English-language setting for considerable lengths of time. I then found that the rate of adjustment was related to education and employment. This led me to consider that the aspiration to social class mobility might be a crucial variable.

SELECTIVE ACCULTURATION AND ETHNICITY

The relocation of groups of individuals entails much more than simple geographical mobility, especially when those moving transfer to a location where there is a change in

---

*This research was made possible through a grant from the Social Science Research Council, Fall 1977.

the ethnic composition of the social group into which they are integrating. The accommodation to a new way of life and to different expectations necessitates changes—some immediate, most gradual. Yet, not every aspect—by far—of one's way of life, or culture, will be modified. The individual experiences new situations and observes different behaviors; yet the person does not lose the lessons and adaptive responses accumulated through previous experiences. New realities will be assessed according to the values and attitudes that are the products of those prior experiences. The term "acculturation" has been used in anthropology to define the process; yet the conceptualization and extensive utilization of this term have been based on limited analysis of the ongoing process.

By selective acculturation I mean that an individual chooses to modify her behavior in those areas where accommodation to the majority culture is seen as imperative and/or is facilitated by certain personal or situational factors. Therefore, acculturation implies that there are individual differences in the areas and degrees of participation in the majority culture.

Migrants from Mexico experience two levels of acculturation, one affected by the Mexican American[1] culture and the other by aspects of the Anglo or majority culture. Mexican American culture is a hybrid that combines elements of values and social relationships from traditional Mexico as these have been impacted by the culture and social system of the United States and Mexican Americans' own individual and group adaptations. The kind of selective acculturation experienced by individuals from Mexico depends on the housing, working, and schooling situation in which they find themselves. Some will experience more contact with fellow Mexicans, others with Mexican Americans, and a few with Anglos. These contacts can be specifically chosen or sought or they may be determined by circumstances.

To be successful in economic terms, Mexicans and Mexican Americans living in the urban United States must either Anglicize or be bicultural. Being bicultural is analogous to being bilingual. That is, one must be able to interpret cultural clues and share codes of behavior with at least two culturally distinct populations. Situational and circumstantial variables require that an individual be able to understand and function effectively in an Anglo setting and also be able to use a different set of behavioral patterns to function effectively among Mexican Americans. A short review of six cases will familiarize my readers with some of the women with whom I am here concerned. The first four came from Mexico, the latter two from United States sites.

SIX CASES

Rosa had been in Houston 4 months. She came to join her husband from a city in Mexico where she had worked as a chemist. They had no children but hoped to have some soon. She was attending an English class, and on her second attempt was able to understand enough to pass the test in order to get a driver's license. She went to English-language movies with her husband and was excited that she was beginning to follow the dialogue. She missed her family and the familiarity with a city she knew well. She had been slightly ill and attributed it to the lack of fresh food that she was accustomed to buying daily. She and her husband would get together with some of his friends from work occasionally.

Irene's father owned a hardware store in Mexico City. He decided to come to the United States with his family. Irene had studied English in school and was certified as a teacher. She had no problem getting a job as a teacher's aid in a private school in Houston. Her husband works with his father-in-law in a small shop they have established here. Irene and her husband have started coaching a Little League baseball team on Saturdays at a park near their home.

Teresa was shocked to find out she was an American citizen 2 weeks before graduating from a Mexican university. She had been born in the United States but raised in Mexico and felt Mexican. She tried to get a job in Mexico, but since she was not a citizen, she could not. She tried to become a Mexican citizen but the red tape was too much for her. She then came to the United States. However, because of her lack of English, she could not use her professional education. She got odd jobs while studying the language and then began taking university courses. She lived with a brother and sister-in-law and dated Anglo boys. She hopes her parents will someday come to live with her in the States.

Silvia swam across the river from Mexico with her husband when she was pregnant. They wanted the child born in the United States so that it would have better opportunities in life than its 3-year-old brother, whom they had to leave in Mexico with his grandparents. Silvia spoke no English and had no plans to study it since she felt she would not be able to learn it. Her husband offered her little companionship, drank often, and sometimes got violent. He usually played cards in the evenings with his friends. Silvia had no personal friends, however. Her brother, who lived downstairs, helped her by buying food occasionally and had offered to take her to the hospital should her 9-month-old baby get sick again. If her brother should decide to go back to Mexico, Silvia thought she would probably leave her husband and return to Mexico herself.

A year ago Louise came to Houston from South Texas with her husband, her four children, and her mother. However, at the time I interviewed her, her husband had just left her, taking the two family cars with him. As a result, she had filed for divorce. She worked as a clerk in an office. Her children, aged 2 to 6, all attended a day-care center. Although they all know English, they speak Spanish at home. She has managed to get help from people in several private and public agencies, but she still seems confused about how to proceed with the divorce.

Maria's husband brought her and their five children to settle in Houston so he could get away from farm work in South Texas. She thinks it would be good to speak English, but she feels it is impossible for her to learn. Her oldest boy, aged 9, speaks English so he talks to his father who understands some. She wishes they could afford to have more children because "then they will stay with you much longer and you aren't alone." She feels people are more hospitable in Mexico. You get out and mingle with the neighbors in the evenings. Here people are all shut inside their homes with air conditioners. Even though she has lived for many years in the United States, her heart is still in Mexico, so they go back frequently to visit.

ETHNICITY AND CLASS

Of the 47 women interviewed, I classify fourteen as aspiring to social class mobility; of these only two had come from places in the United States. My classification is based on: (1) whether individuals or their husbands had jobs other than service workers, or laborers, (2) whether they had held such jobs in Mexico, (3) whether their education had prepared them for such jobs, or (4) whether they indicated that they aspired to such jobs. In contrast, the women I classified as lower class were either employed as domestics or service workers or were married to men who worked as laborers and did not evidence aspirations to upward mobility or what is referred to as "middle-class status." An obvious conclusion might be that the upwardly mobile have more education, more know-how, and therefore adapt or acculturate more easily; however, I believe this conclusion omits significant variables.

Adaptation may be seen as acculturation, which means entering into a process where traditional habits, attitudes, and values are surrendered and replaced by a set of foreign habits, attitudes, and values. This is not an entirely logical process whereby one examines the reasonableness of the alternatives and acts accordingly. One does not easily sacrifice one's cultural code for another code. What I saw was that women aspiring to upward mobility, whether they had come from Mexico or the United States, were ready to change or Anglicize, while Mexican and Mexican American lower-class workers were not. The Mexicans seemed content to acculturate to Mexican American life-styles. The question is why?

The issue is complex, but appears to require that we focus our inquiry on ethnic identity as well as acculturation. Why do lower-class people maintain or insist on a stable ethnic identity, while the upwardly mobile do not? Let us look at ethnicity. My own approach, stimulated and reinforced by my data, is to see ethnicity in the case of migrating Mexican and Mexican American women in terms of the social boundaries conceptual scheme of Barth (1969) and Cohen (1974). However, I do not exclude Hicks' (1977) perspective of ethnicity as an aspect of role behavior.

Barth said that the boundaries were what was important, not what was bounded. He saw ethnicity, not as a commitment to any given series of traditional symbols or cultural values, but "by concentrating on what is *socially* effective, ethnic groups are seen as a form of social organization" (Barth 1969:13 [emphasis in the original]). Many anthropologists and sociologists (that is, Barth 1969; Bell 1975; Cohen 1974; Glazer and Moynihan 1975; and Wolf and Cole 1974) have viewed ethnicity as a means of self-ascription and ascription by others in a polyethnic environment for purposes of social organization.

On the other hand, DeVos takes a psychological perspective saying that "ethnicity, therefore, includes a sense of personal survival in the historical continuity of the group. For this reason, failure to remain in the group leads to feelings of guilt. It is a form of killing inflicted on one's progenitors . . ." (DeVos 1975:17).

Hicks takes still another perspective, which is also sociological. He sees ethnicity as a factor in social organization, but his view is more flexible than Barth's. Hicks states that "ethnicity can most usefully be seen as an attribute of a role. It is thus of the same conceptual order as sex, age, kinship affiliation, political persuasion, religious membership, and so on" (Hicks 1977:2). As such, Hicks sees ethnicity as a defining characteristic only in certain situations that then demand appropriate ethnic role behavior.

These perspectives are not mutually exclusive, and it is only a question of which approach is most beneficial in explaining individual social cases, and whether the universe of such cases more consistently manifests some characteristics rather than others. Spiro was the first anthropologist to suggest that upward social mobility involved a change in self-identity from ethnic community to social class (1955:1244). Cohen, too, sees class consciousness as inimical to ethnic identity: "If status cleavages will cut across ethnic divisions, then the manifestations of ethnic identity and exclusiveness will tend to be inhibited by the emerging countervailing alignments of power" (1974:193). But Cohen sees ethnic identity disappearing in both the working and entrepreneurial classes when class lines internally divide ethnic groups. My data confirm Spiro's theory but contradict the last-mentioned point by Cohen.

Upwardly mobile women in the present sample are not concerned with ethnic identity. They are primarily class conscious. Ethnicity is not an organizing principle because it would exclude them from the organizations of social and economic power as they exist now in the United States society. These women want to learn English, drive a car, belong to Anglo groupings, and get a job that pays well.

The lower-class women are concerned with ethnic identity; they see themselves as Mexican and interact almost exclusively with Mexicans and Mexican Americans. At the same time, these women find themselves isolated from the extended kin and the neighborly relations they were accustomed to in Mexico or the rural United States, and thus they experience the alienation of isolated nuclear families (see Safa 1977).

All this is not to say that ethnicity is not also a middle-class or even an upper-class phenomenon. One need only look at the Boston Brahmins and their claims to blue blood to see how they have manipulated these symbols in the name of social organization. But ethnicity for such peoples is more as Hicks has defined it, an attribute of role to be utilized only when the role is appropriate, and in their case, since they are seldom threatened, rarely.

For the working-class females I interviewed, ethnicity is a role attribute and also more than that. It is a principle of social identity and social organization needed to protect them against the encroachments on their economic and domestic integrity by the omnipresent and voracious Anglo politicoeconomic system. They know they cannot compete on Anglo terms. Also, if left without group support, they know they will be devoured. Their only security is their ethnicity.

I have no doubt that ethnic consciousness will develop among my upwardly mobile interviewees when they find that as they compete successfully, their ethnicity is thrown up to them as a stumbling block. I posit that it will be then that ethnicity ascribed by others will become not only the psychological phenomenon that DeVos talks about but a factor of social organization. When these women recognize their need of support, they will revert to an ethnic identity for which they feel no necessity now.

FACILITATORS OF ACCULTURATION

In order to describe what elements promote acculturation, I have distributed them into four categories: (1) attitudinal facilitators, (2) cognitive facilitators, (3) behavioral facilitators, and (4) brokers. By attitudinal facilitators, I mean those attitudes and values that promote "readiness" in an individual to adapt and accept elements of culture different from one's own. Cognitive facilitators are the information or the means to acquire knowledge that promote familiarity with the majority culture. Behavioral facilitators are activities that promote positive contact with the majority culture. Finally, brokers are persons or institutions that intervene to aid an individual in becoming familiarized with the majority culture.

Attitudinal facilitators

My research among female Mexican migrants reveals the primary role of class aspiration as an attitudinal facilitator of acculturation as I have described in the foregoing. Either the values provided by class membership or the aspiration toward such membership promotes accommodation and the taking of steps to learn about and adapt to the majority culture.

The very act of migrating reveals an attitude of readiness to adapt to a new mode of life but not necessarily to sacrifice values and social relationships. In coming to a new cultural atmosphere, the women were prepared for changes. As one said, "Ya me doy cuenta que el sistema es differente aqui." (I have come to accept the fact that the "system" is different here.) They missed family and neighborly relationships. "Nos sentimos más hermanos allá." (There is a greater feeling of brotherliness over there). But the principal reason for migrating remains an incentive for staying. They come looking for better paying jobs, and they find them. Their children are eating better, and despite the poor and crowded housing, they usually do find a place to live with indoor plumbing and running water. They see that those who have been in the United States for longer periods of time have incomes far superior to what was possible for them in Mexico. Some parents have come seeking improved situations for their children. One mother with a handicapped child came seeking treatment she could not get in Mexico. She found it and would like to stay. She is ready to adapt to life in the United States.

Cognitive facilitators

The most important cognitive facilitator is knowledge of the English language. The greater the ease in speaking and understanding English, the easier it is for the women to move around the community, to participate in activities, to make use of the media, to ask and understand directions, and to make use of social services. Not all who would like to learn the language are able to avail themselves of English classes. Several were not able to study because they were illiterate in Spanish, and all English classes were taught on the assumption that the students know the mechanics of reading and writing. These women say, ''No me da la cabeza.'' (I am not able to learn.) They blame their illiteracy on lack of intelligence instead of on the opportunity for schooling that was denied them as children in Mexico. To be effective, English classes would have to be taught orally or combine adult literacy with language learning. However, knowledge of English alone does not imply automatic acculturation. Some women who speak English because they were raised in rural or small towns in Texas nevertheless maintained themselves isolated from Anglo contacts by moving solely around the Mexican American *barrio* for shopping and entertainment. Thus, they are acculturating to Mexican American urban life but not to the ways of the majority culture.

A second cognitive facilitator is the level of education that had been attained. This is closely related to class status and class aspirations. Those women who had received more than a primary education, whether in Mexico or in the United States, more easily became acquainted with the content of Anglo life-styles and traditions. If they did not know English, they were able to learn it quickly. Some of the more educated younger women dated Anglo men. They went to English movies and watched English TV programs.

Behavioral facilitators

Behavioral facilitators for acculturation include employment and independent shopping. Employment outside the home put women in contact with expanded social environments. One of the reasons men seem to acculturate more readily than women is probably because employment tends to provide more numerous social contacts with the consequent expansion of information sources. When women work in sales, restaurants, or as domestics, they seem to have greater access to information about and contact with Anglo culture. Those who work in tortilla factories or cleaning office buildings are more limited in that they only interacted with fellow Mexican workers. Nevertheless, these women were able to exchange information and expand their horizons. The women who were not employed outside the home were very isolated and unable to acculturate as broadly or quickly as those who were employed.

Those who depend on husbands or relatives with vehicles when shopping and doing errands tend to retreat and become unsure of themselves as they lose hegemony over one of their most important roles in the domestic scene: obtaining and preparing the family's meals and taking care of clothing. Some women have to wait for a weekend to be driven to the Laundromat. This also contributes to isolation from Anglo society.

Cultural brokers

Finally, in regard to the fourth type of facilitator, I identified three kinds of brokers. The most important brokers are children attending school. Mothers with children in school were introduced to more facets of everyday life in the United States. They became familiar with holidays such as Halloween and Thanksgiving and with national heroes like Washington and Lincoln. They picked up some English from their children and were made aware of issues and concerns discussed at school. There is, however, a negative side to children serving as cultural brokers. When parents use them as translators (sometimes even to read their own report cards), there is a danger that respect for parents will erode, and this often leads to discipline problems.

Probably the most disadvantaged of all the women were those whose children were not allowed in school because of lack of residence documents. The 1977 Texas law that requires more than $100 tuition monthly for children who are not legal residents keeps many children out of school. In many cases, this is so even though the Immigration and Naturalization Service had granted residence to fathers and sometimes to mothers but not to children, making them ineligible for free public schooling under Texas law.

Relatives who precede the recent migrants act as brokers for acculturation. They introduce the women to procedures and places. They often accompany them in order to acquaint them with medical facilities, schools, and other services. These relatives are sources of support and information. In the majority of cases I investigated, the husbands had preceded the wives and they became brokers for their wives. In those cases where there are other relatives available, the women have greater access to information. The most isolated women are those who husbands came first and who have no other relative or acquaintance with whom to communicate. Only those who are able to get employment outside the home are able to mitigate the isolation.

Service institutions may also become brokers. One particular institution served this function, the Parent-Child Development Center. It is a research and educational center that investigates parenting and other characteristics of the Mexican American population; it also provides guidance and information for parents and a preschool for the children. Women who are selected to participate in the program are eligible for classes of many types, for example, English, automobile driving, and crafts; more importantly, they are invited to participate in discussion groups. The center acts as a broker by promoting acculturation and facilitating the adaptation of the women to Anglo society.

CONCLUSION

The process of selective acculturation experienced by Mexican female migrants was influenced much more by aspirations of upward mobility than by knowledge of English. Those who did not speak English but aspired to a higher-class status were taking steps to learn English. The lower-class women, whether from Mexico or small-town U.S.A. and whether they spoke English or not, did not feel the need to accommodate to Anglo society but maintained themselves in a greater or lesser degree of isolation from the majority society. Those women who were working were employed in Mexican American establishments or were engaged in service occupations (cleaning) where contact with Anglos was minimal. Aspirations of upward mobility are reflected in the desire to accommodate and engage in contact with the Anglo society. Acculturation for these women is thus a much more thorough and rapid process.

Undocumented status itself does not seem to directly influence acculturation. It does tend to maintain most women in isolation and thus retards efforts at accommodation. However, those who aspire to upward mobility risk detection by going ahead with English classes. They also feel that the more they accommodate, the safer they will be. It is important to note here that only 1 of the 24 undocumented women was uncertain about remaining in the United States. All the rest were planning to remain.

The role of brokers is important first in minimizing isolation and second in facilitating acculturation. Children in school are excellent brokers as they provide information and introduce parents to Anglo traditions and life-style.

NOTE

1. By Mexican, I mean women who were born in Mexico and have recently come to the United States, with or without residence permits. Mexican Americans are United States–born or long-time residents in this country.

REFERENCES

Barth, Fredrik
1969 Ethnic Groups and Boundaries. Boston: Little, Brown & Co.

Bell, Daniel
1975 "Ethnicity and social change." Pp. 141-174 in N. Glazer and D. P. Moynihan (eds.), Ethnicity: Theory and Experience. Cambridge, Massachusetts: Harvard University Press.

Cohen, Abner
1974 Two-Dimensional Man: An Essay on the Anthropology of Power and Symbolism in Complex Society. Berkeley, California: University of California Press.

DeVos, George
1975 "Ethnic pluralism: conflict and accommodation." In G. DeVos and L. Romanucci-Ross (eds.), Ethnic Identity: Cultural Continuities and Change. Palo Alto, California: Mayfield Publishing Co.

Glazer, Nathan and D. P. Moynihan
1975 Ethnicity: Theory and Experience. Cambridge, Massachusetts: Harvard University Press.

Hicks, George L.
1977 "Introduction." In George L. Hicks and P. E. Leis (eds.), Ethnic Encounters: Identities and Contexts. North Scituate, Massachusetts: Duxbury Press.

Melville, Margarita
1978 "Mexican women adapt to migration." International Migration Review 12(2):225-235.

Safa, Helen Icken
1977 "Working class women in Latin America: a case study in Puerto Rico." In June Nash and H. I. Safa (eds.), Sex and Class in Latin America. New York: Praeger Publishers.

Spiro, Melford E.
1955 "The acculturation of American ethnic groups." American Anthropologist 57:1240-1252.

Wolf, Eric R. and John W. Cole
1974 The Hidden Frontier: Ecology and Ethnicity in an Alpine Valley. New York: Academic Press, Inc.

Chapter 11

Cultural styles and adolescent sex role perceptions

An exploration of responses to a value picture projective test

John M. Long and Diego Vigil

If the Mexican American woman faces the double burden of two minority statuses, what of the young Chicana on the threshold of womanhood? As Derbyshire (1968) noted over a decade ago, she (along with her male peers) finds herself in a condition of dual marginality, that of ethnic minority status on one hand and adolescence on the other. The latter condition, of course, universally confronts one with decisions concerning adoption of appropriate sex role behavior. When faced with the often-conflicting Mexican and Anglo American cultural definitions of appropriate sex roles and the recent striking changes in these definitions, how does the Chicana see herself? To what degree does she share her male peers' views of sex, family, and work expectations? In what ways are her perceptions affected by the degree to which she is culturally Mexican oriented or American oriented?

We have examined these questions herein with data derived from projective testing administered to two purposively selected samples of Mexican American and Mexican high school students attending schools in the suburban areas east of Los Angeles. While specific hypotheses were constructed on the basis of the results of an earlier pretesting conducted on a generally similar but much smaller sample of students (1976), we were in general expecting that (1) students with a Mexican cultural orientation would project sex role expectations more in accord with those described by Lewis (1949) or Madsen (1964) than would more acculturated students; and (2) male and female teenagers would differ from each other in their perceptions of appropriate behavior for themselves and for the opposite sex. The results we have thus far obtained have been mixed in regard to both of these propositions.

THE VALUE PICTURE TEST

We have employed in this investigation a value picture test developed under the direction of Walter P. Goldschmidt of the Department of Anthropology at UCLA. Generally similar to instruments previously employed by Goldschmidt and Edgerton (1961) and the Spindlers (1965), the test consists of line drawings and a structured questionnaire

Fig. 6. Who in the family should be in charge of the money and why?

designed, as the Spindlers said of their technique, to tap into "the respondent's cognitive management of perceived social realities" (Spindler and Spindler 1965:21). The test that we have employed differs from the earlier ones in that it specifically addresses behavior related primarily to sex roles and it is designed to be administered in group settings to literate subjects (MacIver 1975). There are ten pictures, each depicting a relatively commonplace event, with each scene peopled by recognizably Mexican or Mexican American figures. The accompanying questionnaire addresses each picture in turn with a brief explanation of the action depicted and a set of forced choice and open-ended questions probing the respondent's attitudes and underlying values.

The following issues are probed in the test:

1. Who in the family should be in charge of the money and why (Fig. 6)?
2. Should a mother without a man to help with her children work, or should she "go on welfare" in order to remain with her children? If she has a man and he is working, then should she work or stay home?
3. Would you like to have a woman for a boss at work? Why?
4. Interethnic dating: this picture has two versions, one of which depicts a "young Mexican woman taking her Anglo boyfriend to meet her parents" (for female subjects) and the other in which a Mexican boy is with an Anglo girlfriend (for male subjects).
5. Should fathers diaper their babies, and if so, should they do it as often as mothers? Why?

6. Apparent adultery: this picture has two versions, one of which depicts a husband discovering his wife and another man embracing (for male subjects) and a second depicting the wife discovering her husband with another woman (for females). The question of "ending their relationship" is specifically probed.
7. Should the man or woman pay on a date, and who should ask for dates?
8. With two small children already, how would you feel about the prospective birth of a third? Would you prefer a girl or boy baby (there are one of each now)?
9. Should women repair auto engines, and if so, to what degree and why?
10. In a situation where the husband's elderly mother has been living with the couple, and it is becoming increasingly difficult for the wife to care for her, should the old woman be placed in a retirement home, and who should make such a decision?

Pretest and formulation of hypotheses

In 1975, Vigil (as part of a larger study) administered the value picture test to twelve Los Angeles area Chicano high school students; these included six each from an urban school and a suburban school. Divided equally by sex, each subsample also included two each from three distinct levels of acculturation (toward Anglo-American culture), as measured by a self-report instrument devised for that purpose. Data from the testing were used initially to illustrate general findings based on other data collected (Vigil 1976). Subsequently, the authors more thoroughly analyzed the responses to determine that the type of information desired was in fact elicited by the instrument (this proved to be the case) and to suggest questions for further research.

In 1978, the test was administered to three purposively selected samples, and this study treats the initial results from two of those samples. (The third group, consisting of active youth gang members, will be included in a later, more complete investigation.) The initial analysis was directed only at responses to those pictures that had elicited (in the 1976 analysis) differential responses by sex or by level of acculturation. (None of the pictures had elicited statistically significant results, owing to the small numbers involved.) Three pictures failed to suggest such differences and were thus not included in this analysis. The 1975 students were in general of the opinion that both husband and wife should have a say in the management of household money because that would be fair and/or it would avert arguments; a minority of each sex felt that the woman should control the money since she would be more aware of household needs. These students were virtually unanimously accepting of a female boss at work, in some cases noting a requirement of either sex for fairness and/or for competency. The majority of both sexes and of each acculturation level also preferred that men pay for dates; a slightly larger minority felt that requesting a date was permissible for either man or woman.

On the basis of responses to the remaining seven pictures, the following hypotheses were developed for further testing:

1. *Female respondents more often than male respondents would opt for a woman re-maining home on welfare rather than leaving a child in another's care in order to work* (see Fig. 7). The hypothesis applied only to choice in the absence of a male provider; in

Fig. 7. Should a woman go on welfare or go to work?

that case, most of the female students in the earlier test had opted for welfare, whereas none of the males did so. Our expectation was grounded not so much in terms of family roles (there is no husband present) as in terms of perceived economic well-being. (The female students and many of the males who chose for the woman to work presumed an economic benefit for them in doing so.)

2. *Male respondents more often than female respondents would express misgivings concerning interethnic dating.* Half of the males had done so in the pretest, while none of the female students had objected. We felt greater male conservatism on this point might stem from the greater chance of their having had more frequent and more overt hostility expressed toward them by Anglos, owing to their presumed greater mobility than the girls would have had.

3. *Mexican-oriented adolescents, and in particular Mexican-oriented males, would be more apt to forthrightly object to fathers diapering babies.* Only a minority of the students tested earlier had clearly favored this, but most—rather than responding no to the forced choice answers—made their answers conditional. Typically, these stressed emergency situations or preparation for the same. The only no responses came from Mexican-oriented students, mostly males.

4. *Male respondents more often than female respondents would suggest or consider divorce in response to finding one's spouse in the arms of another.* Most of the males in the earlier study had done so, while none of the female students had done so. This

appeared to be related to traditional Mexican and Chicano role expectations, and we therefore formulated the following hypothesis.

5. *Mexican-oriented male respondents would more often suggest or consider divorce in such a case*.

6. *Anglo-oriented acculturated respondents would more often express economically based hesitation about a third child*. A majority of all students in the earlier testing had simply welcomed the new baby, but several of the more Anglo-oriented expressed misgivings at the cost. For this item, then, we ignored the forced choice response for the first question and coded only the presence of economic considerations in the responses to the open-ended "why?" question.

7. *Male respondents more often than female respondents would prefer a boy baby*. Only males had expressed a sex preference for the baby, and all but one opted for a boy. (The exception would have a girl because she would be easier to care for.)

8. *Male respondents more often than female respondents would object to women working on cars*. Half of the males had mentioned misgivings about women working on automobiles in the pretest. In most instances, these occurred when a respondent would not say yes or no to the forced choice question but made his objections clear in the open-ended response. For this item, therefore, we coded the open-ended responses according to whether or not they indicated misgivings.

9. *Mexican-oriented respondents would be more apt to forthrightly reject placing the husband's mother in a retirement home*. Only a minority of the earlier test groups had favored such action, but most of the more acculturated gave conditional responses, while most of the Mexican-oriented respondents simply rejected the retirement home.

10. *Male respondents more than female respondents would expect the husband to decide whether his mother should be placed in the home*. Only males in the earlier testing had so indicated. A majority of both males and females had said both husband and wife should be involved. In the retest reported herein, a Spanish translation of the original questionnaire was administered to the Mexican-oriented sample of students. Unfortunately, the option "mother" was excluded in the translated version from the forced choice options to the question of who should make the decision. This failing of course prevents testing of the hypothesis, but we have included it and a discussion of actual responses because we feel them to be of interest.

Sample selection and testing procedure

Two groups of Mexican and Mexican American students were selected from students enrolled in high schools in the suburban areas east of Los Angeles to represent, respectively, culturally Mexican-oriented adolescents and Anglo-oriented students.

The first group consisted of nine males and twelve females enrolled in a special English as a Second Language (ESL) curriculum. All are recent immigrants from Mexico and all speak Spanish much more fluently than they do English. Their self-reported grade point averages (on a scale where 4.0 is equal to "A" and 2.0 would be a "C") was 2.75, similar to the overall G.P.A. for the high school that they attend. Two regular class sessions were used to administer the test, with those who were absent the first time taking the test on the second occasion.

The second group was recruited with the help of school officials at a nearby, quite similar high school. Officials were requested to select students of Mexican descent who were born in the United States, spoke English fluently, had a high grade point average, and were at least moderately active in extracurricular activities in school. These criteria had been associated with Anglo-orientation in Vigil's earlier study (1975). The sample included ten males and nine females, similar in age and school grade level to the Mexican-oriented group. They differed, however, in having a significantly higher G.P.A. (3.24) and in being more fluent in English and less fluent in Spanish. Three sessions with six to eight students were conducted.

Administration of the test differed only in language. Students first filled out a front sheet eliciting demographic data and information about the students' participation in various social and recreational activities. (These were not employed in the present study because of time limitations.) They then were directed to turn to the questionnaire page appropriate for the first drawing; this was held up by the administrator, who then circulated among the students to ensure that each could clearly see the drawing. When all students had completed responses to this picture, the students turned to the next set of questions and a new drawing was presented to them. In the case of the two stimulus pictures that have sex-typed versions, boys were asked to wait while girls responded to the female version, after which the girls awaited the boys' completion of their answers.

Treatment of the data

The forced choice responses to questions concerning each of the seven pictures selected for this study, except the question about welcoming a new baby and the question concerning the propriety of women working on cars, were coded for analysis. In the excepted cases, the written responses were simply coded as indicating or not indicating the variable, as noted in the preceding in conjunction with the hypotheses. Each variable was then cross-tabulated by sex and by group; this procedure allowed for testing of each hypothesis and for exploration of further relationships not hypothesized. Chi-square or (when the total number of subjects involved was less than twenty) Fisher's exact probability statistic was employed to determine the statistical significance of differences between groups or between sexes. Because of the small sample sizes, however, we have not strictly limited our discussion to results that attained statistical significance.

FINDINGS

Three pictures failed to elicit significant differences by group or by sex. Mexican-oriented and Anglo-oriented students of both sexes were overwhelmingly approving of a person's choice for interethnic dating, by approximately a four to one margin in each category. Our hypothesis of greater male conservatism on this issue was clearly invalid. A majority of both sexes and both cultural groups also was unopposed to women working on automobiles; only among the Anglo-oriented females did a bare majority (five out of nine) express misgivings. Our hypothesis of male resistance therefore did not bear out. Mexican-oriented students also did not differ significantly from Anglo-oriented students (as we had hypothesized they would) on the question of placing the husband's mother in a retirement home; about three fifths of each group rejected the proposition. In fact, slightly (but not significantly) more of the Mexican-oriented adolescents *favored* the placement. Responses to the second question for the same picture (who should decide whether the mother should go to the home) are of interest, despite the methodological problem involved. One third of the Mexican-oriented students and one sixth of the Anglo-oriented group felt that the husband ought to decide, with males in each group slightly more apt to favor the husband. Within the Anglo-oriented group (where the option of the mother herself deciding was included among the forced choice answers), two out of three males selected that choice, compared to one in three of the females. Within the Mexican-oriented group, one third of the males *wrote in the choice of mother deciding.* (None of the Mexican-oriented females did so.) Although the stimuli are not completely comparable, it is perhaps worthy of note that when all males' choices are compared to those of females, the difference is marginally significant ($X^2 = 5.73$, d.f. $= 2$, p < 0.10).

The hypothesized greater tendency for females to more often prefer that a mother stay home on welfare rather than go to work was not affirmed. There were no significant differences by sex, and in fact the category most apt to prefer the work option was that of the Anglo-oriented females. A significant difference ($X^2 = 8.55$, d.f. $= 1$, p < 0.05) between Mexican-oriented and Anglo-oriented students was found, but it was clearly attributed to differences between the females of each group ($X^2 = 8.17$, d.f. $= 1$, p < 0.05).

As hypothesized, Mexican-oriented students were more apt than Anglo-oriented students to declare that fathers ought not to diaper babies ($X^2 = 6.78$, d.f. $= 2$, p < 0.05). The majority of the Anglo-oriented group gave a conditional answer to the question; within the Mexican-oriented group, a plurality of the males said no. However, to the question of whether they ought to diaper their babies as often, the responses did not differ by group or by sex, with "no" answers more common than "yes" answers in each category.

Male respondents overall were not more apt to consider divorce in the face of apparent adultery as we had expected them to be; a similar majority of both sexes suggested divorce. There was, however, an interesting interaction of group membership and sex: Females among the Anglo-oriented respondents more often favored separation, but among the Mexican-oriented respondents, males more often opted for divorce. The difference between females of the two groups was not significant, but the males' difference was marginally so (Fisher's exact probability $= 0.07$).

Three out of four of the Mexican-oriented respondents would feel good about the approaching birth of a third child, whereas a slight majority of the Anglo-oriented respondents gave a conditional response to the question. Nevertheless, there is no significant difference in the proportions mentioning economic concerns with regard to the new baby, and our hypothesis is not borne out; most of those expressing hesitation regarding a third child state concerns for the mother's ability to adequately care for the children. As expected, however, males significantly more often prefer male babies than do females (Fisher's exact probability = 0.016). Only two girls, both Mexican-oriented, would prefer a boy baby, and each gives as a reason for this preference the belief that the father would prefer another boy. As a group, the Mexican-oriented students are more apt to express a sex preference than the Anglo-oriented students (X^2 = 4.61, d.f. = 1, p < 0.05).

DISCUSSION

The findings reported here are based on samples purposively selected to represent two extremes of Chicano youth in the suburban areas east of Los Angeles: Those most Mexican in their cultural orientation and those most successfully integrated into the Anglo-American dominant culture of the vicinity. The degree to which findings based on such groups can be generalized beyond these locales is open to question, of course, but the issues addressed here are common to all Chicano populations in the United States.

The young women in our samples did not differ greatly from one another or from their male peers in tolerance for interethnic dating, in regarding women's working on cars with favor or at least equanimity, or in a shared distaste for sending the elderly off to retirement homes. The last is in keeping with traditional Mexican values for family solidarity, but the previous finding seems to mark a generalized discounting of at least portions of traditional sex role expectations. Both groups of girls differed from the males in preferring (if they had a preference) girl babies, although the two exceptions made their choices in terms of the perceived wishes of the husband. Both Mexican-oriented and Anglo-oriented girls apparently expect more of a voice in important decisions such as whether they should be expected to care for their ailing mothers-in-law (although this finding is confounded by a methodological problem).

In terms of who diapers the baby, both sets of young women (along with their male peers) are acceptive of the traditional role of the mother, although Anglo-oriented girls are slightly more apt to hedge in this regard: men should apparently clean the infants when women are not present (but only then). On the question of remaining at home with one's children rather than working, allegiance to tradition is less clear. Mexican-oriented girls much more often select the option of remaining home, and this may reflect traditional ties to the role of mother, while the Anglo-oriented women may be ideologically more in touch with feminist assertions of a right to work. However, it is equally possible that this division represents the girls' respective perceptions of opportunities for a job with good pay and agreeable hours; the English-speaking high achievers may reasonably expect to earn much more working than they would receive in welfare benefits. As for the issue of tolerance of ones spouse's adultery, the Mexican-oriented group responds in accordance with traditional values; the male is outraged and the female patient. But the Anglo-oriented females are similar to the males of the Mexican-oriented group; they suggest divorce in return for such dalliances.

In summary, our general expectations have only partly been met: Mexican-oriented students indicate more traditional values in some regards but not in others; females differ from males on some issues but not others. In important cases, the Anglo-oriented Chicana differs in an opposite direction from the male than is the case among the Mexican-oriented adolescents. The picture that emerges lends little support for stereotyping the young Chicana (or her male counterpart) with traditional values but also differs from the imagery projected by some of the more radical Chicana feminists. The young women surveyed here project a blend of traditional role expectations, self-assertive intentions, and pragmatic values.

REFERENCES

Derbyshire, R. L.
  1968 "Adolescent identity crisis in urban Mexican Americans in East Los Angeles." In E. B. Brody (ed.), Minority Group Adolescents in the United States. Baltimore, Maryland: The Williams & Wilkins Co.
Goldschmidt, W. and R. Edgerton
  1961 "A picture technique for the study of values." American Anthropologist 63:26-47.
Lewis, O.
  1949 "Marriage and the family: husbands and wives in a Mexican village. A study of role conflict." American Anthropologist 51:602-610.
MacIver, A.
  1975 "Sex roles and sexuality among urban college youth." Unpublished research report. The University of California at Los Angeles.
Madsen, W.
  1964 The Mexican Americans of Southwest Texas. New York: Holt, Rinehart & Winston.
Spindler, G. and L. Spindler
  1965 "The instrumental activities inventory: a technique for study of the psychology of acculturation." Southwestern Journal of Anthropology 21:1-23.
Vigil, J. D.
  1976 "Adolescent Chicano acculturation and school performance: the role of social economic conditions and urban-suburban environmental differences." Unpublished dissertation. The University of California at Los Angeles.

Chapter 12

Social networks and survival strategies

An exploratory study of Mexican American, black, and Anglo female family heads in San Jose, California

Roland M. Wagner and Diane M. Schaffer

The portrait of the Mexican American family structure that is usually presented in social science literature focuses on the traditional solidarity within *la familia*, emphasizing the resiliency of ties between relatives dispersed demographically and cross-generationally and their integration into a mutually supportive network. This portrait generally assumes that the nuclear family is the basic component of the kinship structure, and it emphasizes the importance of the male as head of the family. Much of this literature has been based on research in rural areas and agricultural towns, especially in south Texas and New Mexico (for example, Kluckhohn and Strodtbeck 1961; Madsen 1964; Romano 1960; Rubel 1966; and Saunders 1954, to cite only better known sources). The research that has been conducted in larger urban areas is quite limited and is somewhat dated by this point (for example, Clark 1970; Grebler, Moore, and Guzmán 1970; and Tuck 1956). The recent efforts of the Spanish-Speaking Mental Health Research Center (for example, Keefe, Padilla, and Carlos 1977), directed by Amado Padilla, as well as the independent efforts of other researchers (for example, Matthiasson 1974) are filling the gap in needed literature on the rapidly changing Mexican American life-styles, contemporary urban family structure, and patterns of resource utilization.

While the general outlines of the model of the nuclear and extended family structure among Mexican Americans may be accurate as depicted in the literature, significant regional and economic variations have not been adequately explored. Variations in the patterns of cooperation and resource specialization within the kinship network, for example, may be obscured by overemphasis on the uniformity of reciprocity within the kinship network. The assumption of an open flow of goods and services within the network diverts attention from specializations that may, in fact, develop within particular kinship linkages. Gilbert has documented that ". . . the extended family among Mexican Americans is not a unitary and constant configuration nor do norms of obligation unvaryingly extend over the entire universe of kin" (1978:46). She found that "primary" kin (parents, siblings, children) were visited in different frequencies and relied on in different circumstances than "secondary" kin (aunts, uncles, grandparents, cousins, nieces, and nephews). Further research should be done on resource specializations within both of these broad categories of kinship.

The emphasis on the household head status of the male within the family detracts from an adequate understanding of roles women have played in the past and continue to play in Mexican American society today. As is true for all ethnic groups in the United States, the incidence of female-headed families is increasing among Mexican Americans subsisting at poverty-level incomes. Many Mexican American women have, in fact, had to assume the role and responsibilities of "household head" even while they are married. The absence of men for several months out of the year while involved in the migrant labor circuit has created a *de facto* household head status for many of their wives (see Olson 1977 for a study of the impact of the migratory life-style on a rural Mexican village).

Research is needed on the long-term sociocultural adjustment process that women undergo after they become independent family heads and on how this adjustment may be facilitated or complicated by cultural factors. There is a need for detailed studies comparing women of different ethnic groups in the problems they face, their coping strategies, their patterns of utilization of formal and informal helping resources, and possible differences in values, attitudes, and social networks that may affect their social functioning.

In order to explore some of these questions concerning the adaptations of Mexican American women who are family heads and to gain a more detailed insight into the operations of the extended family structure and general social network, the authors conducted two pilot studies on the east side of San Jose, California.

Over the summer of 1976, one of the authors (R. M. W.) conducted research on long-range population trends and social developments in the Mexican American barrios in east San Jose. In addition, a pilot study was conducted on a sample of 38 Mexican American, Anglo, and black female family heads in this area for purposes of refining some of the hypotheses derived from network analysis. The eastern half of San Jose has long been the major concentration of Mexican Americans in Santa Clara county (Sanchez and Wagner 1979). Since the 1960s, single women with dependent children have begun to gravitate into the area in search of lower rent. Households headed by women now comprise from 17 to 26 percent of households in the census tracts in this area. The growth rate of this family type has become so alarming that a recent study has characterized much of this area as a "female ghetto" (Social Planning Council of Santa Clara County 1978).

In 1978, Schaffer conducted a follow-up pilot study in conjunction with Wagner on a sample of 26 single women living in a low-income housing project in east San Jose. This study involved the research assistance of graduate students in the School of Social Work at San Jose State University. A total of thirteen Mexican American and thirteen black women were interviewed.

The joint findings of these pilot studies will be discussed in this chapter. The results must be regarded as tentative because of the limited numbers in the samples in both cases. The women in the first study were drawn largely from job training programs and thus heavily overrepresent the component of the female family head population on welfare.

The second survey samples single women at home during the day in a public housing complex, and thus it also tends to overrepresent the unemployed in the population.

FEMALE HEADS OF FAMILIES: A GROWING COMPONENT OF THE POPULATION

Currently some 13 million households, 22 percent of all households in the United States, are headed by single, separated, divorced, or widowed women (U.S. Commission on Civil Rights, 1974). One out of every three of these women subsists on a below poverty-level income, and the majority of welfare case loads throughout the country consist of single women with dependent children. The social and economic vulnerability of female family heads has long been recognized, but their growing magnitude in the country among all ethnic groups has only recently been documented. It has been hypothesized that a fundamental shift in family types in industrial societies may be occurring and that the proportion of female family heads will continue to increase. The most important factor associated with the growth of families headed by women is the rising divorce rate, but secondary factors include rising illegitimacy rates among teenagers and a greater tendency for women to establish independent households instead of living with relatives (Ross and Sawhill 1975). The average age of female family heads is becoming younger than in previous periods (McEaddy 1976). As the transition occurs away from the traditional "distributive" or father-headed family toward the "egalitarian" family, with a concomitant growth in market integration of the women, conditions favor a higher frequency of female-headed families.

Social science research on families headed by women has tended to focus on macro-level issues that can be explored through national census data. These include the immediate and underlying causes of the growing incidence of this family type (Ross and Sawhill 1975), the socioeconomic characteristics of families headed by women (McEaddy 1976), and the possible negative consequences on children resulting from being raised in this family environment (Duncan and Duncan 1969; Moynihan 1965; Uhlenberg 1972). The focus of this research reflects an implicit value bias against female-headed families. Sometimes it is assumed to be a pathological family type, inimical to mental health and the later economic achievement of children because of inadequate role modeling (LeMasters 1971; Moynihan 1965). Negative consequences on children have been shown to result from marital disruption (Campbell 1975; Duncan and Duncan 1969; Herzog and Sudia 1968; Uhlenberg 1972). This research does not necessarily imply that being raised in a family headed by a woman is intrinsically inimical to mental health and economic success of family members, although the two are sometimes merged into the same theoretical model. The problems associated with families headed by women might not be intrinsic but rather could result from the difficulties of living in a society that is normatively oriented to the monogamous nuclear family and levies economic and social sanctions against alternative family forms.

Significant ethnic differences have been demonstrated in the incidence of families headed by women, not all of which can be explained by economics alone. There is a disproportionately high percentage of families headed by women among the black population at large. As of 1974, the relative figures nationally showed that 33.6 percent of all black households were headed by women, compared to 19.7 percent for whites and 21.6 percent for the total population (U.S. Commission on Civil Rights 1974). Ross and Sawhill (1975) attribute the disproportion to the higher rates of illegitimacy among black teenagers, the relatively low remarriage rates, and especially to the greater marital instability. Marital instability, in turn, strongly correlates with economic factors such as the employment problems of the husband and the relatively low earnings differential between black men and women compared with the white population at large.

Mexican Americans, in contrast to American blacks, have a lower incidence of families headed by women in spite of only a marginally better economic profile. Seventeen percent of Mexican American households were headed by women in 1970 (U.S. Commission on Civil Rights 1974). Currently, the Mexican Americans have one of the lowest percentages of this family type, surpassed only by Filipino Americans and Chinese Americans (13 percent and 12 percent, respectively).

These findings are also reflected in significant differences in marital instability rates for the Mexican Americans. Eberstein and Frisbie (1976), through regional subclassifications and comparison of ethnic groups, concluded that Mexican Americans have a lower marital instability rate than blacks or Anglos and that the Anglo rate has been increasing at a higher rate than the other two groups. These data support the conventional perception of the Mexican American family developed primarily through qualitative anthropological observations (Madsen 1964; Rubel 1966). According to this perspective, the Mexican Americans have highly resilient family ties, the roles of husband and wife are more clearly demarcated, divorce or separation are rarer than among Anglo families (Burma 1954; Eberstein and Frisbie 1976), and this is in spite of their overrepresentation in the lower income categories (Browning and McLemore 1964; Grebler, Moore, and Guzmán 1970; U.S. Bureau of the Census 1971). Variation in socioeconomic status, then, is not entirely responsible for the variation in marital instability rates and in female family heads by ethnic groups. There is a general inverse correlation between marital dissolution and socioeconomic status, but the research suggests that marriages will be stabler and the incidence of female family heads will be somewhat lower for Mexican Americans than for Anglos or blacks in comparable economic circumstances (Eberstein and Frisbie 1976).

FEMALE HEADS OF FAMILIES IN THE MEXICAN AMERICAN COMMUNITY OF SAN JOSE

Statistics for Santa Clara County, the general target area for the two research projects, mirror the preceding discussions for ethnic variation in the percentage of female family heads at the national level. The 1970 census data indicated that 14.7 percent of all Spanish-speaking and Spanish-surnamed household heads were women compared to 18.1 percent for the county population at large (Social Planning Council 1978).

The plight of single women with dependent children is especially acute in Santa Clara County with its unusually high rent and general cost of living. Their economic vulnerability, combined with overt discrimination by landlords against tenants on welfare and/or with children, has resulted in the geographical clustering of female family heads in a few census tracts in the county. A recent study (E.S.O. 1974) has identified seven "female ghetto" census tracts in Santa Clara County, four of which are located close together on the east side of San Jose, the major metropolitan center for the county.

The focal point of Mexican American settlement in the county is also on the east side of San Jose, encompassing some of the seven identified "female ghetto" census tracts. The original barrios or neighborhoods in which Mexican Americans settled in the late 1920s were located on unincorporated land on the fringe of the city limits, an area known today as the Mayfair district (Clark 1970). Since the 1950s, San Jose has undergone explosive growth, mirroring developments in the Bay area at large. Tract house complexes grew rapidly around the original Mayfair barrios. A mixed population of Anglos, blacks and Mexican Americans, with an unusually high percentage of female family heads, developed in the barrios and especially on their periphery (Sanchez and Wagner 1979).

THE PLIGHT OF THE FEMALE FAMILY HEAD

The complex problems that a single woman with dependent children faces are common for all three ethnic groups. Certain themes emerged in the interviews with the Mexican American, Anglo, and black women.

Employment

Female family heads are chronically unemployed or underemployed relative to other elements in the adult work force. Only 5 of the 38 women in the first study were employed, although the sample was biased toward a higher frequency of underemployment because of the focus on those taking part in job training programs. The median gross earned income for female household heads in Santa Clara County in 1975 was only $537 per month, while for the county at large the median household income was $1638 per month.

The causes of the chronic underemployment and unemployment of women with dependent children are varied. Sex discrimination in job placement and career development is deeply ingrained in our male-oriented economic system. The State Commission on the Status of Women in its 1973 survey of California found that "in virtually every field men earn more than women, even in clerical jobs. . . . A California woman makes less than 50 cents for every $1 earned by a man" (ESO 1974:30). In addition to these limitations in the external opportunity structure, women also face internal barriers to economic advancement in their lack of job skills, their own attitudes socialized into them since childhood, and in the familial obligations they must face alone after their loss of or separation from their spouse. The average woman in the first study was around 30 years old with two children. Many of them had married quite young and had limited employment experience or skills. The circumstances of having two young children to raise presented formidable obstacles to their finishing their education or getting job training.

Welfare—AFDC

Since there exist these internal and external barriers to employment, many single women with dependent children are forced to seek public assistance. In Santa Clara County, 77 percent of the AFDC case load consisted of female household heads in 1972. In the first study 35 of the 38 women were currently receiving AFDC. There was a range from $258 to $432 per month in the amounts reported by the women. Almost unanimously the women agreed that life on AFDC was just one step removed from starvation. No realistic allowance was given for essential items such as diapers, school clothing for the children, shoes, toiletries, laundry, personal items, transportation expenses, car insurance, and so on. By the time rent and utility bills were paid, many women had less than $5 left for the entire month to meet these needs. The rent allowance was around $125 per month, which is considerably below the current market cost, and the same is true for utilities allowances as well.

The physical needs of the women and their children were met through MediCal and food stamps. Women with one child paid $32 per month for $92 worth of food stamps. Those with two children paid $64 for $128 worth of stamps, and so on according to the graduated scale.

As deprived as these circumstances are, many women were unable to rise above this level of subsistence in spite of being employed. Because of the low earning potential of women, those receiving AFDC with three children actually could gross almost as much as the average earned income for women workers. In 1974, the maximum AFDC allowance for a woman with three children was $3,840 per year in comparison with the $4,000 per year the same woman would earn working at minimum wage levels. To some extent, then, the welfare system is self-perpetuating.

The emotional and psychological pressure women face while being on AFDC is a constant part of their lives. An institutionalized form of gossip was encouraged through the "community complaint" procedure, according to which a landlord or neighbor could complain to the Department of Social Services about a woman's housekeeping or whether she has a man sleeping in the house with her (ESO 1974:57). The constant official prying and questioning into their personal lives is humiliating for many of the women.

Credit

Since they are on the margin of survival, single women family heads usually are forced to buy many essential household items such as refrigerators on time. Frequently they need small, short-term loans to carry them through the month. Their need for credit is endemic, yet single women are clearly penalized in their ability to satisfy this need. The women in the first study complained of the difficulties of obtaining routine department store charge cards, master charge, VISA, and other such short-range means of credit. Insurance companies reportedly discriminate against single women. In spite of the fact that auto insurance is required by law, many companies do not insure a divorced woman during the first year because she is considered "unstable" (ESO 1974:57).

Housing

One of the first problems many women face after separation from their spouse is finding housing within a price range they can afford. The county Housing Authority, which aids women in their search, was not recommended by any of the women in the first study. The waiting list was long, and none of the women actually obtained housing through this agency. The limited price range affordable by most of the women was further complicated by the fact that many landlords discriminate against single women, particularly if they discover they are receiving welfare and have young children. Upper limit restrictions on the number of children women may have are common in many housing and apartment developments, including those that are HUD sponsored.

Transportation

Contemporary life-styles, particularly in California, are difficult to maintain without access to a car. Visiting, entertainment, and the routine purchase of essentials such as groceries are difficult to accomplish by public transit, especially in view of the large distance often involved. Nine of the 38 women in the first study, or 24 percent, lacked their own automobile. Those owning a car found maintenance and insurance to be a chronic problem, especially since they usually could afford only older vehicles that were in need of frequent repair.

Social

The conjugal family is still the fundamental unit in the social organization of this country. Many social activities are "couples" oriented, and often a single woman finds herself subtly excluded; she may even find old friendships weakening because of the potential threat her altered marital status poses. The woman must once again take the initiative to establish new relations with men and at the same time cope with her role of being a mother. There are many singles clubs today, such as "Parents Without Partners", but only one of the women in the first study participated in their functions. Those on AFDC, even if they happened to own an automobile, frequently mentioned that they simply did not have enough money left for gasoline to enable them to carry on an adequate social life. Poverty breeds a form of social isolation, particularly in California where friends or family may be living many miles away in a congested urban area. The economics and the simple logistics of locating an adequate babysitter at the right time also prevent many women from reengaging themselves in social activities after their separation.

Adaptive strategies

The women reported coping with the circumstances just described in a variety of ways.

Subterfuge. There are varieties of subterfuge to which single, female family heads are forced in order to survive. Most commonly, women discover that it is easier to claim that they are married when filing for department store and gasoline company credit cards. The sheer volume of clients that these companies have prevents them from investigating cases in detail. Many respondents flatly stated that falsification is the only way they could obtain access to these sources of short-range credit. Another common form of subterfuge is to claim that they are married when seeking houses to rent, since single women are commonly discriminated against. Frequently the women will conceal the fact that they are on welfare from their prospective landlord. In one instance the woman had arranged ahead of time for her uncle to falsely claim to the landlord that she was employed as a secretary at his lumberyard.

Women also resort to subterfuge with the welfare department. One of the simplest and most widespread examples is the selling of food stamps. More seriously, one of the women reported her rent to the eligibility worker as being $15 per month higher than it actually was, and her landlord was sympathetic enough with her financial plight to back up her story. Those women who go to school and get a babysitting allowance sometimes arrange with the babysitter to furnish a receipt for an inflated payment. Another common form of "welfare fraud" is for women to move in together as roommates and split expenses, concealing this from the welfare agency. The legal vulnerability of women resorting to these measures increases the level of stress they experience.

Repayment by services. Another adaptive strategy commonly reported by the women in our sample was to repay small financial loans through services. The service most frequently offered was babysitting, which was most compatible with their life-style. Usually they would develop arrangements with friends or relatives who were financially more secure than themselves.

Between women family heads it is common to find exchanges of services and goods of a nonmonetary nature. Those lacking cars, for example, may borrow another woman's car and repay her with babysitting. Frequent borrowing back and forth of groceries and the loaning of food stamps is common. This informal type of barter system was reported as a resource by all respondents.

THE ROLE OF THE KINSHIP NETWORK

The proximity of the barrios offered social and economic resources, primarily family members of the Mexican American women who were not available to the same extent for the Anglo and black single women. In effect, there was a difference between the ethnic groups in the socioeconomic vulnerability of the women within the "female ghetto" census tracts.

Table 12-1 presents a general comparison of the Mexican American women in the first study with the small number of Anglos and blacks. It is apparent that the Mexican American and Anglo women were similar in many respects. Both tended to be in their early thirties, with two children, and had lived in San Jose for approximately the same length of time, a dozen years or more. More of the Anglo women had completed high school. The black women, as limited as the sample is, were younger (in their twenties), had fewer children, and were relative newcomers to the San Jose area. The black community is a comparatively new phenomenon in San Jose and has been growing significantly only since around 1970.

Only three (10 percent) of the 30 Mexican American women in the first study lacked relatives in San Jose, whereas 60 percent or more of the Anglos and blacks lacked relatives. Furthermore, the average size of the kinship network present for the Mexican Americans was strikingly larger compared to that of the other women.

The Mexican American women typically had eleven relatives present in the city (some ranged up to 30 or more), and this was not including their own children living within the household. The Anglos and blacks, in contrast, had a much smaller kinship network (averaging four people). Of the three Mexican American women lacking relatives in San Jose, two appeared to be having emotional problems. Only one of the three seemed comfortable with her circumstances, and she was an older woman (51 years of age) with teenage children on whom to rely.

Table 12-1. Selected social attributes, Mexican American, Anglo, and black female family heads

	Mexican American	Anglo	Black
Total number	30	5	3
Age			
20 years or less	5	0	1
21-30	11	2	2
31-40	8	2	0
40 and above	6	1	0
Mean	31.8	36	23
Education (mean years)	9.9	12.8	12.3
Area of residence			
Mayfair barrio	11	0	0
Outside Mayfair	19	5	3
Place of birth			
Mayfair barrios	2	0	0
Outside Mayfair, in San Jose	6	1	0
Outside San Jose	22	4	3
Years in San Jose (mean)	15.3	12.5	4.6
Number of relatives in San Jose (mean)	11.1	4.4	4.7
Number lacking relatives in San Jose	3 (10%)	3 (60%)	2 (66%)

Table 12-2. Mexican American female family heads and their parents, residence areas

Total living in same neighborhood as parents	24
Both in Mayfair barrios	7
One in barrios, the other in an area close by	12
Both in the same neighborhood on the edge of the Mayfair barrios	3
Both in the same neighborhood in other portions of San Jose	2
Total living in different neighborhoods than parents	3
Neither live in Mayfair barrios	1
One lives in Mayfair, the other in a neighborhood that isn't close by	2
Total number of respondents with parents alive and in San Jose	27

The majority (70 percent) of the Mexican American women lived in matrifocal households separate from their relatives; however, 20 percent lived in extended family households (usually with parents), a considerably higher frequency of this household type than reported for the Mexican American population in Los Angeles or San Antonio (4 percent and 3 percent, respectively) (Grebler, Moore, Guzmán 1970:353). The women residing in extended family households or in joint family households with nonrelatives tended to be younger and to have fewer children than those living in independent matrifocal households.

All but one of the Anglo women lived in independent households, and the one exception was residing with a friend. Among the blacks, two lived in matrifocal households and one in extended family residence with her parents.

Table 12-2 shows that even for the Mexican American women in independent households, the great majority lived in neighborhoods close by their parents. Altogether, 27 out of the 30 women (90 percent) lived either in the same household with their parents or in the same general neighborhood.

Table 12-3 indicates that there is a form of "resource specialization" in the kinship networks of the Mexican American women. Parents are turned to in circumstances of dire necessity such as in illness, when the women might move in with the parents, or more commonly the mother might live with her temporarily, take care of the children, and fix the meals. Parents are also most often relied on for borrowing money. We may assume that parents are usually financially more stable than other members of the woman's kinship network. Siblings and friends tend be of her own age group, are still confronting the multitude of financial obligations typical of younger people with families to support, and would be burdened by these requests from women. Parents are also a prime social link for the women in their regular visiting. The major source of emotional support for the woman usually is her parents.

Siblings tend to be utilized for those problems that are best met through people of

Table 12-3. Resources relied on by Mexican American, Anglo, and black female family heads (''highest incidence'' choice only is listed)

	Mexican American	Anglo	Black
Babysitting	Siblings	Commercial	All equal
Borrowing money	Parents	Parents	Siblings
Loaning money	All equal	All equal	Friends
Transportation (those without car)	Siblings	All equal	Friends
Car repairs	Siblings and commercial services	Commercial	Commercial
Visiting	Parents and friends	Friends	Friends
Household repairs	Landlord	Self	Friends and landlord
Yardwork	Self and children	All equal	Self and siblings
Illness	Parents	Friends	Parents
Advice	Siblings	Friends	Friends and parents

one's own generation. Those women with cars, for example, turn to their brothers as often as to a commercial garage for repairs. In the event that they lack an auto, Mexican American women turned to their siblings for rides or for borrowing a car. Significantly, siblings were turned to for advice (usually a sister) more often than parents. People of one's own generation usually have a more empathetic understanding of problems one may be facing, since they may be confronting similar problems themselves. This could include things such as relationships with men, sources of financial aid, social services, and so on. The women felt too embarrassed to discuss certain problems with their parents, particularly those involving sexual relationships, conflicts with their religious beliefs, and so on. Among people of Mexican heritage, the elder brother *(hermano mayor)* traditionally has an important role to play in caring for his sisters. The elder brother is, in a sense, a surrogate father. Many of the Mexican American women seemed to maintain such a relationship with their male siblings.

The *comadre*, or godmother, was important primarily as a source of advice for the Mexican American women, but only secondary to the siblings and parents. This advice role is traditional in the *compadrazgo* (godparenthood) relationship, since this person is supposed to have input not only in how one raises children but also in the problems of daily life.

The categories that were conspicuously low in frequency for the Mexican American women were their reliance on friends and their use of commercial organizations or social service agencies for other than financial support (AFDC, MediCal, food stamps). There was a definite tendency to rely on the immediate kinship network for satisfying daily problems, both in the social-emotional sphere as well as in limited economic matters such as short-term loans. We may speculate that because the women had great time-depth in the area and many relatives living nearby, they felt little need to develop alternative avenues for aid.

The Anglo and black women, in contrast to the Mexican Americans, relied more frequently on friends for visiting, illness, and advice. Commercial sources were most commonly utilized for babysitting and car repairs. The parents remained important for borrowing money, but the relative frequency with which they were turned to was less than among the Mexican American women. Siblings clearly played a secondary role.

The network resources utilized by the few Mexican American women lacking relatives in San Jose closely approximated that of the Anglos and black women. Since parents and siblings were not available, the reliance on friends, as well as on commercial organizations, increased.

To some extent the Anglo and black women had been forced to rely on nonkin sources of aid to a greater extent than the Mexican American women simply because they lacked comparably large kinship networks in San Jose. In addition, however, cultural differences may enter as a factor in that the Anglo and black women did not choose to reside close to their relatives to the same extent as did the Mexican American women.

THE ROLE OF THE FRIENDSHIP NETWORK

Although the Anglo and black women relied more heavily on friends than the Mexican American women, they did not have larger friendship networks. Most of the women in the first study, regardless of ethnic group, had few friendship relations. The great majority of the women indicated that they had one or two friends they regularly visited, and a few women had no friends at all to whom they felt close. The female family head generally seemed to have a restricted social life, with their relationships beyond the kinship network focused on one or two special persons, generally women who were also female family heads and who often lived close by as neighbors. For the Mexican American women the institution of *compadrazgo*, godparenthood, provided a common avenue for cementing ties with friends. In effect, those relationships beyond the kinship network tended to become formalized into fictive kinship ties. One woman, for example, lived in a duplex and over a period of time became close friends with the woman living in the other half of the building. She cemented their relationship through having the woman become the godmother of her child. They relied on each other frequently for babysitting, small loans of cash, emotional support, and routine household jobs.

STUDY 2

Study 1 focused on a sample of women of mixed ethnic background living in or on the periphery of the core Mexican American barrios of the Mayfair district of San Jose. The Mexican American women had lived in San Jose for an average of 15 years and most had an extensive kinship network present. In Study 2, we turned our attention to a more

Table 12-4. Study 2: characteristics of the sample by ethnic group

	Mexican American	Black
Total number	13	13
Education less than high school (%)	85	38
Number of children in the home		
Mean	2.54	
Range	1-7	
Eldest child (%)	46	76
Under 6		
Ever married (%)	69	23
Median length of separation (yr.)	2.5	1
Born in San Jose (%)	15	8
California (other than San Jose) (%)	23	38
Mother or Father born in San Jose (%)	15	0
Mother or Father born in Mexico (%)	31	0
Length of residence in San Jose less than 3 years (%)	67	30
Less than 1 year in present residence (%)	46	54
Less than 1 year in previous residence (only those who had been in current residence less than 1 year) (%)	25	50
AFDC recipient (%)	92	92
Currently employed (%)	15	38

mobile population of female family heads, a group whose average length of residence in San Jose was less than 3 years.

The severe shortage of low-income housing in Santa Clara county, combined with active discrimination against single women with families, has resulted in a growing concentration of female family heads of all ethnic groups in several high-density apartment areas. The residents of a public housing project in one of these "ghetto" areas were the population from which our respondents were drawn for Study 2. We will call this "Project F." The majority of the residents are from minority ethnic backgrounds, particularly Mexican American and black American.

The characteristics of the Mexican American and black respondents in Study 2 are displayed in Table 12-4. All but two respondents were AFDC recipients, and very few were employed. The ethnic groups were similar in average number of children (approximately 2.5), in length of residence in Project F (median 1 year), and in probability of being native to California (40 percent), but in other areas the two groups differ significantly. Black mothers were less likely to ever have been married and twice as likely to have all children under 6 years of age. Approximately 60 percent of the black mothers (in contrast to only 15 percent of the Mexican American mothers) had high school diplomas, suggesting better prospects of future employment when their children reach school age.

Coping strategies

The sample for Study 2 consisted of women from two different minority groups, women in similar social and economic circumstances.

All respondents discussed in detail the resources available to them and their attempts to meet their family's physical, social, and emotional needs within the constraints of AFDC support. The problems and the strategies for coping revealed in Study 1 were repeated. Particularly common among the residents of Project F was the sharing of apartments with a sister, mother, or other relative.

Network composition

Because of the high density of single parents in the project, we hypothesized that cooperative friendship networks would have developed.

When we examined the composition of the support networks reported by the women in Project F, we found dramatic differences between the two ethnic groups in the extent to which they depended on residents of the project versus kin. Even though both groups reported very limited friendship networks (few had more than two friends), the black mothers were far more likely to report a close friend living in the project (62 percent of the black mothers compared to 30 percent of the Chicanas.) Bearing in mind that the two groups had approximately equal length of residence in Project F, the resource specialization preferences displayed in Table 12-5 are surprising. The differences cannot be attributed to availability of relatives, for we found no difference in the frequency with which the relative to whom the mother felt closest was contacted. More than 50 percent of both Mexican American and black women reported daily contact with their closest relative.

The items selected for Table 12-5 display a trend that was a consistent contrast between the two ethnic groups throughout the interview. For emotional and social support, Mexican American's reported turning to relatives, even though they lived in an environment that provided an unusually high proportion of potential single parent friends. In contrast, the black mothers showed high dependence on friendship networks developed within the apartment complex. For example, for support when "feeling down" and for a male role model for their children, Mexican Americans were far more likely to turn to a relatives than friends, whereas the reverse was true for black women.

The background data on the respondents suggest that the Mexican American mothers' preference for kin resources in solving immediate, short-term problems may be explicable in terms of a different degree of "urbanization" or "mobility adaptation" than is found in the black population. Despite their equally short average tenancy in Project F, the two ethnic groups differed dramatically in their average time spent at their residence previous to Project F. This suggests that the black sample was more mobile and may have the

Table 12-5. Resource specialization: kin vs. friend by problem area

	Chicana (%)	Black (%)
Male to whom children feel close		
No one	23	8
Relative	61	31
Friend	8	46
Ex-husband	8	15
Who do you turn to if you're feeling down?		
No one	8	0
Relative	84	23
Friend	8	77
From whom would you ask advice on childrearing?		
No one	15	23
Relative	70	61
Friend	0	15
Professional	15	0
From whom could you borrow $500?		
No one	8	15
Relative	50	46
Friend	0	0
Loan company or bank	34	31
Number of relatives contributing to daily expenses		
None	69	54
One	31	16
Two or more	0	30

expectation of developing neighbor relationships into friendship networks as a support strategy and as an adaptation to frequent change of residence. Both groups reported moving in the project for financial reasons rather than for being close to relatives; however, the Mexican American women seem more likely to have activated or maintained emotionally supportive relationships with the available network of relatives. We hypothesize that the Mexican American mothers, even though recently arrived in San Jose, had not experienced change of residence as frequently as had the black sample and continued a pattern of dependence developed in more stable communities.

Looking at long-term, persistent needs or those involving larger demands on resources, such as needing a $500 loan or advice on problems with children, both ethnic groups turned primarily to relatives. Thus, their choices in these cases were consistent with the data reported by Litwak and Szelenyi (1969); that is, even in urbanized groups where kin are geographically distant, the kinship network serves as a preferred resource for long-term or high-demand problems. Relationships with neighbors are cultivated and relied on for immediate and short-term needs in areas such as emotional support, child care, and exchanges of the ''barter'' type described earlier.

Future research

In Study 1, our discussion of network utilization focused primarily on resource specialization within the kin network by a stable component of the Mexican American women in the community. In Study 2, we again looked at resource specialization but turned our focus to preferences between friends and kin for the mobile woman. Looking now at the joint results of the two studies, we will briefly examine the implications of our consistent findings on the size of the friendship networks of single mothers.

The finding that the women of all three ethnic groups tended to have restricted but intense friendship networks was surprising, since the assumption is often made that broad social networks are more adaptive for persons in insecure social and economic circumstances. A broad network supposedly maximizes the range of resource persons available to solve any given problem (Horwitz 1977; van den Berghe and van den Berghe 1966). Working-class families have been generally characterized as having broader informal social networks than middle-class families (Bott 1957; Gans 1962).

On the other hand, one of the most common characterizations of the "culture of poverty" (Lewis 1966) is the "social disengagement" of the poor, their lack of extensive social ties to other individuals and especially to formal organizations. It is apparent that the simplistic assumption cannot be made that the social network of friends and relatives is uniformly relied on by socioeconomically disadvantaged populations.

Several considerations seem important in determining one's choice of strategy regarding reliance on the social network and the degree to which it will be enlarged. Foster (1969) has postulated that there is an optimum size to the social network beyond which the balance of losses begins to outweigh the gains in terms of the obligations associated with the maintenance of these ties. A broad network of friendships with women who are of like circumstances would be a burden as well as a source of aid. The single mother would be opening herself up to more frequent requests from a larger number of people unless each of the women in her network was also involved in a comparably large network of her own. Since this assumption cannot be made for some members of the friendship network, and because some simply do not reciprocate the favors they receive, the majority of the women in the sample tended to restrict their friendship activities. They cultivated one or two especially close relationships, usually with other women who were also single household heads, and regularly cooperated with each other in mutually solving the myriad problems of daily survival. Rather than spreading limited resources thinly over a broad network, they chose to concentrate limited resources within the confines of a few dyadic ties.

An additional factor that influenced the size of the friendship network was the limited financial resources of most of the women. They often lacked cars, and those who did own a vehicle had difficulty maintaining it in good working condition and could not afford the considerable expense for gasoline. The population in San Jose and surrounding Santa Clara County is quite dispersed, and access to a vehicle is almost essential for the active social life necessary to form and maintain a broad friendship network. The need for qualified child care was a second economic barrier for these women, for none could afford to pay, and they perceived the choice of a social life for themselves to be possible only at the sacrifice of adequate care for their children.

ETHNICITY AND STRESS: SOME UNRESOLVED QUESTIONS

The preliminary explorations offered by these two studies highlight the need for studies of the effect of cultural background on the stress experienced by the single parent. The extent to which the Mexican American woman may experience single parenthood as more or less stressful than her black counterpart remains unaddressed by our data. In their preliminary report of the data from the Stress and Families Project, Belle et al. report that within a sample of low-income single mothers, white women reported becoming single as a negative and stressful experience, whereas, black respondents did not (Belle et al. 1978:12). How does the Chicana experience compare? On the one hand, she appears more likely to have kin support available; what, on the other hand, are the costs of requesting support at the level she requires as a single parent? What is her status in the Mexican American community should she decide to stay and rely on that support? How does she experience the status of *la soltera*, being a single woman in a community that emphasizes kinship and the nuclear family?

If the Mexican American woman leaves proximity to relatives, how does she develop alternative support structures? Does she suffer greater stress than a woman whose life experience of high mobility has given her the expectation and skills to initiate support networks with neighborhood members?

REFERENCES

Belle, Heborah, et al.
1978 "The plight of low-income mothers and their children." Paper presented at the Stress and Families Conference, Aspen Institute for Humanistic Studies, Aspen, Colorado, July 6, 1978.

Bott, Elizabeth
1957 Family and Social Network, London: Tavistock Publications, Ltd.

Browning, Harley L. and S. Dale McLemore
1964 "A statistical profile of the Spanish-speaking population of Texas." Public Affairs Comment, Institute of Public Affairs. University of Texas, vol. 10, No. 1.

Burma, John H.
1954 Spanish Speaking Groups in the U.S., Durham, North Carolina: Duke University Press.

Campbell, Angus
1975 "The American way of mating: marriage Si, children maybe." Psychology Today 8:37-43.

Clark, Margaret
1970 Health in the Mexican American Culture, ed. 2. Berkeley, California: University of California Press (ed. 1, 1959).

Duncan, Beverly and Otis Duncan
1969 "Family stability and occupation success." Social Problems 16:273-285.

Eberstein, Isaac and W. Parker Frisbie
1976 "Differences in marital instability among Mexican Americans, blacks and Anglos: 1960 and 1970." Social Problems 63:609-621.

Economic and Social Opportunities, Inc. (E.S.O.)
1974 "Female heads of household and poverty in Santa Clara County, San Jose, California." San Jose, California: Economic and Social Opportunities, Inc.

Foster, George
1969 "The dyadic contract. A model for the social structure of a Mexican peasant village." In Jack Potter, May Diaz, and George Foster (eds.), Peasant Society: A Reader. Boston, Massachusetts: Little, Brown and Co.

Gans, Herbert J.
1962 The Urban Villagers. New York: The Free Press.

Gilbert, M. Jean
1978 "Extended family integration among second-generation Mexican Americans." In J. Manuel Casas and Susan E. Keefe (eds.), Family and

Mental Health in the Mexican American Community. Monograph No. 7. Los Angeles, California: Spanish Speaking Mental Health, Research Center.

Grebler, Leo, Joan Moore and Ralph Guzmán
1970 The Mexican American People. New York: The Free Press.

Herzog, Elizabeth and Cecilia Sudia
1968 "Fatherless homes: a review of research." Children 15:117-182.

Horwitz, Allas
1977 "Social networks and pathways to psychiatric treatment." Social Forces 56(1):86-105.

Keefe, Susan E., Amado Padilla and Manuel Carlos
1977 "The Mexican American extended family as an emotional support system." In J. Manuel Casas and Susan E. Keefe (eds.), Family and Mental Health in the Mexican American Community. Monograph No. 7. Los Angeles, California: Spanish Speaking Mental Health, Research Center.

Kluckhohn, Florence and Fred L. Strodtbeck
1961 Variations in Value Orientations. New York: Row, Peterson and Co.

LeMasters, E. E.
1971 "Parents without partners." In Arlene S. Skolnick and Jerome Skolnick (eds.), Family in Transition. Boston, Massachusetts: Little, Brown and Co.

Lewis, Oscar
1966 "The culture of poverty." Scientific American October, 1966.

Litwak, Eugene and Irah Szelenyi
1969 "Primary group structures and their functions: kin, neighbors and friends." American Sociological Review, 34(4):465-481.

McEaddy, Beverly
1976 "Women who head families: socioeconomic analysis." Monthly Labor Review, June, 1976. Washington, D.C.: U.S. Government Printing Office.

Madsen, William
1964 The Mexican Americans of South Texas. New York: Holt, Rinehart and Winston.

Matthiasson, Carolyn J.
1974 "Coping in a new environment: Mexican Americans in Milwaukee, Wisconsin." Urban Anthropology 3:262-277.

Moynihan, Daniel
1965 The Negro Family: The Case for National Action. Washington D.C.: U.S. Government Printing Office.

Olson, Jan L.
1977 "Women and social change in a Mexican town." Journal of Anthropological Research 33(1):73-88.

Romano V., Octavio I.
1960 "Donship in a Mexican American community in Texas." American Anthropologist 62:966-977.

Ross, Heather I. and Isabel V. Sawhill
1975 Time of Transition, The Growth of Families Headed by Women. Washington D.C.: The Urban Institute.

Rubel, Arthur J.
1966 Across the Tracks. Austin, Texas: University of Texas Press.

Sanchez, Armand J. and Roland M. Wagner
1979 "Continuity and change in the Mayfair barrios of East San Jose." In San Jose Studies, San Jose State University, San Jose, California (forthcoming).

Saunders, Lyle
1954 Cultural Differences and Medical Care: The Case of the Spanish-Speaking People of the Southwest. New York: Russell Sage Foundation.

Social Planning Council and County of Santa Clara
1978 Profile '70, A Socio-Economic Data Book for Santa Clara County, San Jose, California.

Tuck, Ruth D.
1956 Not With the Fist: Mexican Americans in a Southwest City. New York: Harcourt, Brace, Jovanovich, Inc.

Uhlenberg, Peter
1972 "Demographic correlates of group achievement: contrasting patterns of Mexican Americans and Japanese Americans." Demography 9:119-12B.

U.S. Bureau of the Census
1971 Selected Characteristics of Persons and Families of Mexican, Puerto Rican, and other Spanish Origin. (Current Population Reports: Series P-20, No. 224). Washington D.C.: U.S. Government Printing Office.

U.S. Commission on Civil Rights
1974 Women and Poverty (Staff Reports, June, 1974). Washington, D.C.: U.S. Government Printing Office.

van den Berghe, P. L. and G. van den Berghe
1966 "Compadrazgo and class in Southeastern Mexico." American Anthropologist 68:1236-1244.

Chapter 13

Health and illness perceptions of the Chicana

Hector Garcia Manzanedo, Esperanza Garcia Walters, and Kate R. Lorig

> Si se alivió, fue la Virgen;
> Si se murió, fue el doctor.
>
> *Old Mexican "Dicho"*

More than 60 million people south of the border belong to a nation to which many of us can relate, either by birth or by descent. It is considered that by 1990, the Hispanic people will not be a minority but the majority in California. Every day, some hundreds of people from Mexico are crossing the border, either legally or illegally, to try to "make it" in *los Estados Unidos*. Each one of those individuals, and those whose ancestors who were here even before the American Revolution started, is the product of a cultural background that includes values, beliefs, and mores from unknown thousands of years of cultural development in indigenous populations in Middle America, three centuries of domination by Spain, and even a sprinkle of African, French, and American influence in different periods of the history of Mexico.

CULTURE AND HEALTH

What is the product of all these elements put together in what we may refer to as "the Mexican culture"? According to Foster, culture can be thought of as "the common, learned way of life shared by the members of a society, consisting of the totality of tools, techniques, social institutions, attitudes, beliefs, motivations and systems of value known to the group" (1962:11). It will be necessary, therefore, to assume that the present Chicano individual, as a member of his society, is a product of a set of environments that include the historical-social background of Mexico. Part of this background consists of ideas, beliefs, and behavioral patterns that are related more closely to those prevalent among bearers of the Mexican culture than the ones prevalent in the United States. In fact, to what extent the ideas, beliefs, and behavioral patterns prevalent in the Southwest are affected by persons of Mexican origin or descent living in this area has been the subject of study for many social scientists like Saunders (1954), Clark (1959), Madsen (1964), Rubel (1965), and Romano (1965) to mention just a few.

As part of the culture that an individual absorbs through his or her growth and development, there is a set of values and beliefs that relate to life, death, illness, and health, values and beliefs that are part of a system where many other values and beliefs related to other aspects of the culture are integrated into a whole. This is an important premise, and it has been found on numerous occasions (Foster 1952, 1962; Paul 1955; Spicer 1952) that changes in a set of values and beliefs also require changes and adjustments in other cultural aspects. For instance, trying to modify people's perceptions about mental illness may be an impossible task unless there are concomitant changes in some values and beliefs held by people with respect to what should be considered "normal" behavior (Cumming and Cumming 1955). Although concepts that are related to health and illness can be identified in the Southwest United States but can be traced to the Mexican cultural background of many persons living in the area, there may be part of a mixture of values and beliefs that also incorporate concepts and ideas of modern medicine. Even the so-called folk medicine from Mexico is in part derived from ideas prevalent during the Colonial period; these ideas were brought to Mexico from Spain as the most modern medical knowledge at the time. Many of the ideas and beliefs that prevail in traditional medicine in Mexico, such as the "hot-cold" concept of disease, were brought by the Spaniards, but their origins can be traced to the humoral theory of Greek medicine (Foster and Anderson 1978).

Not even a decade had elapsed after the fall of Mexico-Tenochtitlán and the conquest of the empire when the Indians Juan Badiano and Juan de la Cruz were recording, in Náhuatl and Latin, the vast reservoir of medicinal plants they used in their healing practices. Thus, it should not be assumed that Mexican folk medicine consists only of the practices, real or fake, of the *curanderos* and the use of a few herbal remedies. It is obvious that there are several centuries of both scientific and popular knowledge in the ideas and beliefs that Mexican people have and, by extension, are held as part of their cultural background by the Chicanas. Studies are needed in order to ascertain to what extent, and in which areas, concepts and beliefs from the Mexican heritage are still present among the Chicano population. Many of the people who came in the past from Mexico belonged to a rural, agricultural background. A rural life-style usually meant limited schooling, no physician, and more often than not a large family to offset the extremely high infant mortality rates in rural settings. Life was perceived by these people as unpredictable, scarcity or abundance determined by the whims of nature. Religion was an important part of life, since it provided the reasons for socializing, enjoyment, and conspicuous consumption during the patron saint festivities.

Tradition was the most important source of wisdom. The elderly were, and still are, especially in Indian communities, the respected leaders of opinion. Among the influential persons in rural communities, it is easy to find that the *curandero* and the *comadrona*, the healer and the traditional midwife, respectively, are holding their own, since in most cases they are the only available "health care providers." Even where physicians can be found nearby, the cost of medical care is still too high for many people to afford. Most important perhaps is the fact that while the patient and his family may communicate by means of concepts and beliefs they share with the curandero or comadrona, the same is not true in most cases for the physician. Lack of confidence, high-cost services, and inability to communicate seem to be reasons why traditional medical practices are still very much alive in rural Mexico.

Are there important differences between the urban, low-income Chicano family living in the *barrio,* and the rural Mexican family in this context? Possibly the most important one is the scarcity of traditional medicine practitioners. The high cost of medical care and the inability to communicate (even if everyone speaks English) with medical professionals may also be present in this situation.

It is impossible to make generalizations about the Chicano population, and every social scientist involved in its characteristics is aware of it. Nevertheless, it is common to find that the image of a farm worker or cannery worker who speaks only Spanish, is Catholic, mingles with his own, and whenever he needs it will seek a curandero for illness problems, is still prevalent among some members of the dominant society. At present, over 80 percent of the Spanish-surnamed population in California is urban; only a small proportion is still monolingual in Spanish (usually the elderly and the most recent immigrants), and, at least in Santa Clara Valley, they may be found now not only in canneries but in the electronics industry and county government as well. Utilization of medical personnel and hospital facilities in common, although frequently their expressions about their dissatisfaction in the way they are treated in those facilities is harsh and critical.

Important differences may be found among the Chicanas and their perceptions about health and illness. These differences may be due to the level of exposure that the Chicana may have had to the dominant culture, as well as to what her Mexican heritage has been. In analyzing these factors, materials from both the Mexicana and the Chicana will be utilized, and hopefully some concerns with respect to the adoption of cultural change will be identified. The discussion that follows will focus on the woman, either the Mexicana in central or northern Mexico or the Chicana mainly in northern California. Central and northern Mexico have been selected because they constitute the most common place of origin for migration to California. The areas to be discussed will center on the values and beliefs related to illness in the cultural realm, followed by the Chicana's position in the family, and the performance of her different roles in the social realm.

THE CULTURAL REALM

Values and beliefs concerning illness have been described by a large number of experts in the field and usually relate to concepts whose origin can be traced to Colonial era medical practices, as well as to indigenous traditions. It would be impossible to summarize those beliefs and concepts that can be found at present in Mexico. Even trying to describe concepts presently found in the Chicano population would be very difficult indeed.

What should be discussed here are the consequences of values, beliefs, and concepts in trying to seek medical care. On the one hand, it may be common to find that an extensive body of knowledge, which usually makes sense in a cultural frame of reference, is present in trying to understand the people's concerns about illness. For instance in Mexico, excess may be a reason for a number of illnesses. Excess in eating causes *empacho,* while excess in smoking, drinking alcohol, or even working, may be considered the cause of tuberculosis. Therefore, persons afflicted must seek to restore equilibrium in order to become healthy again. In the patient's perspective, the way to do it is by resolving the cause, that is, the excesses responsible for the problem in the first place. Elsewhere, in diseases like the ones just described, it is the patient's fault that he or she is sick (Foster and Anderson 1978). However, in some other instances, the person is a victim of events over which he or she has no control but nevertheless will affect his or her health. Some magical concepts associated with diseases like *"mal de ojo"* or *"males puestos"* (witchcraft) could be classified here.

Together with these, there are other factors associated with values about personal behavior. Modesty is an important concern both for the Mexicana and the Chicana seeking medical care. Sex education by the mother was never approached as a part of a young girl's training in traditional families in rural Mexico. However, important concepts related to modesty can be found even in Sahagun's treatise on the New Spain, dating back to 1534. Wearing clothing that appropriately covers the legs and bust is stressed even at present in nonurban areas. Churches in central Mexico posted signs warning visitors to dress appropriately when visiting the church until very recently.

In Guanajuato, for instance, pregnant women usually prepared for the delivery, together with medical supplies, a wide skirt that would hide genitalia from the midwife's gaze, while at the same time allowing her to maneuver and perform the delivery. This same *"enagua ampona"* was used by the parturient to catch the smoke of burning medicinal herbs considered remedies to "cure" the lower abdomen after the delivery.

To what extent are similar concerns about modesty present in California? At least for some respondents in Alameda County (García Manzanedo 1967), this was an important concern in deciding in favor of bottle-feeding instead of breast-feeding: the breasts were not exposed anymore, thereby considering bottle-feeding "cleaner" and "more comfortable." Both Clark (1959) and Cosminsky (1978) mention modesty as an important concern for Mexican American women in Sal-si Puedes and the border area, respectively.

Another aspect that may have changed recently is that of the utilization of traditional medical practitioners, *curandero* and *comadrona.* Although for many years they were the only resources to be found in rural, isolated communities in Mexico, their influence was also felt by the position they held in those communities. Being the repositories of health knowledge, people used the cultural framework they propounded to deal with illnesses. In fact, it is common that patients taken to a physician in rural Mexico will show the type of complaints usually associated with modern medicine, while the *curandero* is still catering to patients suffering from disease entities like *susto, latido, espanto,* and others that will not be found in medical textbooks, at least under those names. García Manzanedo (1978) found in northeastern Brazil that a similar situation existed, and respondents recognized some illnesses that the medical establishment (hospitals, clinics, physicians, nurses) could deal with, while others were to be treated by the local variety of *curandero,* the so-called *rezador*. However, a number of illnesses were considered of a different nature in the sense that the *farmacéutico* (drugstore person usually) could diagnose and cure.

To what extent is utilization of physicians an economic matter? Among Chicano families from Alameda County and the harbor area of Los Angeles, it is common to travel to Tijuana or Mexicali in Mexico to obtain either traditional or modern medical care at prices they can afford and in a language and cultural frame of reference they can understand (García Manzanedo 1967).

THE SOCIAL REALM

The discussion will center on some characteristic features of the woman's roles in the family and how those roles may influence the perceptions and behavior of the Chicana with respect to health and illness.

First of all, the Mexicana has been depicted in the literature as the center of the family's affections. Díaz Guerrero considers that the two most important figures in the Mexican male's world are feminine: his mother and the Virgin of Guadalupe. The Mexicana as a mother has very important specific roles in the family. For the purposes of this discussion, her role of "healer" will be discussed more in depth. Traditional knowledge is part of a woman's upbringing, and knowing which herbal tea is "hot" or "refreshing" must become one of her first tools in keeping the health and welfare of the family. As mother and wife, she is supposed to provide relief, remedies, care, and nurturing to all family members. She must be aware of the types of foods that may worsen a condition and of first aid measures to be taken. In rural as well as urban households, the woman will grow her own supply of *Manzanilla, hierbabuena, ruda, albahaca* and will keep dry bundles of other plants like *gobernadora, prodigiosa,* and *poleo* in a little basket in her kitchen. Home remedies are, possibly all over the world, the first health resource sought by anyone suffering from indigestion, a bad cold, or diarrhea.

A young respondent in Alameda County, a second-generation Mexican American, considered that a pediatrician was the first resource to be used in case of a child's abnormal symptoms, although her husband insisted on her first giving the child some herbal tea or another remedy instead of running to the doctor at the slightest raise in temperature. However, in her own view this was the appropriate behavior in American society, while her husband was still "traditional" in his regard to the child.

In many cases, mothers cannot adopt this role of "healer" because they lack the necessary knowledge or because their access to supportive others may be absent. Some respondents from Mexico who came to Alameda County sought the advice of older, more experienced local women with respect to home remedies. This advice, which would possibly be provided by their own mothers and *madrinas* in their own village, was nonexistent in California. Therefore, these young women sought an equivalent in their new surroundings, and more often than not, those older women in time became the *comadres* of the new ones.

Seeking professional medical care in Mexico is a condition that usually requires the approval of the male head of the household. Expenses to be considered, and the ways in which those expenses will be covered, should be approved by the man in the family. In rural households, sometimes women keep chickens and pigs to be fed with scraps and what little corn the family can afford to spare. Both chicken and pigs represent the woman's "savings account." Emergency funds can be obtained by selling a pig or a hen. Nevertheless, the husband-father must approve the expenses to be made.

Similarly, adoption of the sick role behavior requires the fulfillment of a number of conditions, and in the Mexican family, the decision-making process to validate a family member as ill requires the examination and adoption of a number of conditions. For the woman head of the household to adopt this role it is required that older family members, usually her mother or mother-in-law, validate this role. Responsibility for caring for her husband and children and assuming homemaker's tasks is provided by this validation, and either mother, mother-in-law, or both will share those responsibilities.

What procedures exist for a Chicana mother to resolve this problem? Is validation of the sick role still a matter of family decision making, or is it now an aspect to be decided on by the professional? Are the surrogate homemakers, mother and mother-in-law, being substituted now by persons in the health care and social services field?

Since accepted performance of the sick role behavior requires (1) validation, (2) recognition of temporal disabling conditions, (3) evidence of purpose to recover, and (4) the possibility of expressing pain or discomfort to acceptable levels (Vega and García Manzanedo 1977), each one of those conditions may have to be examined according to the particular social aspects of the family structure. For instance, validation in rural Mexico may be given by older family members or by the healer; in the Chicano family in the Southwest, a professional expert, either physician or nurse, may be required to validate the role. Recognition that the patient will be unable to fulfill her expected tasks while ill is another factor to be considered. In the Mexican family, mother and other family members will fulfill those tasks, while in the Chicano family a different system may exist to resolve this problem: neighbors, friends, or others. Evidence of the desire to make the disabling condition as short as possible may be expressed by the Mexican patient by sulking, trying to obey instructions with respect to diet, resting, and showing preoccupation about his or her condition.

A final aspect to be dealt with in the discussion of the social relationships and the health and disease perceptions of the Chicana is that of her relationships with the healing personnel, either traditional or modern. As was mentioned before, seeking professional medical care will usually require the approval of the head of the household or his counterpart in Mexico, but taking the children to the doctor or the clinic is the Chicana's responsibility. Carrying out instructions about diet, medicines, and restrictions will also be a part of her tasks. In Alameda County and among recent immigrants from Mexico, the husband would usually accompany the woman and the children to the hospital, but not necessarily to the local Child Health Conference. However, if only one car was available, the male would not work that day in order to take the family to a health facility. This behavior is different from that commonly found in Mexico, where mothers will usually visit the clinic by themselves or with their children and only occasionally their husbands will accompany them. Even in cases where the *curandero* visits the home to perform a cure, males will be outside of the house while the *curandero* performs his work. Also, helping the *comadrona* bring a baby into the world may be done by women relatives or neighbors, but it is not common for males to be present while a woman delivers a baby.

CULTURAL CHANGE

So far the discussion has been illustrated by means of examples mainly from Mexico and California. However, it is evident that cultural and socioeconomic differences are present among the Chicana population as well as the Mexican woman in her own country. One phenomenon, however, is almost always present in the woman of Mexican descent living in the Southwest and that is her part of the cultural background from Mexico. Even persons who are third and fourth generation United States citizens may still retain, in varying degrees, the concepts and ideas that are closer to their Mexican heritage. There-fore, a brief discussion about the possible processes taking place among this part of the population should be presented here.

Sociologists recognize at least three different types of processes, and it is our intent to analyze which ones can be considered appropriate to explain the Chicana's perceptions about health and illness: (1) enculturation, (2) acculturation, and (3) assimilation. In the first case, enculturation may be an ongoing process whereby the individual acquires all the values, ideas, and appropriate behaviors in his or her own culture. In the case of the Chicana, however, there may be a mixture of values, concepts, and behaviors that are being learned at home and within the family realm and a different set that is being imposed by the dominant society and its social institutions like school, primary groups, and other similar organizations. In this way, the Chicana may be subject to often contradictory messages, and her values and beliefs may be a mixture of both cultural environments, without necessarily rejecting one in favor of the other. For instance, some women in Alameda County declared that they believed in the "hot-cold" food theory principles, and they had already superimposed in this belief system some products like soda pop, vitamin pills, and others.

Acculturation differs in concept from enculturation in that the existence of two groups, one in a dominant relationship over the other, implies that interaction taking place between them results in the mutual adoption, as well as rejection, of each other's values, beliefs, and behavioral patterns. As explained by sociologists, this process does not necessarily require that the less powerful group adopt those aspects from the dominant one; in fact, the contrary has often been the case. Witness the immediate adoption by the Spanish conquistadores of *tortillas* and other foodstuffs in Mexico or the potato in South America.

The concept of assimilation does not stress relationships of submission-dominance, but rather a "melting" into the host society, something similar to a process of full adoption of all characteristics, values, and behavioral patterns of the society where the immigrant group comes to live. These three processes have been juggled in different ways to explain the relative enculturation, acculturation, or even assimilation of different minority groups. It is evident that, at least for the Chicano families, none of these processes seems to be fully descriptive of the dynamics of the adoption, rejection, or persistence of specific types of values, beliefs, and behavioral patterns. On the one hand, Chicano families show varying degrees of acculturation to the American way of life, while at the same time retaining some of their own traditional Mexican ways. It would be almost impossible, however, to assert that the Chicano population is the product of the assimilation of Mexican individuals to the United States as a dominant society.

For the purposes of this paper, then, the Chicana is the dual product of a traditional Mexican value and belief system, while at the same time she practices behavioral patterns and holds specific ideas and types of knowledge that are mostly found in the dominant (Anglo) population. The culture change process implies the existence, side by side, of elements in her own environment that belong to both the Mexican and the American life styles, value systems, and knowledge bases.

Given these factors, how does the Chicana behave with respect to medical and health care programs and activities? In what ways are her values and beliefs interfering with her health and that of her family? What types of concerns must be addressed by the health planners involved in the provision of health services to the population?

A survey conducted among Chicanas in 1977, in Santa Clara County, may help throw some light on these questions.

HEALTH BEHAVIOR AND VALUES SURVEY
Overview

Whereas generalizations and stereotypes about Chicanas should not be made, health professionals are also in a position of having to provide the community with programs in a culturally sensitive manner. It is for this reason that providers need to determine the prevalent attitudes, values, and behaviors of the community they serve.

In 1972, the authors conducted a survey of the values and behaviors of Chicana women in Santa Clara County with respect to health and cancer. The results of the survey were to serve as a basis for the development of cancer education programs. Following are the results of the survey. However, first an overview of the county should be provided in order to give the reader a glimpse of the area.

Santa Clara County lies approximately 40 miles south of San Francisco. In 1977, it had a population of over 1.2 million and according to the 1970 census over 17 percent of the population was Spanish surnamed and Spanish speaking. There are no indications that this percent is decreasing. Instead, it is more likely to be higher as immigration into California from Mexico increases. Until the 1950s, the area was largely rural and most Chicanos were employed in agriculturally related jobs. However, since then the area has experienced a marked change. Most of the area except for the southern county is urbanized and is commonly known as Silicon Valley. The electronics industry is the largest employer, employing over 26 percent of the county's labor force. Ethnic minorities, especially women, comprise a large number of those working as assemblers.

The survey of 376 women was conducted in the summer of 1977 and concentrated in areas of Santa Clara County with a high percent of Spanish-speaking, Spanish-surnamed residents. Data from the 1970 census were the basis for the selection of the areas.

Findings

The survey findings revealed that age and place of birth had a significant bearing on the preference and behaviors of Spanish-speaking, Spanish-surnamed women interviewed. Whether a woman practiced BSE (breast self-examination) or had ever had a Pap smear test was influenced more by her age than by her place of birth. However, her preference as to the sex and ethnicity of physicians was influenced more by her place of birth than by her age (see Figs. 8 and 9).

Sixty-seven percent of the women born in Mexico preferred a female physician to a male if they were given the choice. Only 7 percent preferred a male physician, and 26 percent had no preference. The preference for a female may be attributed to a woman's values for modesty and communication with other women.

Fifty-seven percent of the women born in Texas also preferred a female physician, but the percentage preferring a male physician or having no preference increased to 14 and 29

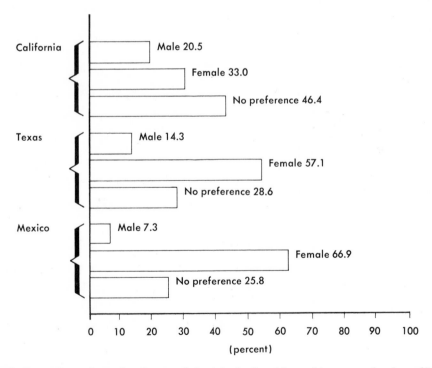

Fig. 8. Comparison of sexual preference of physician by Spanish-speaking women by place of birth, Santa Clara County, 1977.

percent, respectively. The most unexpected results were from the group of women born in California: 33 percent preferred a female physician, 20 percent preferred a male physician, and 46 percent had no preference. Fifteen percent of the total sample chose a male physician, and in that case, the most common reason stated was that respondents perceived him as being more intelligent, truthful, and/or trustworthy. Women who stated their preference for a female physician felt they would be more free to discuss their problems with another woman.

A similar trend to that of sexual preference was evident with respect to the ethnic background of physicians. Women born in Mexico overwhelmingly preferred a Spanish-surnamed physician to an Anglo physician, 78 percent as compared to less than 1 percent for an Anglo physician and 21 percent with no preference. The proportions for women born in California were: 53 percent had no preference, 40 percent preferred a Latino physician, and 7 percent preferred an Anglo physician. The proportions for the Texas-born women fell between those born in Mexico and those born in California.

For the total sample, the Latino physician was preferred by more than half (54.5 percent). The women felt they could communicate better with him/her, whereas the Anglo physician was preferred by only 4.5 percent of the respondents who felt she/he was more efficient, had more contacts, and could explain better in English. However, the rest (41

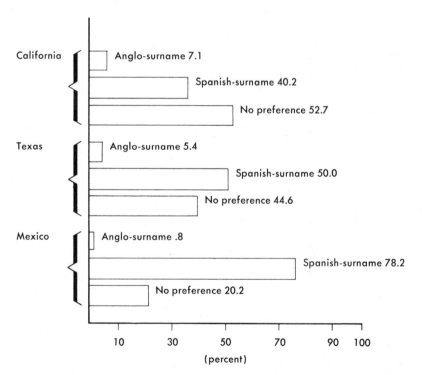

Fig. 9. Comparison of ethnic preference of physicians by Spanish-speaking women by place of birth, Santa Clara County, 1977.

percent) had no preference because they considered both to have equal training, or they could communicate in English.

Age proved to be a factor in determining a woman's knowledge and her practice of breast self-examination. Sixty-eight percent of all the women stated they knew how to examine their breasts, and of those only 53 percent practiced it monthly. The practice of monthly BSE started increasing markedly in the 36 to 40 year age group and peaked at 81 percent at the 46 to 50 year age group, then a sharp decrease occurred. In the older age group (56 years and more), the practice of monthly BSE dropped to 40 percent.

The data for women having had Pap smear tests shows no definite pattern associated with the age groups. For instance, persons in the younger and older age groups had the lowest percentages of those who have had Pap smear tests, whereas the 36 to 40 year age group had the highest percentage (95 percent).

It has long been recognized that, in Spanish-speaking communities, alternative health resources are utilized, including *curanderos* (traditional folk healers), chiropractors, herbalists, spiritualists, and pharmacists. The women interviewed were asked which of these they had utilized in the past to treat an illness for themselves or family members. After their responses were recorded, they were asked to rank each resource according to the level of trust they attributed to each (see Tables 13-1 and 13-2). Two interesting facts were revealed: (1) high utilization and trust of pharmacists, and (2) lower than expected utilization and trust of *curanderos*.

Table 13-1. Utilization of alternative health resources by Latina women in Santa Clara County, 1977 (n = 376)

Resource	Yes (%)	No (%)	No answer (%)
Pharmacist	78.2	21.5	0.3
Chiropractor	28.5	70.7	0.8
Herbalist	21.8	76.6	1.6
Curandero	10.9	87.0	2.1
Spiritualist	5.1	93.6	1.3

Table 13-2. Number of Latina women utilizing selected health resources by level of trust; Santa Clara County, 1977 (n = 376)

Level of trust*	Alternative health resources				
	Pharmacist	Chiropractor	Herbalist	Curandero	Spiritualist
1	160	39	27	21	3
2	75	59	75	32	7
3	25	21	49	48	20

*1 = very high trust, 2 = high trust, and 3 = trust. The fourth and fifth levels of trust have not been included as they represent lower levels of trust.

In addition to the alternative health resources utilized, the project was interested in determining whether a woman would discuss an illness with her husband. Seventy-three percent of the women responded they would tell their husbands about any problems with their breasts or sexual organs. However, in trying to ascertain the reasons for this behavior, most women responded only, "because he is my husband."

This study has several implications for health care providers in both improving effectiveness of service and getting the most health care for dollar spent.

It seems obvious that if the target of any medical program is the Chicana/Latina, the program will be most effective with a Spanish-speaking female physician. However, lacking the ability to find such a person, a female physician would be second choice and the final choice would be a male non-Spanish–speaking physician. Data are not available on the preference between female non-Spanish–speaking and male Spanish-speaking physicians. However, since many Latina women also speak some English, it is felt that a female non-Spanish–speaking physician might be an acceptable alternative.

A second implication of this study is that, when working with Spanish-speaking women, it is important to consider their husbands/partners. More than 73 percent of the women indicated that they would share serious health problems and decisions with their husbands. In order to make such decisions less traumatic and more positive, health care providers should consider including both husband and wife in information and counseling sessions.

It has long been thought that Spanish-speaking people depended heavily for health care on the alternative health care system offered by *curanderos, brujas,* and other types of folk healers. Furthermore, it has been believed that this system was nearly impossible for Anglo health professionals to penetrate. In the past, attempts have been made to explain this system to health professionals, but little has been done to utilize this knowledge in a systematic way.

Also, the survey demonstrated clearly that, for the population interviewed, *curanderos* and similar folk healers are neither highly utilized nor highly trusted. In contrast, it was found that 78 percent of the women chose pharmacies as their entry point into the health care system. Traditionally, pharmacists have been regarded as having a minor role in health education. However, if in fact they are the first point of contact—and often the only point—of entry into the health care system, they and other professionals need to become aware of this health education role.

Further, what was found by our study was that 48 percent of the women interviewed did not practice self-breast examinations, although they knew about the technique and how to practice it. Based on this finding, it is important that health education programs do an evaluation of the knowledge/practice discrepancy in the target population when planning a program. If in fact the knowledge level is low, then the first step in a program should be directed toward increasing this level. However, as was the case in our study, the level of knowledge is relatively high, but the practice level is somewhat low. Further investigation must be done to ascertain reasons for this apparent discrepancy, then a program should be designed to modify this discrepancy.

HEALTH PROGRAMS AND THE CHICANA

As has been pointed out, the Chicana has always had a role in the health and economics of her family and to some extent of her community. However, this has always been in the cultural context that was transported mainly from rural Mexico. The question remains how does she become involved in the preventive health programs prevalent in the United States?

This is a two-edged coin. On one side, many agencies have never made the attempt to obtain Chicana participation. It has always been easy to say that Spanish-speaking women would not participate in certain programs because it was contrary to their cultural norms. This has often been stated for such programs as breast self-examination and Pap smear screening. In fact, since agencies believed that such programs would fail when directed to Spanish-speaking women, they made little or no effort, and even when efforts were made, they became self-fulfilling prophecies.

A change in the revolving door of noninvolvement began in the early 1960s with the Office of Economic Opportunities Neighborhood Health Center movement. Legislation mandated that Chicanas and other minorities from the neighborhood be employed at the centers. Typically they were employed as neighborhood aids, family health workers, laboratory assistants, and in other health-related positions. At the same time, most of the health professionals at these health centers were young idealistic "Kennedy Kids" who had not yet formed their ideas of what could and could not be done successfully.

In California as in other places in the country, the time was right to try new approaches to community health. Assisting in this movement were various community colleges that set up special educational programs and eased entrance requirements. These programs were often linked with some service providers such as neighborhood health centers, mental health centers, and Head Start programs. As a result, for the first time a large number of Chicanas had the opportunity to work in the health agencies and private voluntary agencies.

These new approaches brought about more permanent changes in the system. Plans are no longer made without consideration of the Chicano community; Chicanas can now be treated by Chicana nurse practitioners and even in a few cases by Chicana physicians. The role models for minority females in the health care system are no longer only the cleaning women. At present, community workers, physicians, nurses, dental hygienists, and a whole cadre of other health professionals are of minority descent.

Despite the strides that have recently been made, the fact still remains that the Chicana appears largely outside of the American health care system.

Everett Rogers (1971) has done extensive research, based on the work of Beal and Bohlen (1957), on the diffusion process. This is a strategy for getting new practices and/or information spread through a broad population. This strategy was used by the Special Populations Committee of the American Cancer Society in Santa Clara County, California, in their attempt to get Chicanas to practice breast self-examination. The diffusion process as adapted by the committee involves five steps.

Diffusion process

Awareness. In the awareness phase, the population becomes aware that a new behavior or product exists. This is usually accomplished by the mass media. In the case of Chicanas, television and radio are probably the means by which they become aware of a new product or practice. Unfortunately, there is a tendency on the part of health professionals to believe that awareness assures the adoption of practice. As mentioned previously, in Santa Clara County, the majority of Chicanas who came to breast self-examination classes indicated that they already were aware of the need to examine their breasts. However, less than a third indicated that they were actually practicing breast self-examination. Various health campaigns that used mass media to increase awareness found that media were almost useless in the Chicana community to obtain active participation in health-related activities. However, this should not be discounted. It can be used to raise awareness.

Interest. The practice, program, or product is tried by the innovators in the community. These are the persons who will always try anything new and to some extent establish their reputation based on being first. It should be noted, however, that innovators are not usually community leaders. This distinction is important because if innovators are recruited to disseminate a program, it may fail since the community may view these people as being on the far fringe and thus may be hesitant to follow their lead.

Opinion leader. There is one segment of the population that does tend to follow the lead of the innovators. These are people to whom others in the community come for advice, therefore, the label of "opinion leaders." A person may be an opinion leader in one or several fields. Thus, one might be influenced by one neighbor's politics, by another on where to get medical care, and by a third on her opinion of a new detergent.

These opinion leaders are the key to getting a new idea spread throughout a community. This is especially true of communities that tend to be insular and to depend on friendship and trust for support in the activities of daily living. Thus, the identification of opinion leaders is a key to getting the Chicana involved in health programs. These are the persons who santion, in an informal but powerful way, the participation of others in the community.

In the identification of opinion leaders, there is one caution. Merton (1968) has identified two different types of opinion leaders. The first he designates as "local influentials." Those are leaders who perceive themselves in light of the local community only. They are concerned with knowing as many people as possible and tend to join groups as a means of extending their personal relationships. On the other hand, there are "cosmopolitan influentials," those who see themselves in the light of the greater society. They are concerned with the quality of their relationships and tend to join organizations because of their activities.

In gaining the participation of the grass roots Chicana, it is important to identify local influentials, as they are the ones who can effectively spread the word through the population. The cosmopolitan influentials are much more effective serving on committees and participating in program planning. They tend to be effective as consumers on boards composed of consumers and providers of health care.

Trial. The fourth step in the diffusion process is that of giving the population a chance to try the service or practice. In health care, this is very important, since to a great extent the trial will determine if the practice is continued or rejected. Thus, in urging women to go to a clinic, examine their breasts, or change the food habits of their families, it is important that the service or product be provided in a manner that is both acceptable and accessible. For example, community clinics will not be utilized if the staff is seen as hostile and unaccepting of cultural patterns of the community.

Adoption. At this point, the program has been tried and the women decide to continue with the practice. This step becomes instrumental in decisions of others in the community. Success builds on success.

The program or health practice that has been accepted will need to be reinforced. It is important that the reinforcement not only be planned into the program but also be as personal as possible.

Consciousness raising

A second approach to gaining involvement in health care might be suggested by Freire (1970). In *Pedagogy of the Oppressed,* he outlines a system in consciousness raising in which people become aware of the problems in their community, identify the causes of these problems, and then make decisions about how to overcome the problems. This whole process as seen by Freire is very political and calls for challenging the political and/or other established systems.

In the health field, this approach has been used successfully in setting up shelters for battered women. People are helped to recognize their problems and to act on their own behalf to solve them. While this can be a very successful method it must be used with caution for at least two reasons.

First, it is relatively easy for any charismatic person to raise the consciousness and political awareness of the community and then to manipulate that community to any ends. Therefore, the community in the process of organization must be fully aware of both the benefits and pitfalls of increased activity. While this is a corruption of the Freire ideal, it is a potential danger.

A second issue with the philosophy of Freire is the identification of a common tendency in health organizations to lame the victim. Ryan gives the example of mothers being taught to prevent their children from eating paint because of the danger of lead poisoning. The health establishment, however, blames the lead poisoning on the mother rather than on the landlord. This same logic can be applied to the national campaign to cut down on cigarette smoking while at the same time tobacco companies are being paid to grow tobacco.

CONCLUSIONS

In concluding, it is well to mention several factors that have been shown to make a difference in getting Chicanas and others to participate in health care programs and practices.

1. Programs should meet the health care needs expressed by the community. The only

way that this can be done is by the use of a needs assessment, either a survey or other similar tool to identify needs. Unfortunately, because most health care funding is categorical, it is almost always impossible to take this approach. However, if no resources are available for a formal survey, the next best step is to ask the community what their needs and priorities are within the confines of the program. Thus, a program aimed at cancer screening may find that the needs are for transportation, babysitting, or classes given in people's homes.

2. Programs should involve community members and their participation should be sought in planning, development, and implementation. Too often, community participation is tokenism mandated by the funding source.

3. Programs should be part of the participant's life and not separate from it. People should not have to go out of their way or life experiences to participate in health care programs. This is especially true of education and prevention programs.

4. Programs should, whenever possible, utilize community members as providers. Community health workers can also carry out a variety of health screening procedures such as blood pressure screening and glaucoma screening.

5. The standards to evaluate the success of a program should be set by the community. These standards are often based on the experience in the Anglo community. Such standards for long-established programs for the predominant culture may not be valid for new programs for a "hard to reach" minority. The only way to evaluate programs for Chicana women is by using standards set in conjunction with Chicanas themselves.

REFERENCES

Beal, G. and Bohlen Jr.
1957 The Diffusion Process. Special Report No. 18. Ames, Iowa: Agricultural Extension Service, Iowa State College.

Clark, Margaret
1959 Health in the Mexican American Culture. Berkeley and Los Angeles, California: University of California Press.

Cosmonsky, Cheila
1978 "Midwifery and medical anthropology." Pp. 116-126 in Boris Velimirovic (ed.), Modern Medicine and Medical Anthropology in the United States–Mexico Border Population. Washington, D.C.: Pan American Health Organization.

Cumming, John and Elaine Cumming
1955 "Mental health education in a Canadian community. Pp. 43-69 in B. Paul (ed.), Health, Culture and Community. New York: Russell Sage Foundation.

Foster, George M.
1952 Problemas en los Programas Sanitarios Interculturales. Mexico: Instituto Nacional Indigenista.
1962 Traditional Cultures: and the Impact of Technological Change. New York: Harper & Row, Publishers.

Foster, George M. and Barbara G. Anderson
1978 Medical Anthropology. New York: John Wiley & Sons, Inc.

Freire, Paulo
1970 Pedagogy of the Oppressed. New York: The Seabury Press.

García Manzanedo, Héctor
1967 "Mother, child, and culture: selected problems in maternal and child health in a Mexican-American population. Unpublished doctoral dissertation. University of California School of Public Health, Berkeley, California.
1978 "Estudio sociocultural sobre integración de los sistemas de salud y participación de la comunidad." Boletín de la Oficina Sanitaria Panamericana LXXXIV (3), Marzo.

Madsen, William
1964 The Mexican Americans of South Texas. New York: Holt, Rinehart & Winston.

Merton, K.
1968 Social Theory and Social Structures. New York: The Free Press.

Paul, Benjamin D. (ed.)
1955 Health, Culture and Community: Case Studies of Public Reactions to Health Programs. New York: Russell Sage Foundation.

Rogers, Everett M.
1971 Communication of Innovations: A Cross-Cultural Approach. New York: The Free Press.

Romano, Octavio I.
1965 "Charismatic medicine, folk healing and folk sainthood." American Anthropologist 67:1151-1173, October.

Rubel, Arthur J.
1965 "Understanding the domestic agricultural migrant of Mexican and Spanish descent: his cultural heritage, perception of health problems, and means of meeting health needs. Working Conference on Evaluation of Health Education Materials for Domestic Agricultural Workers of Mexican and Spanish Descent. Ann Arbor, Michigan, March.

Ryan, William
1976 Blaming the Victim. New York: Vintage Books.

Sahagún, Fr. Bernardino de
1947 Historia de las Cosas de la Nueva España. México, D.F.: Editorial Ateneo.

Saunders, Lyle
1954 Cultural Difference and Medical Care, the Case of the Spanish-speaking People of the Southwest. New York: Russell Sage Foundation.

Spicer, Edward
1952 Human Problems in Technological Change. New York: Russell Sage Foundation.

Vega, Leopoldo, y Héctor García Manzanedo.
1977 "Bases Esenciales de la Salud Pública. México, D.F.: Prensa Médica Mexicana.

Chapter 14

The status of Hispanic women in nursing

Anita L. Alvarado

The data included in this paper represent a segment of a larger longitudinal study of the statuses and trends of minorities in the health professions, specifically medicine, nursing, pharmacy, and veterinary medicine. Nursing was selected because (1) it is a traditionally a feminine occupation, thereby eliminating considerations of bias on the basis of sex; (2) it has long been recognized as a vehicle for upward mobility for women from lower socioeconomic strata; and (3) it has been under considerable pressure from activist ethnic nurses to increase proportional representation in the profession in order to correct a long-standing imbalance as well as to provide culturally relevant health care for ethnic minority populations. The focus of this paper is the examination of the status of Hispanic women in nursing as well as the potential of this group for mobility within the profession as compared to other minorities and to nonminority women. The significance of the results of the first stage of this study lies in the fact that while absolute numbers of minority students in nursing are increasing, the assumption of many elites and educators that trends toward improved ethnic balance are occurring is seriously challenged when proportional representation is examined. What appears to be happening is that numbers of nonminorities are entering the profession at a higher rate than that of minorities. Thus, the optimism of those who foresee a slow gradual increase in the percentages of ethnic minorities (U.S. Department of Health, Education, and Welfare 1974a) seems to be premature at present and into the foreseeable future.

Table 14-1 shows a very conservative comparison of selected ethnic minorities and their proportions in relation to the general population. It is conservative in that it is based on the 1970 decennial census in which it is recognized that the proportions of minorities in the population are cited as lower than in reality because of underenumeration. At the same time, the American Nurses' Association has recognized a 20 percent overcount of professional nurses because of nurses' aides and others representing themselves as registered nurses to census takers. Estimates by the Division of Nursing of the Department of Health, Education, and Welfare that are based on data collected by Knopf (1972) and reports by the National League for Nursing (U.S. Department of Health, Education, and Welfare 1974b) reduce the percentage of blacks from 7.5 percent to 5 percent. Unfortunately, there are no comparable figures for Hispanics. However, even if no overcount is assumed for this population, they still comprise less than half of their alleged 5 percent of the total American population. Again, it should be noted that Hispanics are among those groups that the Bureau of the Census recognizes as greatly underenumerated in the general population. A comparison of Hispanics with other ethnic minorities reveals that they are the most proportionately underrepresented group. Interestingly, Asians are overrepresented. This is most likely an artifact of high immigration rates for Filipino nurses. This group comprises 0.8 percent of all registered nurses but only 0.2 percent of the general population. Thus, it is clear the Filipino nurses account for most of the Asian group.

Inasmuch as the data in Table 14-1 represent the cumulative effects of phenomena in past decades, it is necessary to examine data gathered in the 1970s to get a sense of future trends. In order to ascertain which groups are entering the profession, it is most relevant to look at newly licensed nurses who are actually entering the profession. Table 14-2 summarizes the results of Nash's study (1974) of graduates in the early 1970s and is broken down by type of educational program. This is important because graduates of Associate Degree programs and diploma programs are considered undereducated in professional nursing. It is projected that by 1985, the level of entry into the profession will be a baccalaureate degree. At present, a graduate of any of the three programs may take the state boards for nursing. If the graduate passes, he/she is then a registered nurse who may practice professional nursing in any state in which the individual is registered. There are means by which a registered nurse may have reciprocity to obtain a license to practice in another state without further examination, but this is not automatic.

Table 14-2 demonstrates that Hispanics at this time are being educated and graduated at the Associate Degree level only. It is clear that the proportional representation of the group has fallen precipitously, a drop to one fifth of the proportion of the population ratio in Table 14-1. Considering the original underenumeration of the group and the rapidly rising population of Hispanics, the real figures are even more disproportionate. There could therefore be little expectation that nurses educated at the Associate Degree level

Table 14-1. Selected groups, 1970 decennial census

Group	Registered nurses (%)	U.S. population (%)
Hispanics	2.1	5.0
Female	2.0	
Male	0.1	
American Indians	0.2	0.4
Blacks	7.5	11.1
Asians	1.2	0.7
Whites	89.0	82.8
All females	97.3	
All males	2.7	

Table 14-2. Newly licensed graduates

Group	Licensees (%)
Diploma programs (n = 1956)	
Hispanics	0.0
American Indians	1.0
Blacks	2.0
Asians	0.0
Whites	97.0
All females	97.0
All males	3.0
Associate programs (n = 1650)	
Hispanics	1.0
American Indians	1.0
Blacks	6.0
Asians	1.0
Whites	91.0
All females	95.0
All males	5.0
Baccalaureate programs (n = 1150)	
Hispanics	0.0
American Indians	1.0
Blacks	2.0
Asians	1.0
Whites	96.0
All females	98.0
All males	2.0

From Nash 1974.

would be invited to assume positions in decision-making statuses without further education.

Of the other ethnic minority groups, only the American Indians have made gains. Thus, a continuing trend of underrepresentation and undereducation for ethnic minority groups is evident. As a result, the chances for advancement within the profession as well as access to educational and decision-making roles are consequently much lower than their considerably low proportional representation would indicate. There is therefore very low probability for upward mobility within the profession. It should also be noted that males are moving into the profession at a much higher rate than are Hispanics of both sexes at all educational levels. Interestingly, they are educated at primarily lower levels, a characteristic shared with the ethnic minorities.

Table 14-3 shows the totals of newly licensed nurses together with gain or loss for each group. Hispanics show the greatest loss, followed closely by blacks.

The figures on new graduates from practical nursing indicate a higher percentage of ethnic minorities than professional nursing, but this field is also following the general trend toward underrepresentation. Again, males are making a greater demographic impact than Hispanics (see Table 14-4).

In order to evaluate trends for the late 1970s, it is necessary to consider data on admissions to the various types of programs for the academic year 1971-1972 (U.S. Department of Health, Education, and Welfare 1974b). These data show that admissions generally fall considerably below the percentages necessary to achieve proportional representation in the schools (see Table 14-5).

Hispanics fail to reach an average proportionate to their population at all levels and fall below the proportion of registered nurses for the 1970 census. Thus, they continue to lose ground even in terms of admissions. In programs of practical nursing, admission figures confirm a trend toward underrepresentation in this field as well (see Table 14-6).

It would be instructive if recent rates of withdrawals and reasons for withdrawals were available. Knopf (1972) used data from 1962 and constructed categories for whites, blacks, and "others." Her findings are presented in Table 14-7. Withdrawal rates are quite different for the respective groups in the baccalaureate and diploma programs, the baccalaureate programs losing a higher percentage of students except in the category of "others," which nevertheless remains high. In the diploma programs, however, "others" have the highest withdrawal rate.

Reasons that Directors of Nursing gave for students' withdrawals from baccalaureate programs were heavily weighted in terms of scholastic disabilities and unsuitability for nursing in the case of ethnic minority groups (Knopf 1972) (see Table 14-8). While some of the problems involved in scholastic withdrawal may be traced to inadequate secondary school systems in ethnic minority neighborhoods, it is striking that one fifth of whites were said to have withdrawn for scholastic reasons, while three fifths of the others withdrew for the same reason. At the same time, the directors of baccalaureate programs found a considerably higher percentage of nonwhites "unsuitable for nursing."

Compared to directors of baccalaureate programs, directors of diploma programs gave slightly higher percentages of blacks as failing in scholastic and suitability characteristics but rated whites much higher in terms of scholastic disabilities as well as unsuitability for nursing. "Others" were rated higher on scholastic disabilities but lower on lack of suitability for nursing. Thus, in the case of diploma programs, we find whites withdrawing, according to their directors, in much higher percentages for scholastic reasons and unsuitability for nursing, while figures for nonwhites remain high in both categories. This indicates that nonwhite students seem to have the same handicaps in both types of programs and/or are perceived with the same biases by directors who are likely to be highly instrumental in shaping the students' decisions to withdraw. White students, however, are perceived differently by the directors of the two types of programs. The data would seem to indicate that white students entering diploma schools either have different scholastic and personal capabilities than those who enter baccalaureate programs or that a relatively high percentage of them are perceived differently by the directors. There is indeed data that indicate that the diploma students' parents come from lower social status

Table 14-3. Total percent of new licensees (gain/loss)

Group	Licensees (%)
Hispanics	0.3 (−1.8)
American Indians	1.0 (+0.8)
Blacks	3.3 (−1.7 from corrected figure of 5)
Asians	0.7 (−0.5)
Whites	94.7 (+5.7)
All males	3.3 (+0.6)

Adapted from Nash 1974.

Table 14-4. New graduates, practical nursing programs by percentages

Group	Graduates (%)
Hispanics	2.0
American Indians	2.0
Blacks	9.0
Asians	0.0
Whites	87.0
All females	96.0
All males	4.0

From Nash 1974.

Table 14-5. Admissions for academic year 1971-1972

Group	Admissions (%)
Hispanics	
Baccalaureate programs	2.4
Diploma programs	0.6
Associate programs	2.8
Average	1.9
Blacks	
Baccalaureate programs	8.8
Diploma programs	3.8
Associate programs	9.6
Average	7.4
Asians and American Indians	
Baccalaureate programs	1.6
Diploma programs	0.4
Associate programs	1.0
Average	1.0

From U.S. Department of Health, Education, and Welfare 1974b.

Table 14-6. Admission figures, practical nursing programs by percentages

Group	Admission (%)
Hispanics	3.2
Blacks	13.8
Asians and American Indians	1.1

From U.S. Department of Health, Education, and Welfare 1974b.

Table 14-7. Withdrawal rates for 1962

Group	Withdrawals from programs (%)
Blacks	
Baccalaureate programs	70.2
Diploma programs	40.9
Whites	
Baccalaureate programs	48.6
Diploma programs	31.7
Others	
Baccalaureate programs	41.7
Diploma programs	52.6

From Knopf 1972.

and educational levels than do those of the baccalaureate students (Knopf 1972). Because these data are not broken down by ethnicity within the white population, there is no clue as to whether these students may come from white ethnic groups. Given the fact that Hispanics were often included previously in "white" categories or alternately put in "other," these differences may have significance for understanding the data. It would certainly be enlightening to learn whether white withdrawals are more common among those students who come from white ethnic groups and/or culturally distinctive groups. This points up the necessity of gathering complete data, a task whose difficulty is sometimes compounded by the reluctance and even outright vocal opposition of some Hispanic individuals to being classified as other than "white."

All of the data presented unequivocally demonstrate that the status of Hispanics in nursing is extremely poor in terms of proportional representation and chances for upward mobility within the profession. The trends in the foreseeable future are even more dismal as proportions drop drastically among those entering the profession. No hopeful view can be gleaned from recent admission statistics if dropout rates continue to soar at 50 percent or above. The proposed level of entry in the profession with a terminal degree at the baccalaureate level will cut even deeper. The Associate Degrees are often granted in community colleges, with their flexibility of scholastic program and nearness to home as well as their often relatively low financial costs, and will undoubtedly continue to attract ethnic minority women in general and Hispanic women in particular. The graduates of

Table 14-8. Reasons for withdrawals given by directors by percentages

Group	Withdrawal from programs (%)
Blacks	
Baccalaureate programs	
Scholastic reasons	63.9
Unsuited for nursing	3.7
Other	32.4
Diploma programs	
Scholastic reasons	67.2
Unsuited for nursing	4.7
Other	28.1
Whites	
Baccalaureate programs	
Scholastic reasons	20.5
Unsuited for nursing	2.2
Other	77.3
Diploma programs	
Scholastic reasons	37.4
Unsuited for nursing	6.6
Other	56.0
Others	
Baccalaureate programs	
Scholastic reasons	64.3
Unsuited for nursing	7.1
Other	28.6
Diploma programs	
Scholastic reasons	70.7
Unsuited for nursing	4.9
Other	24.4

From Knopf 1972.

these programs have been found to be much more likely to be married and have young children under the age of 6 (Nash 1974). Expectations that young women will marry and have children early are not uncommon. Another effect is likely to be the significant reduction of the rate of entry for males.

The fact that most of the nursing school dropouts come from ethnic minority groups underscores the need for research and action in this particular area. Knopf (1972) issues a stinging indictment of nursing education when she asserts that there is generally a lack of evidence concerning a conscientious and consistent effort to stem the failure rate of nursing students. On the other hand, in one instance with which I am familiar, such an effort has indeed been made at the baccalaureate level through the employment of minority faculty, recruiters, and counselors over a considerable time span. The result has been a shrinking of the minority dropout rate to match that of the nonminority population. The program, however, is funded on ''soft'' money that is running out. It remains to be seen whether the university that houses the program will pick it up. At the same time, the discouragement of the major funding agencies that have frequently been the backbone (and sometimes the only bone) of support for such programs is understandable when the institution funded is unwilling to pick up part or all of an already developed and proven enterprise. As a result, this resource may be significantly reduced or eliminated.

Clearly the admission data indicate that many Hispanics aspire to become nurses. Presumably ethnic minorities in general are admitted with the same credentials and expectations of successful completion by selection committees as are nonminorities. Research is needed to ascertain the reasons why these expectations are so poorly fulfilled in the case of ethnic minorities as compared to nonminorities. Even the latter have very high withdrawal rates, indicating an enormous waste of human and economic resources in the schools. There is a need to compare selection and retention programs in nursing with those of the other health professions, which preliminary research indicates may be lower in attrition. At the same time, a similar phenomenon to that which affected women in medicine in the past may be striking nursing as a profession. For example, with the disappearance of women's hospitals, wards, and clinics concomitant with the rise in acceptability of treatment of women by male physicians together with the reduction in segregation of women, the percentage of women physicians in Boston dropped from a peak of 18.2 percent in 1900 to 9.7 percent in 1920, then to a nadir of 5.8 percent in 1960 (Walsh 1977). Thus, the thrust toward integration of ethnic minorities may have had the effect of reducing or eliminating the number of programs that educated them exclusively, while at the same time ethnic aspirants were forced to compete for relatively scarce seats in the dominant society institutions, as well as having to learn to inspire trust and security in a general population that had little familiarity with them and a great deal of historically derived prejudice against them.

Certainly the heady days of the decline of ethnic nurses' associations in response to the expectation of integration of personnel and health care interests are gone forever. Ethnic nurses are either instituting or reestablishing ethnic nurses' associations whose goals are the raising of the levels of health and health care provision for their respective populations, and they are pushing very actively toward the establishment of effective affirmative action. The National Association of Hispanic Nurses is one of these organizations, representing the interests of nurses and clients of the culturally diverse Hispanic ethnic groups in the United States.

Nursing is perhaps the most dynamic of the health professions, rapidly expanding its roles in an effort to provide better health care for all populations including the traditionally excluded. It is unlikely to be as successful as it could be in a culturally pluralistic society unless sufficient numbers of professionals are educated who understand both nursing and the culturally distinctive ethnic populations it attempts to serve. The relatively small proportions and necessarily superficial cross-cultural education modules that are now being increasingly developed to make students more culturally aware of the needs of their patients cannot be considered as a total solution. This chapter is intended to bring into perspective the very real problems of declining proportional representation and declining prospects for future trends of entry and upward mobility of Hispanics in the profession.

REFERENCES

Knopf, L.
1972 From Student to RN. Report of the Nurse Career-Pattern Study. Washington, D.C.: U.S. Government Printing Office.

Nash, P.
1974 Evaluation of Employment Opportunities For Newly Licensed Nurses. Washington, D.C.: U.S. Government Printing Office.

U.S. Department of Health, Education, and Welfare
1974a Minorities and Women in the Health Fields. Washington, D.C.: U.S. Government Printing Office.
1974b Source Book. Nursing Personnel. Washington, D.C.: U.S. Government Printing Office.

Walsh, M. R.
1977 Doctors Wanted: No Women Need to Apply. New Haven, Connecticut: Yale University Press.

Chapter 15

Feminism: The Chicana and Anglo versions

A historical analysis

Marta Cotera

The relationship of the Chicana to the women's movement, including the suffrage movement in the United States, has been marked by complex factors affecting the development of both groups from 1848 to the present.

There is evidence that a relationship between Chicanas and the women's movement has existed at least for the past 80 years. There is evidence, too, that this relationship has been affected by the same factors affecting women's interaction with black women, white ethnic women, and working-class women because the Chicana is a minority woman and is considered an immigrant. In addition, a great percentage of Chicanas are in the working-class at the lowest occupational scale.

Chicanas' involvement with the women's movement in the 1890 to 1920 period was limited by the barriers that impeded all women with similar backgrounds: the antilabor, antiminority attitudes of the leadership of the women's movement. They were affected also by the antisocialist and anticommunist attitudes of the movement in the early twentieth century, since many Chicana workers and leaders were ardent socialists.

The greatest victory for the women's movement was no victory for minority women. The suffrage amendment did not enfranchise Chicanas and black women. Chicanas were affected by the aftermath of the suffrage amendment when women's movement activities slowed down, because white women achieved their desires, but Chicanas, like other minority women, had to continue to struggle for mere survival. They were affected when middle-class women were given preferential treatment in war industry, but blacks and Chicanas had to continue with unskilled, low-paid agricultural work and other service occupations. Chicanas were affected when white middle-class women went back home in the fifties but minority women did not, and Chicanas, to boot, continued to suffer repression and deportation for their continued labor and civil rights advocacy. Chicanas have been affected when their community and their own gains in the 1960s have taken a back seat to the women's movement just as the black movement and black suffrage took a back seat to the suffrage movement in the latter part of the last century.

Minority women, whether black, native American, Asian American, Chicanas, or even white ethnic women, are ambivalent about the promise of the present reemergence of the women's movement. One can even say they largely lean to the negative. Their ambivalence and apprehension are based on negative experiences suffered in contact with the movement over the past 10 years. Few minority women have read feminist archives nor the current classics; these historical analyses of the movement would definitely reinforce their apprehensions. But for those few minority and working-class women who have done extensive research, history does indeed seem to repeat itself. What is sad is that most minority, radical, and working-class women do need the movement.

THE WOMEN'S SUFFRAGE MOVEMENT AND MINORITY WOMEN, 1848 TO 1900

This early period of the women's movement was both glorious and inglorious. The movement had started out to promote radical and lasting changes in the situation of all women in the home and in society. Even as the movement continued after 1848 and focused mainly on suffrage, the ideals remained solid. The basic premise among suffragists in the 1850s, 1860s, and 1870s was that the vote is an intrinsic human right. When that ideal was abandoned for expediency's sake and restrictions were recommended to cut off the vote from the undesirables, minority women must have felt as did many in the early 1970s when the present movement decided that "women's liberation" was too drastic a term and we must focus on and call our movement a women's rights movement. Many wondered, "rights for *which* women?"

Mexican American women, as part of ethnic groups of late arrivals to the national scene, had only limited participation in the women's movement in the 1848 to 1900 period. This potential for participation was further curtailed by the movement's ideological shift in the late eighteenth century against immigrants and the working class. In 1848, the very year of the historical Seneca Falls meeting when the "Declaration of Sentiments" was issued under the leadership of early feminists Elizabeth Cady Stanton and Lucrecia Mott, Mexican American women were incorporated into the United States through conquest and the addition of Mexican territory.

During the first two decades of feminist activity in the United States, Mexican American women were struggling along with the "social" bandits of the period like Joaquin Murrieta and Nepomuceno Cortinas to liberate Chicanos and Chicano territory. One of the first Chicanas to come into contact with the suffragist movements in the 1880s was Lucy González Parsons, a Chicana socialist labor organizer. Lucy González was born in Johnson County, Texas. As a young woman, she moved to Austin, Texas, where she worked in the state capitol and met Albert Parsons. She married Parsons and in the 1880s they moved to Chicago where they became deeply involved in the struggling labor movement. They worked with the Workingman's Party and founded a labor newspaper, *The Alarm*. Lucy contributed to the paper as writer and editor. Her interest in labor organizing turned toward the organization of women workers. At the time of the famous Hay Market Riots in 1886, when her husband was accused as a conspirator, Lucy was involved in organizing women garment workers. During her husband's imprisonment and after his execution, Lucy continued her activities with the labor movement. In June 1905, she was listed as one of the leaders and founders of the Industrial Workers of the World (Cotera 1976:73).

There is evidence that numerous attempts were made to bring labor organizers like Lucy Parsons and Emma Goldman into the fold of the women's movement, especially by leaders like Jane Addams and Florence Kelley, who were heavily involved with social work efforts to benefit working-class and immigrant women. Both Addams and Kelley spoke eloquently about the fact that these women needed the vote to effect changes in the home and on the job more desperately than did middle-class white, native-born women. Jane Addams and others spoke and acted on behalf of women labor leaders like Lucy Parsons, assisting them in rallies, providing bail when they were arrested, and using their tremendous power and influence on behalf of working women.

Unfortunately for poor and minority women, there were not enough "social" feminists to shift the suffragist movement away from a narrow human rights and universal voting rights platform. The ideals that were born within the abolitionist movement were cast aside to make way in the 1890s for a narrower goal of suffrage for white women at all costs. Two strategies were developed that adversely affected minority, immigrant, and working-class women and men. In the North, from the late 1880s to the early 1900s, suffragists advocated the vote for white middle-class women as an effective counter to the vote of workers and the foreign born. In the South, suffragists advocated enfranchising white women to dilute the effects of the fourteenth amendment and the votes of the newly enfranchised black men. It is true that in following these expedient strategies the suffragists attempted to diffuse attacks by the antisuffragists, that through suffrage black women and "ignorant immigrants" would be enfranchised. They attempted also to please politicians like President William Howard Taft who told the National American Woman Suffrage Association (NAWSA) that he was not supportive of woman suffrage because the intelligent and patriotic might not take advantage of it, but the undesirable classes might become political constituents (Cotera 1976:72).

In 1889, at the NAWSA Convention, Elizabeth Cady Stanton called for literacy tests to abolish the ignorant vote. Carrie Catt's statement from the *Woman's Journal,* December 15, 1894, expresses alarm at the great danger faced by the United States:

> That danger lies in the votes possessed by the males in the slums of the cities, and the ignorant foreign vote which was sought to be bought by each party, to make political success.
>
> There is but one way to avert the danger—cut off the vote of the slums and give it to the women. (Quoted from *Woman's Journal,* December 15, 1894, by Kraditor 1968:261).

Elizabeth Cady Stanton's own testimony to the House Committee on the Judiciary in 1896 presented the contrasting picture of drunken, illiterate, newly arrived immigrants trading votes for bribes, while women professors, writers, and teachers were deprived of the vote (Kraditor 1971:109).

Stanton's plan also promoted the use of educational qualifications and literacy tests for voting. A resolution passed as early as 1893 at the NAWSA Convention read as follows:

> *Resolved,* That without expressing any opinion on the proper qualifications for voting, we call attention to the significant facts that in every State there are more women who can read and write than the whole number of illiterate male voters; more white women who can read and write than all negro voters; more American women who can read and write than all

foreign voters; so that the enfranchisement of such women would settle the vexed question of rule by illiteracy, whether of home-grown or foreign-born production (Kraditor 1968:260).

An exception to the suffragist's mainstream was Mrs. Stanton's own daughter, Harriet Stanton Blatch, who wrote an open letter to her mother protesting the proposals for educational and literary requirements. Her letter was published in the *Woman's Journal* (Kraditor 1971:113).

At the 1899 convention, Mrs. Lottie Wilson Jackson would not support a resolution about black women having to ride in smoking cars. Susan B. Anthony spoke against the resolution in terms that have become very familiar to minority women today (Hymowitz and Weissman 1978:276). After all, according to her, they were only powerless women and they could not very well get involved with any issues such as those. By 1903 the majority of the NAWSA members supported educational requirements for voting, and there was a final separation of the women's suffrage movement from the black movement.

Although many social workers like Jane Addams, Florence Kelley, and Sophonisba P. Breckenridge and socialists like Emma Goldman advocated the rights of immigrants and working women, in most instances during the 1890 to 1910 period their advocacy had little or no effect on the suffragist movement's attitude toward minority or working-class women (Kraditor 1971:121).

Historian Aileen Kraditor analyzes this situation as a harsh indictment on white middle-class women. According to her analysis, women apparently did not feel humiliated when governed by white men, but if foreigners and blacks governed them, especially if they were of the lower classes, it was unbearable. Kate M. Gordon, suffragist from Louisiana, proposed that only white women be granted suffrage. Others quoted extensive statistics to demonstrate that the votes of white women would offset the strength of black votes (Hymowitz and Weissman 1978:276). White women objected to being governed by their former slaves (Kraditor 1971:106).

Because of this classism and racism, the arguments of the need for universal suffrage and the negation of the superiority of the male sex over the female sex were set aside (Kraditor 1971:107). The abandonment of these two principles has lived to haunt all women to this day. Further, the promotion of barriers to universal suffrage such as literacy and educational requirements disenfranchised black women, Chicanas, and poor and immigrant women until the passage of the Voting Rights Act of 1965.

With all the anti-immigrant, antislum, and antilabor agitation, it is no wonder that the suffrage movement had almost no labor support by the end of the nineteenth century.

LABOR, SOCIALISM, AND SUFFRAGE, 1900 TO 1920

Historian William O'Neill documents impressive gains in education, employment, and club organization work achieved by white middle-class women by the 1900s. Other minority and working-class women apparently had not benefitted greatly from the movement carried on in the name of all womankind in the United States. And, according to O'Neill, white middle-class women went to college in impressive numbers and monopolized the good positions that became available (1976:148-149). Yet universal suffrage had not been achieved.

Fortunately for the suffragists, organized labor was no longer dominated by the foreigners and dirty masses of the 1870s; with their more articulate female leadership and better economic status, it became a more acceptable ally for their efforts.

On their part, suffragists concerned with the plight of the working woman did much to win labor support through the activities of the Women's Trade Union League (WTUL) organized by wealthy women. Perhaps this union, along with the work of social workers Florence Kelley and Jane Addams, made the greatest contribution to labor-suffrage coalition building. The WTUL at least put rhetoric into action from 1903 to 1909, when it rendered woman power and fund-raising support to the shirtwaist makers strike in New York City (Altbach 1974:106).

There were still two problems to be overcome: the nagging race issue that continued to keep minority women at arm's length and the problem of socialism in the feminist ranks and in the labor movement.

Black women in 1913 and 1919 continued to suffer direct humiliations from the movement. In 1913, for example, the NAWSA and Congressional Union organizations held a Suffrage Parade in Washington, D.C. NAWSA leaders asked Ida B. Wells Barrett, a black suffragist and vice president of the Black Woman's Suffrage Club, not to march with the Chicago delegation because southern women refused to march in a parade with delegations that were racially mixed. As late as 1919, the Northeastern Federation of Women's Clubs wanted a black organization to wait for their cooperative membership until after suffrage was won (Kraditor 1971:168).

As black women were affected through exclusion, Chicanas suffered the same fate, especially in the southwestern states. Whether they were concerned or not with actively participating in the suffrage movement, it is a fact that their participation at any level has been absent from history. However, there are apparently a few pamphlets in Spanish from the 1900 to 1920 period in the Sophia Smith Suffrage Collection.

Chicanas in the early part of the century were largely visualized as objects of charity and not as equals in any struggle, as were the black women. On their part, Chicanas were apparently too involved in surviving lynchings, corporate takeover of their lands, and exclusion from the educational systems to be concerned with what the suffrage movement thought and believed.

In Texas, although Chicanas were strongly involved in civil rights and labor organizing activities, and although they had their own organizations such as the Club Leona Vicario, Liga Femenil Mexicanista, and the Hijas de Cuauhtemoc, there is very little evidence of coalition-building involvement with the state's feminist leaders like Mary Eleanor Brackenridge, Jane Y. McCallum, and Minnie Fisher Cunningham.

Socialism is the second factor that kept minority women from the suffrage movement. The mainstream of the women's movement feared the image of close ties with socialism that were promoted through the active participation of socialists like Florence Kelley, Jessie Ashley, Lucy González Parsons, Andrea and Teresa Villarreal, Maria Talavera, and Elizabeth Gurley Flynn. Socialists, on their part, did not entirely trust a movement with such unrealistic expectations as that of bringing about a total turnaround in government policies, considering the nature and background of the women in leadership positions and the very weaknesses of the political system (Goldman 1970:61).

Through the words of an active socialist and feminist leader, Jessie Ashley, one can see that women concerned with socialist ideals and activities were only halfway welcomed in the movement. On January 20, 1912, Jessie Ashley wrote what she called her swan song in the *Woman's Journal,* explaining that her 1911 articles had created fears and protests from the suffragists who feared that the movement would be identified with socialism. Like other suffragists who had advocated for greater and more humane vision in their approach to achieving suffrage, Ashley calls for attitudes that will produce real democracy and the true inheritance that women should have. The middle-class mainstream again silenced the more ardent socialists in the movement. In the words of historian Aileen Kraditor, although some of the socialists did become suffrage platforms, the women's movement still remained primarily middle class (Kraditor 1971:125-127).

Chicana feminist activity during the 1900 to 1920 period resembles the dynamics of the present Chicana feminists. Like Chicanas today, the early feminists were struggling for survival and for their development as individuals. Like Chicanas today, they had to work within their own movement and community. They had to attempt also to interact with a woman's movement that was directed toward fulfillment and not survival. And like Chicanas today, the women found, then, that while few battles were won in civil rights on behalf of their communities, fulfillment and the gains of the women's movement were never their gains. The suffragist movement had been manipulated since the 1870s to benefit those that eventually benefitted from it and no one else.

Chicana feminist activities in the 1904 to 1920 period were channeled through civil rights activities and labor organization work. Some outstanding women were Jovita Idar, a journalist and civil rights worker from Laredo, Texas; Soledad Peña, orator and educator; María Renteria; and María Villarreal. These women were speakers and participants in a historical civil rights conference, the Primer Congreso Mexicanista. On October 15, 1911 they also founded the Liga Femenil Mexicanista. The group's goals were to struggle on behalf of the Mexican American and to educate and develop women (Cotera 1976:82).

Mexican American women from Texas to California worked through the Partido Liberal Mexicano (PLM), a political organization under Enrique and Ricardo Flores Magón, socialist organizers exiled from Mexico. Through PLM and many widely circulated publications such as *Regeneración* and *La Mujer Moderna,* Chicanas raised the consciousness of other women in the Mexican American community on matters relating to women's development and feminism. Some of the outstanding Chicanas of the period were involved as writers, advocates, and speakers for the organization. Modesta Abascal, Silvina Rembao de Trejo, Andrea and Teresa Villarreal, Francisca Mendoza, and Maria Talavera were among the most active. One excellent example of the feminist contests of *Regeneración* is the famous essay *A la Mujer,* which has been translated and reissued by California Chicana feminists. Contemporary Chicanas have seen in this essay evidence that within the worker and civil rights activities of the Chicano community there have been serious and progressive statements on women's rights. In this essay, Ricardo Flores Magón urges women to work for revolution and change, outlining some of the conditions they have to fight.

> . . . [T]hough women work more than men, they are paid less, and misery, mistreatment and insult are today as yesterday the bitter harvest for a whole existence of sacrifice.

Women, he explains, are

> . . . humiliated, degraded, bound by chains of tradition to an irrational inferiority, indoctrinated in the affairs of heaven by clerics, but totally ignorant of world problems. She is suddenly caught in the whirlwind of industrial production which above all requires cheap labor to sustain the competition created by the voracious 'princes of capital' who exploit her circumstances. She is not as prepared as men for the industrial struggle, nor is she organized with the women of her class to fight alongside her brother workers. . . . (Magón 1974:5).

Other Chicana feminist organizations that raised money for worker activities were the Club Liberal "Leona Vicario" and the Liberal Union of Mexican Women.

In 1920, with the overwhelming support of labor and the big city vote, the suffrage amendment was passed granting women the vote. Once this happened, the women's movement virtually came to a standstill. According to historian Edith Hoshino Altbach, the increased educational opportunities, leisure employment opportunities, and social and political contacts made it possible for white middle-class women to make it on their own. The remarkable networks of the white middle-class organizations like the American Association of University Women, American Federation of Teachers, National Federation of Business and Professional Women's Clubs, and the League of Women Voters (the former National American Woman Suffrage Association) stayed on to further develop the power base for white American womanhood (Altbach 1974:121). While white women entered the flapper era uneducated about their mothers' struggle for enfranchisement and content to be conspicuous consumers, minority women, especially Chicanas, faced new and awesome tasks. Large corporations and the courts broke up generations of ties to the land, and many Chicanos became the migrant peon class described so disparagingly by anthropologist Ruth Allen. Lynchings of Chicanos kept civil rights advocates on 24-hour detail, and the breakup of Mexican schools put professional Chicanos and Chicanas on the streets.

Chicanas apparently had no time to bask in gains made in the name of womanhood in the United States. The most important gain of all, enfranchisement, was almost as universally denied to her as it was to black women. Actually, the right to vote for Chicanas was not to become a reality until the passage of the 1974 amendments to the Voting Rights Act. Working-class women and Chicanas got a taste of some of the barriers recommended by the suffragists in the 1890s to keep undesirables from exercising the right to vote. Chicanas were barred through poll taxes, which were a burden to the poor, and by requiring proof of citizenship, which many second- and third-generation citizens were afraid to put to a test because of the frequent deportations. They were submitted to literacy and educational tests and to intimidation by law enforcement agencies who guarded the purity of the polling places by keeping Mexicans of both sexes out. Polling places in the southwestern states were almost always on the Anglo side of the tracks, where Mexicans were allowed for domestic work or other service jobs only. In Austin, Texas, as late as 1970, Mexican Americans were denied the vote because they were not allowed to enter the private home where the polling place was located.

Apparently, then, once the suffrage was won for white middle-class women, there were few occasions for contact between white women and minority women.

In retrospect, the passage of the suffrage amendment had little effect on the lives of minority women. According to historian William O'Neill, the expected improvements in the quality of American life did not materialize and much of the blame has been placed on the suffragists themselves, who lost track of the moral issues involved and behaved like any other interest group, trading off principles for advantages until the basic values of the effort were invisible (O'Neill 1976:125). Altbach attributes this problem to the middle-class base of the women's movement, which tended to equate women's oppression with the denial of positions of responsibility, to being relegated to the home and to being considered a sex object, whereas working-class and minority women looked to the movement as an effort that would substantially change their lives (Altbach 1974:104). It was the age-old conflict of fulfillment versus survival—never resolved then and still unresolved today.

The efforts of white middle-class women to formalize the gains made were directed through the club women's movement. By 1920, there were approximately 2 million women in NAWSA and another 25,000 in the Woman's Party. There were millions in the other women's clubs, many of which denied membership to black women. According to Altbach, the leadership in these organizations could relate to black women only as the objects of their charity (1974:115-116). For all of their activities and charitable efforts, they alone, and not the poor, benefitted. These clubs gave women a social outlet and a reason to be with other people. They brought them out of the house and provided the ''graduate'' education and profession they did not have (Altbach 1974:120).

The attitudes of even the strong feminists like Alice Paul did not encourage minority women about their future after 1920. June Sochen, in *Herstory,* indicates that after the suffrage amendment passed in 1920, reformers wondered about the fate of over 2 million black women in the South who most assuredly would be disenfranchised like black men were. Apparently, when this was brought to Alice Paul as a continuing concern for the Woman's Party, she replied that 1920 was not the time to discuss this issue. Consequently, black women suffered through reading tests, intimidation, and violence at the polls (Sochen 1974:279). And, of course, in Texas and many other states they were denied voting rights in the state primaries.

REPATRIATION AND WAR, 1930 TO 1950

The 1930s for Chicana and black women were really no easier than the 1920s had been. Chicanas continued as agricultural workers, domestics, and as workers in agribusiness, like the pecan shelling industry in San Antonio, Texas. Historians record that black women suffered terrible discrimination from the New Deal and that their wages were in pennies, if they actually got to work. In the case of Chicanas, repatriation to Mexico was a constant spectre whether or not they were on relief rolls. Despite the depression, there was no respite for the Chicano community in the areas of civil rights and labor organizing.

One of the few statements to be made about Chicanas, suffrage, and the women's movement in the 1930s is made by Guzmán. He says that the Chicana in this period was not recruited into the women's movement because of the low opinion that white women in the movement had about them. Chicanas were considered too passive and too submissive to their men and families (Guzmán 1974:25).

These passive and submissive Chicanas were apparently too involved in leadership roles and advocacy to read the social science literature that abounded, proclaiming them and their kind as the worst problem ever to hit the country. In the 1970s, Chicano and Anglo social scientists have analyzed the damage done to Chicano psychic development by the literature of the 1930s, which became part of the basis for massive repatriations to Mexico of American citizens of Mexican descent. Through it all, Chicanas played a major role in both civil rights and labor, often coordinating activities with progressive and communist intellectuals to advance their cause.

Chicana labor leaders and politicians, like Denver's Dolores McGran Gonzalez, testified before congressional committees, ran for local office, and served as national delegates to the Progressive Party Convention in the late 1930s. Isabel's writings, in particular, expressed ideals that included women's rights, human rights, and workers' rights.

Other women who have become models of female-inspired activities of the period are Dolores Hernandez, who was killed on October 10, 1933, during a strike of 15,000 farm workers in Visalia, California. Another woman labor union leader made history in 1936 when she led pecan sheller strikers in San Antonio in a successful strike effort. Emma Tenayuca Brooks, then a 17-year-old labor organizer and orator, became a beacon of hope to beleagured workers throughout the United States. For her efforts, she has had to live 40 years in obscurity and anonymity. In civil rights and educational reform, a strong women's advocate, María L. Hernandez of Lytle, Texas, worked tirelessly throughout the 1930s demonstrating, speaking, and protesting the educational status of Mexican Americans in the United States. This illustrious woman published a remarkable treatise on the political responsibilities of government and the governed. Although the treatise was directed to the Mexican nation, the political ideals María expounds for a liberating democracy are the ideals she has advocated in this country throughout her life.

The war effort in the 1940s affected Chicanas as they were recruited to occupy more service and domestic positions left vacant by the fortunate black women who were recruited to work in the war industries. There is some evidence, however, that as much of the garment industry moved to the Southwest during this time, Chicanas took up these jobs. After the war, they were able to keep their place in this particular job market, while other women in heavier and better paid industry were sent home. War activities, repatriation in the 1930s, and the looming spectre of military conservatism did much in the 1940s to discourage civil rights and labor advocacy, which had been the forums for female development in the Chicano community. However, the effort that women put forth, the extreme patriotism displayed by Chicano males, and the contact they established with the Anglo power bases yielded some seeds for the development of activism that was to come in the late 1940s and 1950s. The new activism among women was no longer the socialist and communist inspired advocacy of the early decades but a more subdued, club woman reformist approach channeled through female auxiliary groups sponsored by the League of United Latin American Citizens (LULAC), founded in 1929, and the American G.I. Forum, founded in the 1940s. These new activities centered around educational reform, voter education, and employment opportunities. And, although the gains achieved were meager, an important factor is that they kept Chicanos and Chicanas involved in community development through the repressive anticommunist McCarthy era.

THE CHICANO MOVEMENT AND THE WOMEN'S MOVEMENT, 1960 TO 1970

Chicanas were actively involved from the very beginning of the Chicano civil rights movement in the 1960s. They were involved on behalf of the communities they represented and on their own behalf to speak about their community needs and their own needs as women. Some of the women who led the movement in its early days were Dolores Huerta of the United Farm Workers Organizing Committee, Alicia Escalante with the Welfare Rights Organization, and Gracia Molina de Pick and Anna Nieto Gomez with feminist activities. Women politicians like Virginia Muzquiz of Crystal City, Texas, Mariana Hernandez, and Grace Davies put Chicanas in the political forum. Like these women, there have been hundreds of others who, in the 1960s and 1970s, have proved that Chicanas have come of age politically in this country.

In the mid-1960s, Chicanas were actively working for community and individual progress when the current women's movement loomed on the horizon. Chicanas felt as ambivalent about the new movement as the early twentieth century Chicana socialists felt about the suffragist movement. The new wave of the women's movement was firmly anchored in Alice Paul's Woman's Party platform of achieving an equal rights amendment. Again, white women were bringing forth a movement with a very attractive carrot. Who in their right political mind is going to challenge an equal rights amendment? Especially not minority activist women who were already heavily involved in a human rights movement.

In a blissful state of mutual ignorance about the history of the women's movement, the history of minority women, and our mutual relations, we went on to repeat the history of 1910 and 1920. Too much has occurred since 1968 to recount all the problems that have accompanied the clumsy attempts of the women's movement to incorporate minority and working-class women into the fold. As we have seen in the foregoing historical analysis, Altbach is right, there are too many unresolved issues brought over from the 1920s. Working women, housewives, and minority women's needs were not addressed then (Altbach 1974:122). There is no evidence that they will be addressed by the present leadership. Unfortunately, the documentation of the legacy of the past is not easily available to instruct us and help us formulate a better future, but it is here to plague the present movement with the same attitudes of opportunism and power mongering.

There is no evidence in the writings or behavior of the white women's movement to demonstrate that their attitudes have changed. Minority women are still characterized as objects of charity. There is evidence that employment and power, and not human rights, are the primary concern of the white women's movement. There is plenty of evidence to indicate that many will go to great lengths to achieve these goals. Few will give one vote to achieve human rights, especially for minority and poor women. One cannot find one minority women's organization that will give unqualified support to the women's movement. Nor is there one piece of literature by minority women—black, native American, Asian American, or Chicana—that will praise white women's efforts to work for personal power rather than women's liberation.

Working women also have strong reservations about the present movement. For example, the Coalition of Labor Union Women (CLUW) was formed when the leading labor union women heard the news that the National Organization of Women (NOW) was going to discuss working women in the AFL-CIO with President George Meany. They were incensed that NOW would bypass them and talk directly to male union leadership (Albert 1976:54). Working women and minorities alike have found that professional women in the women's movement will place their own welfare above principle. When the clerical women workers went on strike at Barnard College in 1974, the strikers waited in vain for support from feminist professors (Albert 1976:53). Working women, too, have suffered from intellectual rhetoric and put-downs from the movement's leadership. The constant put-downs of secretarial jobs and garment and industry jobs, by the Vassar, Wellesley, and Radcliffe graduates who control so much of the movement, alienate working women to whom these jobs are important and who have raised families in dignity by doing these jobs well.

Minority women could fill volumes with examples of put-downs, put-ons, and out-and-out racism shown to them by the leadership in the movement. There are three major problem areas in the minority-majority relationship in the movement: (1) paternalism or maternalism, (2) extremely limited opportunities for minority women in the movement, and (3) outright discrimination against minority women in the movement (for detailed instances, see Cotera 1977). Paternalistic or maternalistic attitudes have kept white women from viewing minority women as anything but quaint, inarticulate ethnics, largely from the lower class. This has forced accomplished minority leaders out of the movement and has created a small group of blacks, Chicanas, and other minority women who want to be accepted so badly by the movement that they will shuffle and "yes m'am" to them to stay in favor. The power of these minority women is diminished accordingly, both in the movement and outside of it.

Opportunities for development for minority women within the movement have been very limited. Affirmative action resolutions for minority recruitment in the major organizations like the Women's Equity Action League, National Organization for Women, and the National Women's Political Caucus have been scarce, and when they have been won after heated floor fights, they were either overthrown in subsequent conventions or not implemented at all, especially at the local level. Opportunities for development are very limited, even once the women are in. Rhea Mojica Hammer, the chairwoman of the Chicana Caucus of the National Women's Political Caucus, is bypassed when critical information is forthcoming, excluded in meetings, insulted, ignored, and ridiculed by many of the women who have sat on the policy council with her during the past 8 years. Rose Marie Roybal, who worked with the National Office of the International Women's Year (IWY) Commission, was encouraged to seek a position elsewhere when it was discovered that she was giving information about IWY activities to Hispanic and other minority women. This information pertained to the fact that state committees were already in the planning processes and that by December 28, 1976, planning meetings had already been held in Texas, for example, without any type of contact with minority women.

The basic premise with this type of exclusion, as from many of the activities planned for the U.S. National Women's Agenda and with the International Year of the Child activities in 1979, is that minority women are given observer status. Anytime they advocate for meaningful involvement to benefit their communities, they are tagged as divisive by women leaders. The involvement of minority women in the International Women's Year activities was fought by white women from the very beginning. Yet in Texas, it was the Coalition of Chicanas and the radical women who worked with Chicanas, who gave Texas a pro-ERA delegation. This would not have been possible had the state IWY Committee not been forced to concede inclusion of Chicanas and had Chicanas not spent $10,000 of their own money. The shame of it is that $100,000 was allocated to the Texas conference; yet the committee spent less than $4,000 on minority women and insisted on a registration fee and "fee waivers"—a move that embarrassed poor women and kept many housewives and farm worker women from participating in the conference.

The same exclusion and discrimination exists in many women studies courses, foundation-funded programs, minorities and women recruitment programs, "herstory" research, publishing, and women's service institutions. Activists and feminists who are trying to incorporate minority women into the ERA process for the sake of maintaining the gains made by ERA and to assure its passage have a losing battle. So intent are the women in power on keeping the doors shut to minorities and the poor that they seem to prefer defeat than to give in—shades of the 1910s!

CHICANA CONFERENCES AND SEMINARS, 1970 TO 1975

On a more positive note, Chicana feminists have continued undaunted, mostly outside the women's movement, now and then establishing ties and coalitions with it, to develop their own power base for the achievement of Chicana liberation and to provide increased opportunities for Chicanas. Some of the historical feminist activities[1] in the past 10 years have been the following:

Chicana Workshop, Denver Youth Liberation Conference, March 1970 (held at the Crusade for Justice in Denver, Colorado), well known because the women supposedly indicated they did not want to be "liberated," which more than likely meant that they were not ready to take a stand on the issue of Anglo feminism; Enriqueta Vasquez of Española, New Mexico, has written extensively on this workshop.

Raza Unida Conference in Austin, Texas, July 1970 (an informal Chicana caucus led by Marta Cotera, who spoke of presenting women's needs at the next statewide meeting).

Women's Workshop of the Mexican American National Issues Conference, October 10, 1970, Sacramento, California (this workshop was organized by Francisca Flores and Simmie Romero Goldsmith and resulted in the creation of the Comision Femenil Mexicana).

Women's Caucus, Raza Unida Conference, Houston, Texas, winter 1970 (informal session among Texan Chicanas; discussion on the fact that there were no women speakers or workshop leaders; among those present were Yolanda Birdwell, Carmen Lomas Garza, Gloria Guardiola, Marta Cotera, Alma Canales).

Chicana Regional Conference, May 8, 1971, Los Angeles, California.

La Conferencia de Mujeres Por la Raza, May 28-30, 1971, Houston, Texas, YWCA. (This conference is sometimes referred to as the National Chicana Conference and is historical because, as far as is known, it is the first national conference ever held for and by Chicanas in the United States. It was organized by Elma Barrera and the staff of the Magnolia Park Branch YWCA. Speakers and workshop leaders included the most active Chicanas in the nation. Keynote speakers were Grace Olivarez, lawyer, and Julie Ruiz, School of Social Work, Arizona State University.)

HEW Women's Action Program, Research Recommendations, July 1-2, 1971, Washington, D.C. (mostly Chicanas). A consultation organized by Lupe Anguiano for the purpose of establishing research and program priorities for Chicanas. Some of the women present included educators Cecilia Suarez, Grace Molina de Pick, Mirian Ojeda, Teresa Aragon de Shepro, Vera Martinez, sociologist Deluvina Hernandez, and community persons Paulina Jacobo, Esther Martinez, and Marta Cotera. This group organized the National Chicana Foundation.

Spanish-Speaking Coalition Conference, Women's Caucus, October 23-24, 1971, Washington, D.C. (Spanish-speaking women).

Eastern Region National Spanish-Speaking Women's Caucus, December 15, 1971, New York City (Spanish-speaking women).

Midwest Region "Mi Raza Primero," Women's Caucus, February 22-23, 1972, Muskegan, Michigan (Spanish-speaking women). Some of the organizers were Olga Villa, Jane Gonzalez, and Rhea Mojica Hammer.

Southwest Meeting, February 22, 1972, San Diego, California (mostly Chicanas).

Washington, D.C., Spanish-speaking women employed in various federal and non-federal agencies, February 23, 1972, Washington, D.C. (Review of Women's Action Report).

League of United Latin American Citizens, Women's Affairs Committee, March 11-12, 1972, Phoenix, Arizona (Spanish-speaking women).

Chicana Caucus, Texas Women Political Caucus State Convention, Mesquite, Texas, March 11, 1972. A caucus of close to 100 very politicized Chicanas organized within the TWPC and resolved to work within the National Women's Political Caucus so that the national and state groups would act on Chicana issues; Marta Cotera was one of the keynote speakers for the conference.

Chicana Caucus, National Chicano Political Conference, San Jose, California, April 21-23, 1972.

Midwest Spanish-Speaking Women's Political Conference, May 6, 1972, Notre Dame, Indiana (Spanish-speaking women).

Chicano Studies/MECHA Conference, California State University, Northridge, California, May 1972. (This conference supported a resolution introduced by Chicanas to require all Chicano studies majors to include at least one course of La Mujer.)

Women's Auxiliary, American G.I. Forum, July 26-29, 1972, Washington, D.C. (special women's meeting).

National Chicana Caucus, National Women's Political Caucus, Houston, Texas, February 9-11, 1973. (Over 100 Chicanas from all states in the United States gathered to strategize and pass resolutions on issues relating to the Chicana. Among those in attendance were Alicia Escalante, Rhea Mojica Hammer (who won a national office with NWPC), Lupe Anguiano, Maria Cardenas, Evey Chapa, Lydia Serrata, and Marta Cotera.) Many Anglo women like Sally Andrade and Jeanette Lizcano were part of the caucus and helped in the floor maneuverings.

Chicana Curriculum Workshop, University of California, Los Angeles, California, June 18-22, 1973. (This workshop, headed by the best-known Chicana academicians, resulted in the first Chicana curriculum adequate for colleges and universities and adoptable for high schools, entitled *New Directions in Education: Estudios Femeniles de la Chicana,* edited by Anna Nieto-Gomez.)

Mujeres Pro-Raza Unida Statewide Conference, San Antonio, Texas, August 4, 1973. (Organized by women active in Texas RUP politics—Irma Mireles, Juanita Luera, Ino Alvarez, Evey Chapa, Chelo Avila, and Marta Cotera—the conference resolved to work for the development of women within the party.)

Institute to Prepare Chicanas in Administration, Washington, D.C., July-August 1973. (This institute was headed by Corine Sanchez and involved women from throughout the nation; courses of study included the curriculum previously developed at U.C.L.A.)

Chicana Educational Conference, Austin, Texas, at St. Edwards University, February 23, 1974. (Sponsored by Olga de Leon and Imelda Ramos, the conference was statewide and issues included bilingual education, employment, day care, welfare, rape, and revenue sharing.)

Mexican American Business and Professional Women of Austin, Steering Committee and Organizational Meeting, Austin, Texas, March 1974. First annual meeting was held in June 1974. (Organized by Austin Chicanas including Annabelle Valle, Amalia Mendoza and Marta Cotera to work locally on Chicana issues.)

Chicana Symposium, Texas Southern University, TSU Week, Houston, Texas, April 22, 1974.

Conferencia Chicana Estatal, Jose Antonio School, Montezuma, New Mexico, August 23, 24, 25, 1974. (Purpose of the conference was to involve more barrio women in the movement, and to focus on women's issues, food stamps, child care, school systems, housing, and sex discrimination.)

Chicana Symposium held during Chicana Month, University of Texas at El Paso, October 4, 1974.

Chicana Seminar, University of Notre Dame, Notre Dame, Indiana, spring 1975. Participants and workshop leaders included Olga Villa (Midwest), Lydia Espinosa (Texas), Evey Chapa (Texas), Gracia Molina de Pick (California), and Gloria Gutierrez Roland (Texas).

Chicana Week Seminar, University of Texas, Austin, Texas, May 1975.

Mexican American Business and Professional Women of El Paso, Texas Conference, August 1975.

National Chicana Foundation Meeting, Tucson, Arizona, August 8, 1975.

National Chicana Foundation Meeting, Los Angeles, California, October 15, 1975.

Chicana Identity Conference, University of Houston, Houston, Texas, November 15, 1975. Organized by Mujeres Unidas of Houston, Texas, including Luisa Vallejo, Chris Vasquez, and others. This conference was statewide in scope and topics were both academic and community oriented with history, education, labor, and politics as main concerns. Keynote speakers were Anna Nieto-Gomez, Northridge, California, and Marta P. Cotera, Austin, Texas.

Formation of Mexican American Women's National Association, Washington, D.C., 1976.

Founding of Scorpion Press, Phoenix, Arizona, 1977.

Chicana Advisory Committee for I.W.Y., a statewide advisory committee organized in Texas, which reached 2,000 Chicanas about the International Women's Year activities; also coordinated activities with other states, 1977.

Current Chicana feminist organizations are actively pressing for their communities' development through advocacy in political activity at the local and national levels. Some of the major organizations are: Nacional Femenil (California), Chicana Service Action Center (California), Mujeres Unidas (Colorado), Mexican American Women National Association (MANA, Washington, D.C.), Mexican American Business and Professional Women (Texas), and Mexican American Women Political Caucus (Texas).

CHICANA PUBLICATIONS

Chicanas also have expressed their feminism and their needs through their own journals like *Regeneracion, Encuentro Femenil, Hijas de Cuauhtemoc, La Comadre, Fuego de Aztlan, Imagines de la Chicana, Hembra, Tejidos, La Cosecha (De Colores),* and *Hojas Poeticas.* Other popular journals like *La Luz, Nuestro, El Caracol,* and *El Grito* often feature feminist writings that are helping to raise the consciousness of Chicanas to women's development. A major publishing effort is Scorpion Press of Phoenix, Arizona, which is oriented 100 percent to publishing Hispanic women's works.

Chicana feminist literature and ideology have pressed on beyond the dynamics of Anglo-Chicano relations to a more positive stance. More effort is being placed on restructuring Chicana images in order to develop positive Chicana role models for youth and on planning strategies for eradicating Chicana style, sexism, and for liberating relationships between men and women. Chicana scholars from the northwest coast to Texas are concerned about the family and feminism, competency and feminism, and creating institutions that are humanistic and can accommodate values that are considered female.

Feminism has come easily for Chicanas because of the woman's traditional role and strength as center or heart of the family. It has been easy to move from one position of strength to the other on the job or at school. The tradition of activism inherited from women's participation in armed rebellions in Mexico and in the political life of Mexico has also strengthened the Chicanas' position. Their history of struggle for feminist civil rights and labor organization testifies that many generations of Chicanas have been kept out of the home and on the picket lines. Advocacy, activism, and politics have become their second nature. These become evident when feminist papers have to be written, journals have to be published, or speeches have to be made on women's behalf. This tradition has trained Chicanas to analyze their ideals, their position in life, and their relationships to others.

TAKING STOCK

The Chicana is "together" but her progress is not commensurate with her potential or her goals as a woman.

The two great barriers to her achievement are (1) the opportunism in the women's movement that has forced lower priorities to be set on public policy and governmental programming for minority populations and the poor, and (2) the conservatism of Chicano males.

Chicanas secretly hope that white women will quickly get the powerful positions that they want so that the movement can move on to more substantial changes in the overall status of women, especially for those in the lowest socioeconomic scales. In the meantime, Chicanas do intend to maintain a very alert posture to monitor and claim allocations and gains made on behalf of womankind, especially those that utilize taxpayers' money, and to ensure Chicana participation at all levels. The Chicana input at the International Women's Year National Conference is a good example of this.

In regard to conservatism among Chicano males, Chicanas have had a decade of frustration. It is always easier to battle strangers than one's family. Chicanas have been remarkably restrained about accusing Chicanos publicly of discrimination and imposing barriers. And yet the Chicanas' growth is often stultified at home with fathers, brothers, and husbands who do not realize that this is wrong, that what they are doing is inhuman. Often their conservatism comes from belief in the macho myths spread by university sociologists in the 1930s. This conservatism often comes from ignorance about the roles that women have played in history and in the community. Many times Chicano males are not aware that for a minority woman to achieve her potential in this society, she must excel, work hard, and be mobile. As a matter of fact, Chicanas do accomplish this, a la Houdini with locks and straps and bars imposed by the men in their families and Chicanos at their place of work. For years Chicana feminists have hidden the fact that the males in our lives impose horrible standards and barriers that only superwomen could overcome. For the sake of unity they have gagged themselves to silence. Unfortunately, this has not been taken by the males as a sign of their commitment, but rather as a sign of acquiescence with the repression they impose.

Chicano males, like the white women, will demand commitment and support for their causes, and they will get it. Sometimes Chicanas break both their doors down to offer themselves solely for the sake of experience and participation. Yet, when Chicanas need political support, assistance in return or a recommendation for appointments or projects, both claim repression, powerlessness, impotence. Both are potent enough and successful enough when they need to achieve something for themselves.

As feminists, Chicanas have more and more been left to their own devices—to rely on their own unity and strength. This is evident in the forceful poetry of Chicano journals and feminist literature. Perhaps it needs to be expressed next in ideological and academic terms, as well as on a one-to-one basis with the men in their families, without apologies. In order to complete their liberation, Chicanas will have to express their needs, not to strangers but to their own community. Like mothers liberating themselves from the often psychotic martyr complex, Chicana feminists will have to shed their group martyrdom and no longer tolerate Chicanos who have for decades taken advantage of their accommodating behavior. This courageous action, for those that survive it, will provide all Chicanas with the freedom to be equal with men who can appreciate human liberation, human value, and dignity—the real bases for the Indo-Hispanic Mexican culture.

Where are Chicana feminists today? Like other minority women and working-class women, Chicanas would like to coalesce with the movements that affect them, such as the civil rights movement and the women's movement. Given the need for minds and bodies in the civil rights movement, there is great opportunity for coalition with male-dominated groups. Chicana feminists can attempt to strengthen their input and have their needs as women addressed once they stop playing ''mother'' to grown men and begin bargaining for real power.

Coalitions with the women's movement are also desirable and are constantly called for by blacks, Chicanos, Asian Americans, and native Americans. Chicana feminists are desirious of real coalitions such as those advocated by activist Ralph Smith in his discussion, ''Does the Woman's Movement Compromise the Struggle of Minorities?'' (1977:32). This ideal coalition is one where groups recognize their respective interests; they operate from independent power bases, and they agree and disagree freely and converge when there is a need to converge.

So far the cry for coalition building is all on the minority side, while the women's movement rolls right along, without response or regard for Chicana appeals. Basically, the problem is that whereas minorities think coalitions with the women's movement are necessary, the women's movement knows they are not. Whereas minority groups need to coalesce with the women's movement, or feel that they need to, the leadership of the women's movement knows it needs not coalesce with anyone.

As black activists and Chicana feminists have stated in conferences, these women in the leadership are the million strong club women. They are the wives, daughters, and lovers of those in power. These women do represent a handy movement to have so that government monies and Rockefeller Foundation monies can be diverted with impunity from the poor and minorities back to the white pocketbooks of their wives, the newest and largest minority. The leadership of the women's movement cannot publicly proclaim its antiworking women or antiminority peoples strategies as it did in the 1910s. But, privately, women in bureaucracies have expressed their unhappiness at having to work under minority people who have been promoted through affirmative action plans of the late sixties. The actions of white feminist organizations who discourage the participation of minority women also speak eloquently about the ideals of the movement. Under these conditions, there will be little or no coalition building between movements. In the meantime, black, brown, and native American feminists consistently have to ask, ''Why insist where you are obviously not wanted?'' *Because the movement is carried on in the name of all womankind*. This is a minority and poor woman's country also. *Because they are not "observer women."* They, too, are women. Programs are planned and executed with hard-earned taxpayer monies. Foundations give monies made from corporate profits from hard-working men and women of the lower middle class and of all ethnicities. Because if minority women default on what is rightfully theirs through a false sense of pride, they would not do justice to their intellect or to their commitment to develop their families and communities. If many women now involved in the women's movement are not ashamed to take what they did not struggle for in the job market or on the pickets from 1920 to 1970, then minority and working women are adamant about claiming what is rightfully due to them and to their communities.

Albert, in her article "Trade Union Woman," speaks eloquently for working women and white ethnic women, who also feel the need to coalesce with the leadership of the women's movement. She considers that the most important contribution the movement can make is in terms of bringing women of diverse ethnic groups together; that all women will come together not out of some do-gooder philosophy but because women feel they really need each other to gain power (Albert 1976:56).

The documented history of the women's movement in relation to human rights and minority rights is strongly indicative that this did not happen in the past. The short 10-year history of the new movement is strongly indicative that it may never happen.

NOTE

1. This section was compiled from program and conference notes in my personal files.

REFERENCES

Albert, M.
 1976 "Trade union women." In B. Peters and V. Samuels (eds.), Dialogue On Diversity: A New Agenda For American Women. New York: Institute on Pluralism and Group Identity.
Altbach, E. H.
 1974 Women in American. Lexington, Massachusetts: D. C. Heath & Co.
Cotera, M. P.
 1976 Diosa y Hembra. History and Heritage of Chicanas in the U.S. Austin, Texas: Information Systems Development.
 1977 The Chicana Feminist. Austin, Texas: Information Systems Development.
Goldman, E.
 1970 The Traffic in Women and Other Essays on Feminism. New York: Times Change Press.
Guzmán, R.
 1974 "The function of Anglo-American racism in the political development of Chicanos." Pp. 19-35 in F. C. Garciá (ed.), La Causa Politica. A Chicano Politics Reader. Notre Dame, Indiana: University of Notre Dame Press.
Hymowitz, C. and M. Weissman
 1978 A History of Women in America. New York: Bantam Books, Inc.
Kraditor, A. S.
 1968 Up From the Pedestal: Selected Writings in the History of American Feminism. New York: The New York Times Book Co.
 1971 The Ideals of the Woman Suffrage Movement, 1890-1920. Garden City, New York: Doubleday & Co., Inc.
Magon, R. F.
 1974 A la Mujer. (Translated by Prensa Sembradora.) Oakland, California: Prensa Sembradora.
O'Neill, W. L.
 1976 Everyone Was Brave: A History of Feminism in America. New York: The New York Times Book Co.
Smith, R.
 1977 "Does the woman's movement compromise the struggle of minorities?" Women's Right and Law Reporter 4(1), Fall.
Sochen, J.
 1974 Herstory: A Woman's View of American History. New York: Alfred Publishing Co., Inc.

Chapter 16

The nonconsenting sterilization of Mexican women in Los Angeles

Issues of psychocultural rupture and legal redress in paternalistic behavioral environments

Carlos G. Velez-I.

In late September 1977, I received a telephone call from a lawyer who represented a civil suit against one of the major metropolitan hospitals in Los Angeles for allegedly permitting sterilization procedures to be conducted on nonconsenting "Chicana"[1] women. The lawyer and I agreed to meet. On November 1, 1977, the two attorneys and I discussed the effects of alleged unconsented sterilization procedures that had been conducted on ten Mexican women in Los Angeles, California. I had heard comments regarding the case in other contexts but had not paid a great deal of attention, since from my own personal bias this sort of institutional behavior was not unexpected. Both lawyers presented the case from the perspective that ten Chicanas had been sterilized without their consent. They asked for my assessment of possible cultural and social ramifications of such practices on the ten women.

I replied that I could not offer an informed judgment without analyzing the case and the women. However, I felt able to venture an opinion, an educated one at best. I suggested that quite a variable response could be expected dependent on the behavioral contexts in which these women had been a part, their cultural histories, and their present support networks. Furthermore, at that time, I postulated, and it must be emphasized that it was merely a postulate, the following. If the women had been born in Mexico in rural contexts or in the United States in equivalent circumstance, then sterilization could have severe psychocultural and social results even beyond those expected of other women in the United States. Also, I suggested that the degree of damage could vary with the background of the women. Thus, if the women were urban Chicanas and part of lower-class sectors, their reaction could also be severe, but perhaps their social beings may not be as importantly related to the potential for bearing children. In either context, the severity of a nonconsenting sterilization on the women would be dependent on a variety of exogenous and endogenous variables including class, ethnic maintenance, social networks, work experience, and the psychological well-being of each woman prior to the sterilization procedure.

The lawyers then asked me if I would be willing to serve as a consultant on the case in order to test the postulates that I had suggested. I explained that I could not entertain any a priori conclusions in regard to the women, but that I would be willing to undertake a basic field study of the individuals involved and the circumstances of their sterilization. From the data I would submit an informed opinion of the effects, if any, of the surgery. Consequently, I agreed to serve as a consulting cultural anthropologist for their clients, with the stipulation that whatever conclusions I reached would have to be validated by empirical findings.

THE CULTURAL STRATEGIES OF THE WOMEN

From November 1, 1977, through May 30, 1978, the field studies of these women and their families were designed to gather accurate data that would "place" them in relation to a heterogeneous Mexican population. The studies sought to establish the "subcultural strategies" that these women shared within the cultural boundaries of the Mexican/Chicano population in the Southwestern United States. Using participant observation, unstructured interviews, and questionnaires, it was determined that in fact the women shared subcultural rural Mexican strategies that were adaptive in urban contexts. These findings even surprised the lawyers who themselves had not quite known what to make of the reactions that these women had expressed in regard to the sterilizations.

The data showed that nine of the ten women were born in small rural communities such as *rancherias* or *ejidos*[2] and had been socialized in such environments through the age of 14. In Mexico, these women had fulfilled agricultural chores from milking cows to planting and sowing corn. The one woman who had not been born in a rural Mexican setting was born in Dallas, Texas, but had adopted equivalent strategies in Mexican barrios. We can infer that their socialization experiences from early ages were strictly divided according to sex. Also, among other adaptive patterns, they learned high values on childbearing and strict divisions of labor.

In such social environments, fictive kinship, extended familial networks, and dense friendship networks assisted emotional survival. In urban Los Angeles such extensive and intensive networks had been generated by all of the women and their spouses. Thus, *compadrazgo* relations were shared by all the women. All ten women prior to sterilization had extensive fictive kinship ties for the four traditional occasions in which such ties are generated: baptism, confirmation, communion, and marriage. For some of the women who had four children, compadres and comadres alone had numbered eighteen persons. Five of the ten women had maintained extended generational ties so that a three-generational tier was valued and experienced.

In addition, the mean number of children in the women's families of orientation was 7.5 and in their spouses families of orientation it was 9.5. Thus, not only were they from large families, but these consanguineous relatives could be regarded as possible network supports. Visitations between consanguinities was intensive, and Sundays were generally the days in which the gathering of both fictive, consanguineous, and ascending generational relations would meet for commensal activities or for the celebration of birthdays or feast days. Another means of network expansion was that generated through *amistad* (friendship). Their functions were not only primarily affectionate but also material. The males assisted each other and reciprocated repair and construction work, the women visited and exchanged information, and in all, they formed borrowing and lending networks for household goods. In addition, all of the women and/or their spouses had participated with their families in *tandas* or revolving credit associations.

Such consanguineous, fictive, and amistad relationships had been identified as rewarding or not, based on *"sentido familiar"* (familial sentiment). That is, persons who did not generally reciprocate in exchange relations within these various networks were considered to be lacking in *sentido familiar*. This *sentido familiar* had as its basis, however, two core elements as organizing principles: first, marriage and children mark adulthood and responsibility; and second, as a social corollary for the first principle, is the internalization of the social identity of *"una mujer"* and *"un hombre."* For the women in the case, although having had ritual markers through *"quinceañera"* (debut) to announce the passage from adolescence to adulthood, in fact adulthood was defined once marriage had taken place and children had been procreated. Without such circumstances and regardless of statuses gathered in other contexts such as professional standing or educational achievement, a female was not considered privy to the councils of discussion among women on such topics as sex, behavior of men, or topics of seriousness such as death, and other aspects of the life cycle. It is interesting to note that as long as one of the female lawyers in this case was not married, she in fact had no access to the discussions these women shared regarding their marital difficulties experienced as the aftermath of the sterilization procedures. It was not until the lawyer married that she gained access to their discussions.

While marriage marks entry into adulthood, as a ritual it also legitimizes sexual intercourse for the specific purpose of propagating children. While all of the women were Roman Catholics, it was not only specific Church doctrine to which they pointed as the rationalization of this central principle. Rather, they adhered to a belief that sexual relations were the mechanisms for bearing children and not for the distinct pleasure of the male and female. Thus, the potential for bearing children and concomitantly the potential for siring children were given expression in the belief that sexual relations were primarily for the propagation of progeny. This potentiality quotient was the main vehicle by which continuity of all relations could be assured through *sentido familiar*. As long as children were likely to be born, reciprocal relations were likely to be generated, and the various social networks in which these women and their spouses participated could be assured of continuation.

The social corollary of the first organizing principle that defines adulthood through marriage and children is that the social identities of the women, and in part that of the males who were their spouses, were measured not just by the potential for bearing and siring children but by their actual manifestation. The actual manifestation of childbearing for these women of this subcultural strategy was the means by which their adult status was reinforced and articulated within the domestic group. There these women received prestige and were recognized as valued adults because of the potential and ability to bear children, a potential and ability that was reinforced by the continued presence of small children in the household. To be *"una mujer"* was to have children. During the various network activities previously described, the private domestic value of the women's social identity as *"una mujer"* was assured by the adult female members of those various networks. Constant references during social intercourse about the ages of the children of the women present, the short spacing between children in order to ensure maximal peer relations and caretaker roles available, and in fact the various household duties assigned to females during such network activities as cooking, serving, washing dishes and feeding children contributed to a total domestic social identity.

For males, on the other hand, prestige among cohorts and within the network activities was indirectly associated with the potential for siring children. This potential took a slightly different political avenue for men because it was also used as the measure of political control over the female within the domestic household. Within the networks, a pregnant woman was the symbolic presentation of the male ability to control her social existence within the domestic household. Therefore, *"un hombre"* was able to control *"una mujer"* through impregnation. In addition, *"un hombre"* was assured continued existence through his progeny, since they bore his name. They assured also the efficacy of the various social networks to which he belonged. As will be seen, for males this control of the female and of her continued social existence was one of the central social principles that was greatly compromised as the aftermath of sterilization.

For the most part, then, social identity of these women was closely associated to the domestic group but more importantly to the potential for bearing children and the potential for their spouses to sire children as domestic group political leaders. Certainly, within the domestic group activities, such relations were expressed in the division of labor not only of the spouses but in the division of labor of their children. For the most part, male children had distinct responsibilities from that of female children, with the latter primarily fulfilling caretaker household duties including feeding and caring for younger brothers and sisters. For the most part, male siblings were assigned protective roles, regardless of age, and tasks unassociated with the household. Gardening, collection of garbage, and permissive explorations were largely in the hands of male siblings. When asked at one point during the course of the work as to why none of the male children were observed participating in kitchen tasks, the general response from the women was that their husbands did not want them to be *maricones* (effeminates).

For the most part, then, such qualitative findings pointed to a subcultural rural Mexican strategy for both spouses, since all husbands had been born in small towns in Mexico except for one spouse who was born in rural Imperial Valley in California. Certainly the composition of their past networks had been very much in keeping with traditional means of support and help. They had generated fictive kinship, *amistad* relations, maintained intragenerational solidarity, and planned for large numbers of children.

The socioeconomic characteristics indicate the following: at time of sterilization the mean age of these women was 32.6 years with a range of 24 to 39 years; they had 3.6 mean number of children and a mean income of $9,500 per year, which was the median family income for that of the total United States population; a mean education of 8.5 years which is only 0.6 years below that of the median Mexican females in the United States; and stable housing and employment characteristics. In no way could a "culture of poverty" be suggested as the core of behavioral principles.

THE HOSPITAL AS THE BEHAVIORAL ENVIRONMENT[3]:
THE CONTEXT OF STERILIZATION

Within the confines of a public hospital these Mexican women were selected for nonconsenting sterilizations. In part, such an abuse is greatest in public hospitals, such as the Medical Center* in which the sterilizations of these women occurred, because these are institutions where the poor are regarded as practice cases for medical students. Interns gain status by the number of operations they perform, so it is unlikely that they would turn down the surgical opportunities that a dependently oppressed minority represents. According to one source, a doctor told a group of physicians training at a Southern California county hospital as part of their entry into obstetrics:

> I want you to ask every one of the girls if she wants her tubes tied, regardless of how old she is. Remember, every one who says yes to getting her tubes tied means two tubes (practice) for some resident or intern and less work for some poor son-of-a-bitch next year. (Kennard 1974:66)

In addition, there is a general neomalthusian ideology that permeates the medical profession. Dr. H. Curtis Wood, Jr., a medical consultant and past president of the Association for Voluntary Sterilization indicated this point of view:

> People pollute, and too many people crowded too close together cause many of our social and economic problems. These in turn are aggravated by involuntary and irresponsible parenthood. As physicians, we have obligations to the society of which we are a part. The welfare mess, as it has been called, cries out for solutions, one of which is fertility control (Wood 1973).

At the Medical Center where the ten women were sterilized, Dr. Bernard Rosenfeld, co-author of a Ralph Nader Health Research Group study on surgical sterilization and one-time Ob/Gyn resident at the Center stated:

> Surgical teaching programs are having increasing difficulty in finding patients because they have traditionally had to rely upon the availability of indigents. With the increase of third party payments (insurance), the number of indigents has decreased, causing the medical center to resort to 'selling' and various forms of coercing patients into consenting to surgery.
>
> I estimate that while I was at the Medical Center, between 20 to 30 percent of the doctors pushed sterilization on women who either did not understand what was happening to them or who had not been given the facts regarding their options (Interview quoted in Siggins 1977).

---

*The public hospital in which the sterilizations were carried out will be referred to as the "Medical Center."

Another "insider" also commented on the coercive practices at the Medical Center at the time that the sterilizations of the ten women were taking place:

> I saw various forms of actual physical abuses used to force women in labor to consent to sterilization. There were incidences of slapping by doctors and nurses. A syringe of pain-reliever would be shown to a woman in labor and she would be told 'we will give you this and stop the pain if you will sign' (Benker, press conference 1975).

THE CASE IN POINT: THE STERILIZATION OF MEXICAN WOMEN IN THE LOS ANGELES MEDICAL CENTER

The evidence illustrates practices by the Medical Center staff (nurses and doctors) to pressure these women into signing consent forms during intensive labor stages by withholding medication, not soliciting consent for sterilization, or not informing the patients of the permanency of such procedures. In addition, some husbands were pressured to sign consent forms for their wives without their knowledge. Even though there were no medical indications for such procedures to be performed, consent was obtained from the husbands after their wives had refused to sign the consent forms. There was even a recorded refusal by one woman to submit to sterilization, which appears on her medical chart at 5:00 A.M.; after having been given Demerol, consent forms appear to have been signed by 6:28 A.M.—the time at which the surgical procedures were performed. One woman was told falsely that a tubal ligation was necessary because the state of California did not allow more than three cesarean sections. Her third child was to be born in this manner as had her two previous children. According to her physician, conception of a fourth child had to be avoided since this one would also have to be delivered by cesarean section.

It is a remarkable fact that among the ten women, four did not learn of the sterilization procedures until after they had sought birth control devices. One woman did not become aware that such a procedure had been performed until 4 years later during a medical examination.

In each case the Medical Center reflects the basic characteristics of a paternalistic behavioral environment. In fact, a stay in any hospital exposes an individual to a condition of passivity and impotence not often replicated easily in other environments, except perhaps in judicial contexts. Certainly, in each woman's case, the consent of sterilization was not informed because of the unusual pressures applied and the specific physical conditions most of the women were suffering. Furthermore, their lack of knowledge regarding the irreversibility of the procedures, the sedated condition of some of the women who did sign, and the total lack of written consent of three of the women all point to a "neutralization" of the women as human beings and the objectification of the practice as a necessary one because of population rationalizations, surgical practice procedures for the interns, or for the "social good" of the patient. Such practices led to the rupture of subcultural strategies, the fracture of social networks, and the psychological generation of acute depression as the following section describes.

THE STATE AND STRESS OF THE SUBCULTURAL SYSTEMS
OF THE STERILIZED WOMEN

From the knowledge gained of the manner in which the social and cultural systems had worked before sterilization, it was then necessary to ascertain the ''state'' of the socio-cultural systems after sterilization. On a social level, it was discovered that most of the women had gone through a process of social disengagement, beginning with the husband-wife dyadic relationship. Two of the husbands remained highly supportive of their spouses and no appreciable damage seemed to have resulted in their relationship. One of the two husbands, however, compensated for the loss of his wife's ability to procreate by showering her with gifts at most inopportune times. The other remained a saddened, but not bitter, male who counseled his wife and was extremely supportive of her. The other eight relationships to different degrees suffered irreparable damage. Three couples filed for divorce prior to the completion of the judicial procedures on July 7, 1978. The other five relationships were marked largely by jealousy, suspicion, and in two cases, physical violence and abuse. Jealousy and suspicion arose in three of the husbands because of the change they perceived in their political control over their wives' sexuality. Basically, they feared that their wives would avail themselves of the sterile state, or that other males would make overtures toward their wives once their sterile state was revealed. In this regard, their wives' social identity had changed from respectable woman to possible libertine.

The relationships between mothers and children for eight of ten women shifted as well. Physical punishment of children had increased to the point that, in at least five of the cases, children sought to remove themselves from their mother's presence at every opportunity. Children themselves had begun to express anger to their own siblings so that sibling conflict had also increased. Aggression between mothers and their children and between siblings shifted the qualitative relationship from affection and nurturance to that of fear and violent reaction.

In all cases fictive and *amistad* relations suffered and visitations that germinated such relations decreased dramatically. Saints days, parties, fiestas, and Sunday exchanges have been largely avoided by all the women through withdrawal from fictive and *amistad* relations. For the most part, the women agreed that it was less painful to withdraw from these relationships than to answer questions regarding either the sterilizations or the reason why more children have not been sired since the last born were at this time at least 4 years old. To inquiries about future pregnancies, the retort that they were ''guarding against pregnancies'' was short-ranged. Such questions were exceedingly painful since, of the ten women, five had already chosen names for their future progeny. For the most part, these were names of paternal or maternal grandparents.

Consanguineous relations were also affected. Six of the women did not share the fact that they had been sterilized with immediate siblings and in three of the cases with their own mothers. This denial of course could only take place if social relations were themselves withdrawn by the women in order to avoid the topic altogether. In addition, this also meant that their spouses' consanguineous relatives were also avoided so that this provided another source of conflict between husbands and wives. Such conflict became so endemic that in three of the relationships the husbands lost their employment, two became alcoholics, and one left the family and has not been seen for 4 years from the date of the sterilization.

The degree of cultural disruption has been immense. The basis of social identity and self-image has been largely eliminated for all of the women. In the place of the culturally constituted social definition of self, a substitution of what can be termed the "mula (mule) syndrome" has been generated. The "mula syndrome" refers to the cultural redefinition of the women as "unnatural," "insufficient," or "incomplete women" for they are no longer of domestic value. One woman expressed her situation: "I can no longer be a companion to my husband." Cultural symbols of self-worth were negated and in their place symbols of self-deprecation and self-blame took hold. Of course, these led to feelings of guilt, shame, worthlessness, and self-blame. They blame themselves for what has occurred and are blamed in part by some of the husbands for not resisting sterilization; they then turn in anger against themselves. This situation has been expressed in an acutely vivid dream content. One woman dreamt she found herself traveling to Mexico without her children and on arrival becoming embarrassed when asked by relatives where they were. Another has nightmares in which her children have been stolen, killed, and eaten by unidentified figures. Others have dreamt of finding themselves alone with dead persons, or totally alone and lost without their children or husband, while others recall seeing their children drowning in lakes.

The sense of personality loss and worthlessness, all part of the grief reaction to the sterilization procedures, led to acute depression. For each woman her sense of continuity with the past had been fractured, her sense of self-worth had been shattered, self-blame had been internalized, and a new social identity of impotence had been generated. Each women in fact is now stigmatized. The sterilization procedures stand as visible and permanent marks of humiliation that they can never remove. The greater the effort at denial, the greater the anger and self-hate generated. The greater the anger and self-hate, the greater the necessity of expression on themselves or on others. The greater the expression, the greater the increase in conflict, social disengagement, and cultural disruption. The final effect was acute depression.

These findings and the verified hypotheses were presented in a court of law as part of the evidence in behalf of a law suit these women had filed in federal court. As will be seen, it is ironic that the very evidence used to illustrate the damages done to the social and cultural systems of these women was, in fact, partially used by the court to rationalize a decision against them.

MADRIGAL VERSUS QUILLIGAN: THE TRIAL AS A BEHAVIORAL ENVIRONMENT

On May 31, 1978, a civil suit for damages began in the United States District Court of the Central District of California. The complaint was entitled *"Dolores Madrigal, et. al.,*

Plaintiff, versus *E. J. Quilligan, et. al.''* The action was brought against Dr. E. J. Quilligan, chairman of Medical Center's Department of Obstetrics and Gynecology, and eleven other doctors on behalf of the ten women previously mentioned. In order to appreciate the final outcome of the suit, however, we should recall the central contention that "paternalistic behavioral environments" foster differential treatment of Mexicans when the efficient conditions are present. The trial will be treated as such a behavioral environment and the efficient conditions articulated.

The courtroom was very much like most in that spaces were defined in proper domains for the judge, the plaintiff's attorney's and the defendants' attorneys. Since the trial was a nonjury type, the focus of all the attention by the attorneys on both sides was on the judge. Neither the trial per se nor the judicial arguments will be detailed, since both are much beyond the scope of this work. Instead, the contrasts within the confines of the trial will be addressed in order to understand the behavioral environment within the total context of the social question involved.

These contrasts are most immediately apparent in the attorneys. The plaintiffs' two Chicano lawyers came from the local poverty legal centers who represented their interests. Of the two plaintiff's lawyers, the male was a 35-year-old person who had graduated well at the top of his class a few years previously. He was legally blind from a childhood disease so that the enormously thick glasses accentuated and distorted his dark brown eyes. For the most part this soft-spoken, medium-sized, and slightly pudgy man, shuffled as he moved between the plaintiffs' table and the podium that sat squarely in the middle of the room facing the judge's panelled bench. The other lawyer was a recently graduated Chicana from the same poverty legal center and, like the other lawyer, had been working on the case for 4 years. Dark, thin, and well-dressed, the young female lawyer moved assertively between the plaintiff's table and the podium. She spoke with clear, clipped, and slightly accented diction. They differed little from the ten plaintiffs in court, except for variance in quality of dress.

In opposition, the defendants' lawyers were the best that money could buy for this sort of civil action. Both the male and female lawyer were from one of the more prestigious Beverly Hills law firms and both seemed quite relaxed in their roles in the courtroom. She moved assertively and quickly from the defendants' table even though she was about 30 pounds overweight. This well-dressed, articulate, and quite polysyllabic Anglo woman did not, in fact, actually present any of the defendants nor did she cross-examine witnesses. Instead, she was largely responsible for making legal motions, registering legal requests, and seemed to assist her partner. He was like his fair-haired counterpart, fiftyish, well-groomed, articulate, and quite polysyllabic without the stuttering that seemed to mark the presentations of the plaintiffs' lawyers. Both in hue and in presentation of themselves, there were obvious contrasts that seemed to divide the courtroom into the Mexican side and the Anglo side. The judge seemed to sit in the middle, or so it seemed.

The judge, the Honorable Jesse W. Curtis, a white-haired 70-year-old person, seemed like the stereotype of the paternalistic figure commanding the courtroom. Firm-jawed, angular faced, with piercing blue eyes set beneath profuse eyebrows that moved in unison in mostly frowns, this Nixon-appointed judge to the federal bench was known by reputation as largely a conservative judge who lived aboard his yacht in Newport Beach, one of the most prestigious areas in Southern California. He and the defendants' lawyers were obvious analogues and stark contrasts to the plaintiffs and their lawyers. The judge did not in fact sit in the middle.

For 2½ weeks the plaintiffs' lawyers presented evidence that under duress, after hours of being in labor, and under medication the plaintiffs could not have given informed consent. Dr. Don Sloan, an internationally known gynecologist and obstetrician, testified that given the circumstances surrounding the sterilization procedures none of the women could have provided informed consent. Each woman in turn provided her testimony in Spanish in which the context of her sterilization was detailed. A handwriting expert examined the signatures of those women who had signed consent forms and concluded that in fact each woman had been suffering great distress and stress at the time. Dr. Terry Kuper, the plaintiffs' psychiatrist, presented his evidence of the effects of the sterilization procedures on each woman and concluded that to different degrees each woman had suffered irreparable psychological damage and that long periods of psychotherapy would have to be undertaken by each one. I offered the data discovered in this work in much the same manner and development, except initially the judge was not going to permit my testimony. When Judge Curtis was made aware of my impending testimony, he remarked from the bench that he did not see what an anthropologist was going to say that would have any bearing on damages and that if I were getting paid, my testimony would not be worth a "plugged nickel." He concluded that after all "We all know that Mexicans love their families." Nevertheless, I was able to present the data contained and except for minor cross-examination, no opposing expert was presented to refute my testimony. Of interest to note, however, were the concluding questions that Judge Curtis addressed to me that would be of significance in the final opinion.

After having concluded my testimony, the Judge asked me how long I had spend on the case. I answered that I had spent 450 hours of time between field work, creating the instrument, selecting the control groups, and ascertaining what the effects had been on the women's sociocultural systems. He then asked me if I would have undertaken the study in any other manner. I responded that I would not have since ". . . as an anthropologist to have done otherwise would not have been worth a hill of beans." He repeated the same question again, slightly rephrased, and I answered that professional ethics would have prevented me from coming to the conclusions that I did unless I rigorously followed the methodology I had used. The judge thanked me and I stepped down.

The defense presented no rebuttal of expert witnesses and did not cross-examine the plaintiffs. Instead, they called each one of the doctors in question and from the plaintiffs' medical files commented on the medical procedures contained therein. At no time did any of the doctors recall any of the women, but they all asserted that their "custom and practice" was not to perform a sterilization unless a woman had consented and understood what she was doing. When cross-examined as to whether they spoke Spanish well enough to detail the procedures, they responded generally that they knew enough "obstetrics

Spanish" to get them by. When pressed for details about the individual women, they all answered that they could not recall them as patients since they were so many.

The final decision was handed down June 30th before Judge Curtis left for a lengthy Scandinavian vacation. It stated rather succinctly that the judgment was entered for the defendants. The women lost, but the judge's rationalization is interesting and informative because it, in fact, verifies the theoretical position that underlies this exposition—that in paternalistic environments in which Mexicans are differentially treated in a negative manner, the "ideology of cultural differences" will be used as a rationalization for the structural and asymmetrical characteristics of the environments.

The Judge's remarks are as follows:

Communication breakdown

This case is essentially the result of a breakdown in communications between the patients and the doctors. All plaintiffs are Spanish-speaking women whose ability to understand and speak English is limited. This fact is generally understood by the staff at the Medical Center and most members have acquired enough familiarity with the language to get by. There is also an interpreter available whose services are used when thought to be necessary. But even with these precautions, misunderstandings are bound to occur.

Furthermore, the cultural background of these particular women has contributed to the problem in a subtle but significant way. According to the plaintiff's anthropological expert, they are members of a traditional Mexican rural subculture, a relatively narrow spectrum of Mexican people living in this country whose lifestyle and cultural background derives from the lifestyle and culture of small rural communities in Mexico. He further testified that a cultural trait which is very prominent with this group is an extreme dependence upon family. Most come from large families and wish to have large families for their own comfort and support. Furthermore, the status of a woman and her husband within that group depends largely upon the woman's ability to produce children. If for any reason she cannot, she is considered an incomplete woman and is apt to suffer a disruption of her relationship with her family and husband. When faced with a decision of whether or not to be sterilized, the decision process is a much more traumatic event with her than it would be with a typical patient and, consequently, she would require greater explanation, more patient advice, and greater care in interpreting her consent than persons not members of such a subculture would require.

But this need for such deliberate treatment is not readily apparent. The anthropological expert testified that he would not have known that these women possessed these traits had he not conducted tests and a study which required some 450 hours of time. He further stated that a determination by him based on any less time would not have been worth "beans." It is not surprising therefore that the staff of a busy metropolitan hospital which has neither the time nor the staff to make such esoteric studies would be unaware of these atypical cultural traits.

It is against this backdrop therefore that we must analyze the conduct of the doctors who treated the plaintiffs in this case.

Doctors' custom and practice

Since these operations occurred between 1971 and 1974 and were performed by the doctors operating in a busy obstetrics ward, it is not surprising that none of the doctors have any independent recollection of the events leading up to the operations. They all testified, however, that it was their custom and practice not to suggest a sterilization unless a patient asked for it or there were medical complications which would require the doctor, in the exercise of prudent medical procedures, to make such suggestion. They further testified that it was their practice when a patient requested sterilization to explain its irreversible result and they stated that they would not perform the operation unless they were certain in their own mind that the patient understood the nature of the operation and was requesting the procedure. The weight to be given to such testimony and the inferences to be drawn therefrom will be determined in the light of all the testimony relating to each doctor's conduct.[4]

The Judge's final opinion also excluded the testimony by the handwriting expert, the psychiatrist on the case, and refuted the testimony by Dr. Sloan, the gynecologist and obstetrician, by saying that his statements ". . . completely defy common sense." Why they do so, he did not explain. His conclusion, however, is quite enlightening in that he admits that in fact all of the women had suffered. He states:

> This case had not been an easy one to try for it has involved social, emotional and cultural considerations of great complexity. There is no doubt but that these women have suffered severe emotional and physical stress because of these operations. One can sympathize with them for their inability to communicate clearly, but one can hardly blame the doctors for relying on these indicia of consent which appeared to be unequivocal on their face and which are in constant use in the Medical Center.
>
> Let judgment be entered for the defendants.

Jesse W. Curtis
Senior United States District
Judge (19)

CONCLUSIONS

First, it must be obvious that within paternalistic institutionalized behavioral environments, Mexicans have a high probability of being negatively treated. Certainly the medical sterilizations and the legal judgments uphold this fact. Regardless of the overwhelming evidence to the contrary, the judge disregarded evidence and testimony presented and chose instead to consider the "custom and practice" of the doctors rather than following rules of evidence.

Second, his misuse of the anthropological data in which he identified the women as belonging to a "relatively narrow spectrum of Mexican people" was not presented as empirical evidence. Instead, this commentary was used to illustrate the "atypicality of their cultural traits." In other words, the women were so culturally different that the doctors could not have known that the sterilizations would have affected them in so adverse a manner. This belief removes the legal and moral responsibility for their actions. The "ideology of cultural differences" then is used as the very basis for an unjust and detrimental decision against a group of largely defenseless Mexican women. After all, how could the doctors have been aware that the sterilizations would have such an effect on Mexican women, since the hospital in which these operations were carried out is in the middle of the largest Mexican barrio outside Mexico City. The judge legitimized the doctors' actions and his action against the women by noting that the doctors were too busy to note these cultural differences, and even more importantly, they were so different that the doctors could not have known the effects of sterilizations unless they had carried out studies similar to the one I carried out in the case.

Third, all the work that went into the presentation of this material is still very much in the "meliorative and reformists attempts" of the well-intentioned liberal establishment. I, too, blundered and in fact was responsible for providing the judge with exactly the knowledge he needed to utilize the "ideology of cultural differences." Ironically, while fairly objective empirical findings of effect were presented, which were too overwhelming to ignore on the record, the judge's only recourse was to utilize the data against the women since it could not be refuted.

Fourth, and last, all of the activities that made up this work occurred within the confines of an industrial capitalist state in which the diversity of culture is organized and controlled by a national prism, reflecting a dominant ethnic group of Anglo-Saxon Americans. Both the sterilization of the physical ability of a group of ethnic minority women to procreate and the resultant cultural sterilization of the same group of women were, in fact, provided legitimitization by the court. The decision reinforces that national prism and ensures the superordinate ethnic group of Anglo-Saxon Americans continued domination by whatever means.

NOTES

1. I use the term "Chicana" to designate American-born women of Mexican heritage who are socialized within industrially structured population centers in either agricultural or urban contexts. Cultural specifics from language to belief systems are "distributed" according to class and occupational sectors. "Mexican" is the term I use to designate Mexican-born persons who are socialized within rural or urban contexts and in a possible variety of structural settings from industrial to small village "closed corporate" communities. Cultural specifics from language to belief systems are "distributed" according to class and occupational sectors. The differences between populations will be both cultural and structural; however, similarities will also be reflective of cultural specifics arising from equivalent structural conditions. The term "working-class" Mexican denotes little specifically and assumes a homogeneity of experiences that is ahistorical in content.
2. *Rancherias* are small agricultural settlements in which the population density of the residential area is equal to the area used for subsistence. *Ejidos* are communal lands assigned to a community by the Mexican federal government.
3. I utilize the concept of behavioral environment as an important construct that may be fruitful in designating those situations that promote negative differential treatment. Some environments can be considered "paternalistic" when the cultural constructs demand extreme deference articulated through a routinized and elaborate etiquette; titles of reference and superiority; a specialized argot or jargon; differentiated costumes and attire; allocated physical spaces; segregated activities; and when social relations are based on dependence asymmetry, social distance, and ascribed status differentials without vertical mobility for the client population. "Clients" are perceived as immature, childish, ignorant, and underdeveloped so that the controlling figures in the environment have political control over them and economic access that commands the allocation of valued resources, services, material goods, or information. Enforcement is based on the withdrawal or threatened withdrawal of such resources so that ultimately the roles fulfilled by "clients" vis-á-vis their "patrons" are based on "coercive" support. "Legitimate" support is based on value consensus. For a complete discussion, see Marc J. Swartz (1968).

   Yet, "competitive behavioral environments" in comparison to paternalistic ones are marked by factors of achievement, affective neutrality, mobility, legitimate support, and are legalistic, representative, and "earned." The relations between participants, although hierarchical, are not passive-dependent but active-interdependent. These may be asymmetrical, but all concerned here expect change and development through participation. Competition is designated within boundaries, and conflict is defined and agreed to within parameters that do not threaten the relations between members in the environments. There is a general value consensus without coercion, and resources are allocated to those who can best meet the goals of the behavioral environment. Both "paternalistic" and "competitive" models are polar types and operationalization is still to be developed.

The basic notions of paternalistic and competitive relations are owed to Pierre Van den Berghe's two fine basic works in ethnic and race relations: *Race and Racism* (1967) and *Race and Ethnicity* (1970). In these two works, the author uses the characteristics of paternalism and competition as independent and dependent societal variables that mark the nature of the relations between dominant and subordinate groups within a developmental polar model. I contend that, regardless of larger societal developments, paternalistic and competitive behavioral environments will coexist in even the most "competitive industrialized" social contexts. In the most rational of institutionalized bureaucratic contexts, paternalistic factors may very well mark most relations between participants.

4. See Judge Jesse W. Curtis "Opinion," (No. CV 75-2057-JWC, United States Federal Court, June 30, 1978, pp. 1-19).

REFERENCES

Benker, Karen
  1975 Statement made before a press conference at the Greater Los Angeles Press Club, December 6.
Curtis, Jesse W.
  1978 Opinion, June 30, No. CV 75-2057-JWC:1-19.
Kennard, Gail
  1974 "Sterilization abuse." Essence, October, 66 ff.
Siggins, Richard V.
  1977 "Coerced sterilization: a national civil conspiracy to commit genocide upon the poor?" Unpublished manuscript. Loyola University, School of Law.
Swartz, Marc J.
  1968 "Introduction." In Marc J. Swartz (ed.), Local-Level Politics. Chicago, Illinois: Aldine Publishing Co.
Van den Berghe, Pierre (ed.)
  1967 Race and Racism: A Comparative Perspective. New York: John Wiley & Sons, Inc.
  1970 Race and Ethnicity. New York: Basic Books, Inc., Publishers.
Wood, H. Curtis Jr.
  1973 "Statement of address." Contemporary OB/GYN. January. Quoted in Kennard "Sterilization abuse," *Essence,* October:86.

Chapter 17

To be aged, Hispanic, and female

The triple risk*

Richard C. Stephens, George T. Oser, and Zena Smith Blau

In recent years, there has been an increase in interest in the problems of the elderly. Partially, this new interest has been due to significant changes in the age structure of the United States population, with a substantial increase in the number of persons over 65 years of age and a concomitant heightening of sensitivity to institutional forms of age discrimination as in mandatory retirement. Nevertheless, almost no empirical work has been oriented to the aging Mexican American, particularly the female. We have, as the goal of this chapter, the provision of some empirical data on this neglected group.

Specifically, we hope to test the hypothesis, suggested in some of our previous work, that the Mexican American female is at triple risk as she ages (Blau, Oser, and Stephens 1978). First, she suffers from the problems that most aged people face—the increase in health problems and the loss in income and social status. Second, she must still encounter the legacy of traditional prejudice towards Mexican Americans that is often complicated by poor facility in use of the English language. And third, she has to contend with the additional problems created by the socially defined lesser status of being a woman. Thus, the aging Mexican American female may be at triple risk because she is aged, a member of a minority group, and female.

This hypothesis will be tested by exploring how the Mexican American female fares in a number of different areas of life. We will look at those areas of life that seem particularly important to the elderly—economic conditions, health status, morale, and involvement in the community. We will compare the older Mexican American female (aged 65 years or older) to several other groups in order to test our hypothesis. First, we will compare her to the Anglo female of the same age and social class. In this way, we should be able to determine the risk of being a minority group member while controlling for the two important variables of age and social class. Second, we will compare older Mexican American females with a younger cohort of Mexican American women aged 55 to 64 years. Again, we will control for social class. In this way we can, to some limited extent,

---

*This study was funded by the Texas Department of Human Resources (contract 527-02-R-00).

determine the effects of being "old," while ethnicity and social class are controlled. Third, we will compare the Mexican American female with Mexican American males, while controlling for age and social class. In this way, we should be able to determine the "cost" of being female.

SOURCE OF DATA

The data for this study are drawn from a statewide telephone sample and interviews of the elderly in Texas. The sample of noninstitutionalized persons aged 55 years or older was drawn using the following procedure. First, a current list of all telephone prefixes in Texas was compiled. Next, through cooperative arrangements with local telephone companies and the use of criss-cross directories, the list was purged of dedicated business or commercial, coin-operated, and empty banks of telephone numbers. Finally, a computer-generated random suffix was appended to the remaining prefixes or banks within prefixes. On confirmation (by direct telephone contact) of a telephone number as residential, a household screen was administered that obtained a variety of demographic characteristics for all members of the household. If the household contained one or more people 55 years of age or older, one of those persons was randomly selected to be the respondent to a 45-minute telephone interview. After this initial sample was used, the state was divided into the twelve Texas Department of Human Resources service regions. For those regions that did not contain approximately 400 respondents, further sampling was undertaken to reach that number. It is these augmented regional data that are used herein to assure sufficient sample sizes for the proposed analysis. Because it is this sample that is being used, we cannot generalize to the state population as a whole. However, except for the possibility that these data overrepresent female-only households and may slightly overrepresent less populated areas of the state, we feel no other significant skewness in the data is present.

The numbers of subjects in each of the groups used in this analysis are presented in Table 17-1.* The sample is divided into three social class groups that we have labeled lower (principally unskilled workers and domestics), upper-lower (semiskilled and skilled workers), and middle (clerical, sales, technicians, and so on). These classifications are based on the 1979 U.S. Census Occupational Codes categorization of the occupation of the head of the household in which the respondent resides (we use the husband's longest held occupation in the case of widows). The classification of occupations is more fully described in Bryant (1979). No professionals or executives are included in the analysis because so few Mexican Americans in the sample could be so classified.

The survey instrument administered to these groups contained questions covering a wide range of issues bearing on the needs and quality of life of aging men and women.

---

*Because the numbers of subjects in some cells are not large, the results must be interpreted with some caution. Such small numbers may explain some of the anomalies found in the data. Also, because of disparity of number (N) sizes, no statistical tests of significance will be applied to these data. Additionally, because of space limitations, Ns will not be reported in subsequent tables. However, they approximate the Ns presented in Table 17-1.

Table 17-1. Number of subjects in each of the study groups

Social class	Anglo females over 65	Mexican American males over 65	Mexican American females	
			55-64	over 65
Lower	162	31	77	84
Upper-lower	388	47	68	54
Middle	749	13	28	24

Such issues included health, economic factors, housing, living arrangements, morale, and a number of other topics.

FINDINGS

In presenting the findings, we will look at several major central concerns in the lives of the elderly—economic factors, health, morale, and involvement in community activities.

Economic factors

Certainly one of the basic conditions for well-being is some sort of economic security. While wealth does not guarantee contentment, it certainly is much more difficult to be happy without some minimal amount of economic security. The chief indicator of economic well-being is income.

Table 17-2 shows that the older Mexican American female lives in households with decidedly lower per capita incomes than older Anglo females and younger Mexican American females. The differences between older Mexican American females and older Anglos are especially pronounced. Older Mexican American females in the lower and middle classes have higher household per capita incomes than do Mexican American males, probably as a result of debilitating job conditions attendant to the male Mexican American labor market.

Another indicator of economic well-being is the individual's own assessment of the adequacy of this income. Table 17-3 presents data on the percentages of respondents who report their income as inadequate. The data generally show that, compared with both Anglo females and Mexican American males, older Mexican American females more often describe their income as "inadequate." Differences in relative deprivation may explain the interesting fact that the older Mexican American female less often describes her income as inadequate when compared with younger Mexican American females.

Related to both income and adequacy of income is education. In general, the greater the education, the greater the ability to increase one's income and, in the case of these samples, the greater the ability to assure one's self of economic security in old age. Table 17-4 shows how profoundly disadvantaged older Mexican American females are in terms of formal education when compared with Anglo females of similar social class. Older Mexican American females are markedly less educated than younger Mexican American

Table 17-2. Mean per capita income of households for selected groups

Social class	Anglo females over 65	Mexican American males over 65	Mexican American females	
			55-64	over 65
Lower	$3614	$1646	$2074	$2079
Upper-lower	$3582	$2109	$2369	$1880
Middle	$5875	$2785	$4771	$3298

Table 17-3. Percentages of respondents reporting income as "inadequate" for selected groups

Social class	Anglo females over 65	Mexican American males over 65	Mexican American females	
			55-64	over 65
Lower	33.8	37.9	34.2	35.8
Upper-lower	30.5	20.8	47.7	30.9
Middle	19.2	18.2	44.4	29.2

females. In fact, the educational attainment of older Mexican American females only exceeds that of older Mexican American males and for the middle-class older Mexican American is less than the lower class for Anglos.

Another indicator of economic stability is home ownership. Table 17-5 shows the percentage of persons who are buying or own their homes. These data show that older Mexican American females fare well when compared with the other groups. Older Mexican American females own homes more frequently than their Anglo counterparts, and the home ownership rate for Mexican American males is only about 5 percent higher. When compared with younger Mexican American females, the picture is somewhat complicated. Older middle-class Mexican American females own their houses more frequently than their younger counterparts, but this relationship is reversed for the two lower and upper-lower groups.

While older Mexican American females compare favorably to other groups on the variable of home ownership, the condition of their housing is definitely worse. Table 17-6 shows the percentages of respondents who report their residence as requiring "many repairs." We can see that many more older Mexican American females report their houses as needing many repairs than Anglo females of the same social class. Similarly, in most cases, more older Mexican American females report poorer housing conditions than do Mexican American males or younger Mexican American females.

In summary, the data on the economic variables generally support the contention that older Mexican American females are worse off than the other ethnic age and sex groups.

Table 17-4. Percentages of respondents who have a high school education (or greater) for selected groups

Social class	Anglo females over 65	Mexican American males over 65	Mexican American females	
			55-64	over 65
Lower	20.4	3.4	1.4	1.3
Upper-lower	34.3	6.4	9.2	12.0
Middle	58.7	9.1	32.1	18.1

Table 17-5. Percentages of respondents who are buying or own their houses for selected groups

Social class	Anglo females over 65	Mexican American males over 65	Mexican American females	
			55-64	over 65
Lower	63.6	77.5	75.3	72.6
Upper-lower	76.3	80.8	82.4	76.0
Middle	76.4	100.0	92.8	95.9

Table 17-6. Percentages of respondents who report their house as requiring many repairs for selected groups

Social class	Anglo females over 65	Mexican American males over 65	Mexican American females	
			55-64	over 65
Lower	11.3	20.0	17.3	18.3
Upper-lower	8.4	12.8	23.5	15.1
Middle	6.2	7.7	10.7	16.7

As might be expected, they fare worse when contrasted with older Anglo females and are somewhat worse off than males and younger females of Mexican descent.

Health

Another indicator of well-being, and one that is particularly important to this age group, is health. In this section, we will look at measures on an objective health scale and the respondent's own assessment of his/her health. The first health status indicator is the General Health Status scale. This scale, developed by Haney, et al. (1979), is an assessment of health problems and is based on self-reported medical symptoms and the respondent's self-reported inability to carry out simple tasks (such as climbing stairs and so forth). The scale is scored such that the greater the score, the worse the health.

Table 17-7 shows that, in general, the older Mexican American female has poorer health when compared with the other three groups. In fact, only in the case of the lower-class older Mexican American female vs. the older Anglo female does the older Mexican American female evidence better health. Several anomalies appear in these data: these include the substantially more healthy appearances of Mexican American males and the decrease in health status of older Mexican American females as social class increases.

In addition to attempting an assessment of the actual state of the respondent's health, we also asked for their own assessment of their health. They were asked to rate their health from "excellent" to "poor." Table 17-8 contains the percentage of respondents who rate their health as "good" or "excellent." Analysis of these data show that Mexican American females describe their health as "good or excellent" much less frequently than do the Anglo females and the lower and middle-class Mexican American males. Interestingly though, the upper-lower and middle-class older Mexican American females describe their health as "good or excellent" more often than do the younger Mexican American females.

In summarizing the health data, we can say that older Mexican American females by and large both have poorer health and subjectively evaluate their health as worse than do the other groups. The exception to this rule seems to be the younger Mexican American females who subjectively evaluate their health as worse.

Table 17-7. Mean general health status scores for selected groups

Social class	Anglo females over 65	Mexican American males over 65	Mexican American females	
			55-64	over 65
Lower	6.76	3.03	6.60	6.13
Upper-lower	6.20	4.24	5.39	6.53
Middle	5.68	3.64	3.57	6.4

Table 17-8. Percentages of respondents describing their health as excellent to good for selected groups

Social class	Anglo females over 65	Mexican American males over 65	Mexican American females	
			55-64	over 65
Lower	49.1	64.6	41.6	39.8
Upper-lower	55.2	50.0	47.1	54.6
Middle	64.5	69.3	39.3	47.8

Morale

Having measured some of the physical factors of life for the older Mexican American female, such as income and health, the next question to ask is how do these women perform on the psychical correlates of such factors?

Respondents were asked, ''How do you think of yourself as far as age is concerned?'' Table 17-9 presents the data on the percentage of respondents who said they thought of themselves as old. The results are truly noteworthy. Older Mexican American females of any social class are much more likely to describe themselves as old in comparison with every group save upper-lower class Mexican American males. These findings are especially significant given the wide percentage differences between the older Mexican American females and the other groups.

Given these large differences in age self-concept, it is not surprising to learn that older Mexican American females exhibit more self-alienation. Table 17-10 presents mean alienation scores for the various groups. The alienation score used here contains four Likert-type items (feeling life isn't useful, no point to living, things getting worse, and regret chances missed to do a better job of living). The standard deviation of the scale is 2.6, and the coefficient alpha is 0.63. For every comparison, save one, the older Mexican American female displays greater alienation than the other groups. As in some of the previous analyses, differences in the scores of the older Mexican American females are greater when compared with Anglos and Mexican American males and are less pronounced when compared with younger Mexican American females.

Table 17-9. Percentages of respondents describing themselves as old for selected groups

Social class	Anglo females over 65	Mexican American males over 65	Mexican American females	
			55-64	over 65
Lower	18.2	20.0	17.3	36.7
Upper-lower	14.2	40.4	15.4	34.0
Middle	14.3	25.0	11.5	43.5

Table 17-10. Mean alienation scale scores for selected groups

Social class	Anglo females over 65	Mexican American males over 65	Mexican American females	
			55-64	over 65
Lower	7.92	8.00	8.07	8.07
Upper-lower	7.70	7.42	8.18	8.30
Middle	7.66	7.33	8.16	8.50

Table 17-11. Mean depression scale scores for selected groups

Social class	Anglo females over 65	Mexican American males over 65	Mexican American females	
			55-64	over 65
Lower	9.26	7.58	9.41	8.61
Upper-lower	9.22	7.83	9.52	9.21
Middle	8.46	8.38	9.11	9.35

Another variable that has been shown to be important in understanding the elderly is depression (Stephens, Blau, Oser, and Millar 1978). The depression measure used here is a five-item scale (unhappiness, loneliness, boredom, restlessness, and upset by criticism) with a standard deviation of 2.7 and a coefficient alpha of 0.70. Examination of Table 17-11 shows that there is little consistent relationship between depression and the variables we have been examining. Older Mexican American females are more depressed than Mexican American males. However, older Mexican American females are less depressed than at least one category of Anglo females and two categories of younger Mexican American females.

In summary, older Mexican American females generally have lower morale than the other comparison groups, at least as measured by age, self-concept, and alienation. However, the older Mexican American females do not seem as depressed as the women in the other two comparison groups.

Social integration

The final generic life area that we will examine is social integration. That is, we will look at how involved these respondents are with the people around them. In order to measure the level of involvement, we will examine interaction with family and friends, two important social groups.

The Child-Centered Participation Scale (Table 17-12), scored only for people with children, is a seven-item scale with a standard deviation of 1.82 and a coefficient alpha of 0.68. It has items that measure active involvement in children's lives (helped child in last year, gave or loaned money, performed some service or chore, helped with grandchildren, helped when child was ill, offered advice on major decision, confided in child). These data are very interesting. First, they both confirm and deny some of the cultural stereotypes we have of Mexican American culture. Older Mexican American females score higher than Anglo females. But older Mexican American women score lower than both younger Mexican American women and, more notable, than Mexican American men. Thus, while it appears that, at least on this variable, older Mexican American women score more favorably, they score less favorably than the other Mexican American comparison groups. This finding would suggest that they are less involved in their children's lives than is commonly assumed.

Table 17-12. Mean child-centered participation scores for selected groups

Social class	Anglo females over 65	Mexican American males over 65	Mexican American females	
			55-64	over 65
Lower	2.42	2.95	4.07	2.81
Upper-lower	2.74	3.35	3.83	3.02
Middle	2.83	3.62	4.10	3.08

Table 17-13. Percentages of respondents who have no close friends in the community for selected groups

Social class	Anglo females over 65	Mexican American males over 65	Mexican American females	
			55-64	over 65
Lower	10.1	25.8	13.0	20.2
Upper-lower	5.7	8.3	16.2	20.0
Middle	6.2	7.7	10.7	20.8

Besides the family, interaction with friends is also a source of social integration. Table 17-13 presents data on the percentage of respondents who report having no close friends in the community. As can be seen, the Mexican American female, by rather large percentages, reports having no close friends more frequently than all but the lower-class Mexican American male. Thus, these data, combined with the family interaction data, indicate that the Mexican American females appear more isolated and less involved in social relationships.

DISCUSSION AND SUMMARY

When one looks at the data as a whole, several conclusions can be drawn:
1. On almost every variable, the older Mexican American female appears more disadvantaged than the older Anglo female even when social class is controlled.
2. On most variables, the Mexican American female appears to be in a worse position than does the Mexican American male for each social class grouping.
3. On most variables, the older Mexican American female fares worse than the younger Mexican American female. However, the young Mexican American female, in many analyses, is similar to the older Mexican American female. Part of this similarity can be explained by the fact that the "younger" Mexican American women in our sample are not really that much younger than the older women. In many cases, much less than a decade separates their ages.

These three conclusions, taken as a whole, generally support the triple-risk hypothesis advanced at the beginning of the chapter. The older Mexican American female truly suffers from the circumstances of being old, Mexican American, and female.

While much more could be written on the policy implications of these findings, we would like to make a few suggestions that seem appropriately derived from these data. First, the living standards of the aging Mexican American female need to be raised. Obviously, a higher income needs to be provided, not only for the female but the Mexican American male as well. Second, more health resources need to be put at the disposal of these groups. And third, greater efforts need to be made to increase the social integration of the older Mexican American female. These data would suggest that the family, the traditional bulwark against adversity among Mexican Americans, is not operating successfully in the later part of the life cycle for Mexican American women. Outreach programs, designed especially for older Mexican American women, organized by churches and other community centers, might supplement the activities of family and friends. We would hope that such attempts at further social integration might not only provide better access to needed community services and resources but would also improve the morale of the aging Mexican American female. Without such efforts, the problems are likely to persist; this fact is attested to by the many similarities of the older to the younger Mexican American female. These younger females will soon provide a new and larger group of older and disadvantaged Mexican American females.

REFERENCES

Blau, Zena Smith, George T. Oser and Richard C. Stephens
  1978 "Aging, social class and ethnicity: a comparative study of Anglo, black and Mexican-American Texans." Leon and Josephine Winkelman Lecture. School of Social Work, University of Michigan.

Bryant, Joseph M.
  1979 "Social structure and 'lebenschancen:' an assessment of class and racial and ethnic stratification approaches." Unpublished masters thesis. University of Houston.
Stephens, Richard C., Zena Smith Blau, George T. Oser and Melanie D. Millar.
  1978 "Aging, social support systems and social policy." Journal of Gerontological Social Work 1 (1):33-45.

Index

A

Abascal, Modesta, 222
Abdominal distention in infants, 80-81
Abortion(s)
  Chicana use of, 33-50
  clinics and, 45-48
  doctors and, 36
  hospitals and, 43-45
  nontherapeutic, right to, 34
  patients and, 36
Acculturation, 149, 197
  and ethnicity, 155-156
  facilitators of, 160-162
  knowledge of English language and, 160-161
  levels of, 156
  selective, 8, 156
    and ethnicity, 155-156
    of female Mexican migrants, 155-163
Aceite de comer, 64
Aceite de oliva, 63
Actos about Chicana women's movement, 97-101
Adaptations to postpartum traditions by Mexican American women, 76
Adaptive strategies of female family heads, 179-180
Addams, Jane, 219, 220, 221
Additives to milk for infants, 79
Adolescent sex role perceptions, cultural styles and, 164-172
Adoption in diffusion process, 205
Adultery, divorce because of, attitudes concerning, 167-170
Afterpains, medicinal substances to prevent, 64
Aged Hispanic females, 249-258; *see also* Mexican American women, older
Aid to Families with Dependent Children, 178
Aires, 60, 75, 136
Albaca, 64
Alcanfor, 64
Alvarez, Ino, 230
Ambrosia ambrocoides, 63
American Psychological Association
  Division of Population Psychology, 18
  Task Force on Psychology, Family Planning and Population Policy, 18

Andrade, Sally, 230
Anemia, medicinal substances for, 64
Anemopsis californica, 63
Anglo female family heads
  exploratory study of, 173-189
  resources relied on by, 183
  selected social attributes of, 181
Anglo feminism
  and Chicana feminism, contrast between, 105-107
  symbolic strategy in, 102-105
Anglo version of feminism, 217-234
Anguiano, Lupe, 229, 230
Anil, 64
Anthony, Susan B., 220
Aragon de Shepro, Teresa, 229
Artemesia mexicana, 56, 64
Artemesia rhizomata, 55, 63
Ashley, Jessie, 222
Assimilation, 197-198
Atole, 59, 75
Attitudinal facilitators of acculturation, 160
Avila, Chelo, 230
Awareness and diffusion process, 204
Azahar, 57, 64

B

Babies
  fathers diapering, attitudes concerning, 167, 170
  of migrants, Mexican-born and Houston-born, duration of lactation among, 77
  sex preference for, attitudes concerning, 168, 171
Baby shower, 56-57
Bacchans pteronoides, 60, 64
Barba de elote, 64
Barrera, Elina, 229
Barrett, Ida B. Wells, 221
Behavior
  breast-feeding, macro pattern in, according to social class, 67
  of Chicana with respect to health and illness, 195-197
  health, and values survey, 198-202
Behavioral environments, paternalistic, issues of psychocultural rupture and legal redress in, 235-247
Behavioral facilitators of acculturation, 161

259